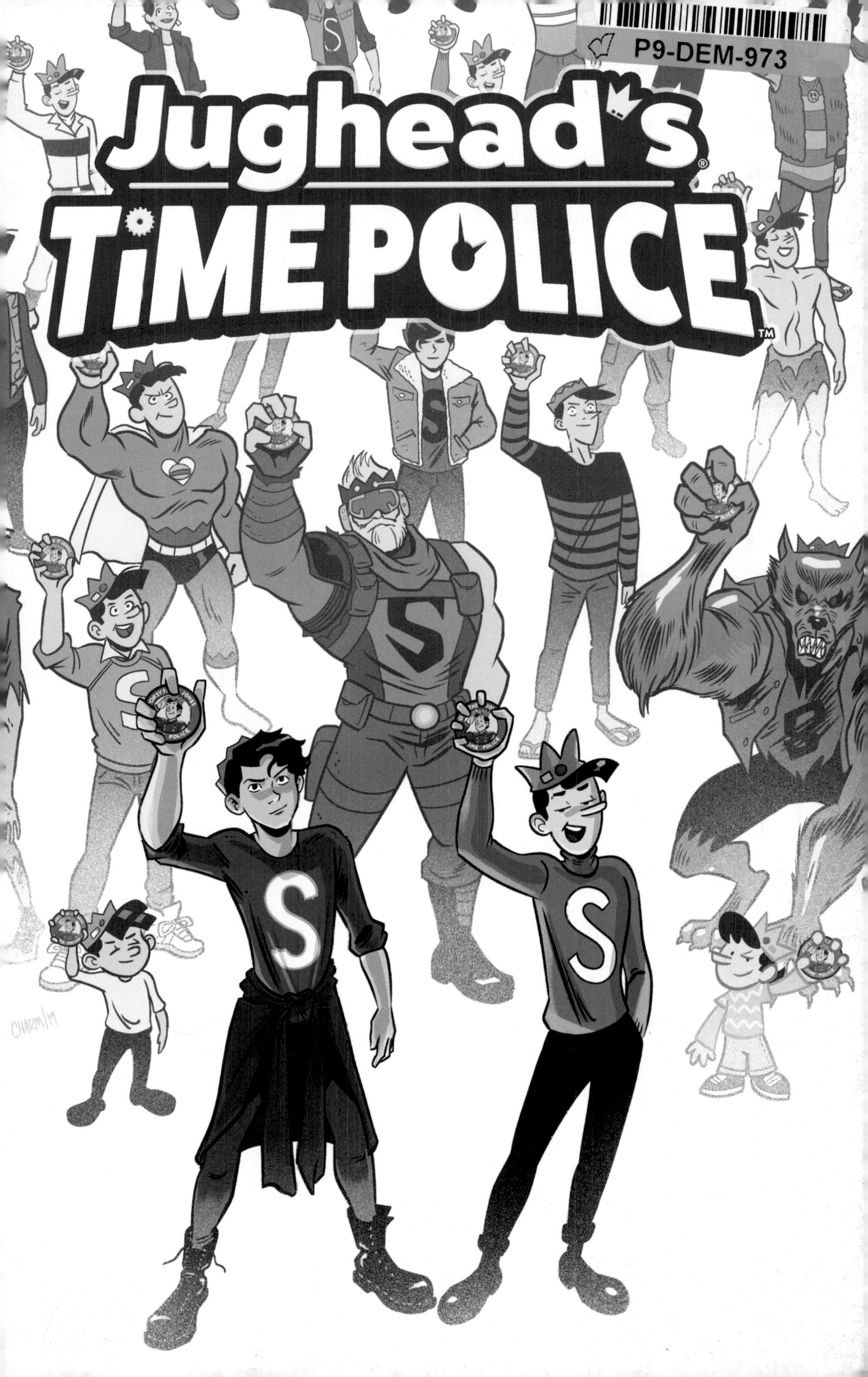
Jughead's®
TIME POLICE™
TIME POLICE
CHARM/19

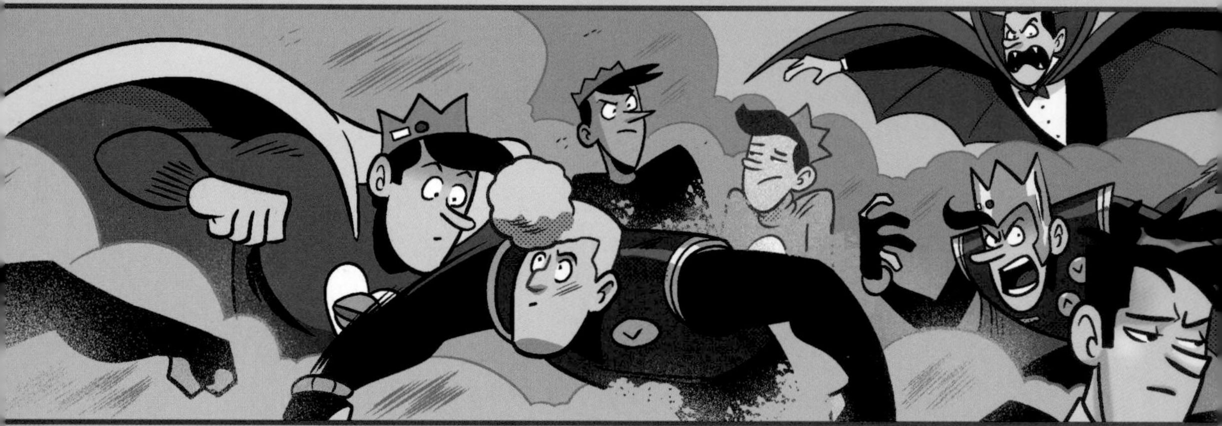

STORY BY
SINA GRACE

ART BY
DEREK CHARM

LETTERING BY
JACK MORELLI

COLORING BY
MATT HERMS

EDITOR-IN-CHIEF
VICTOR GORELICK

PUBLISHER
JON GOLDWATER

EDITORS
ALEX SEGURA AND
VINCENT LOVALLO

ASSOCIATE EDITOR
STEPHEN OSWALD

ASSISTANT EDITOR
JAMIE LEE ROTANTE

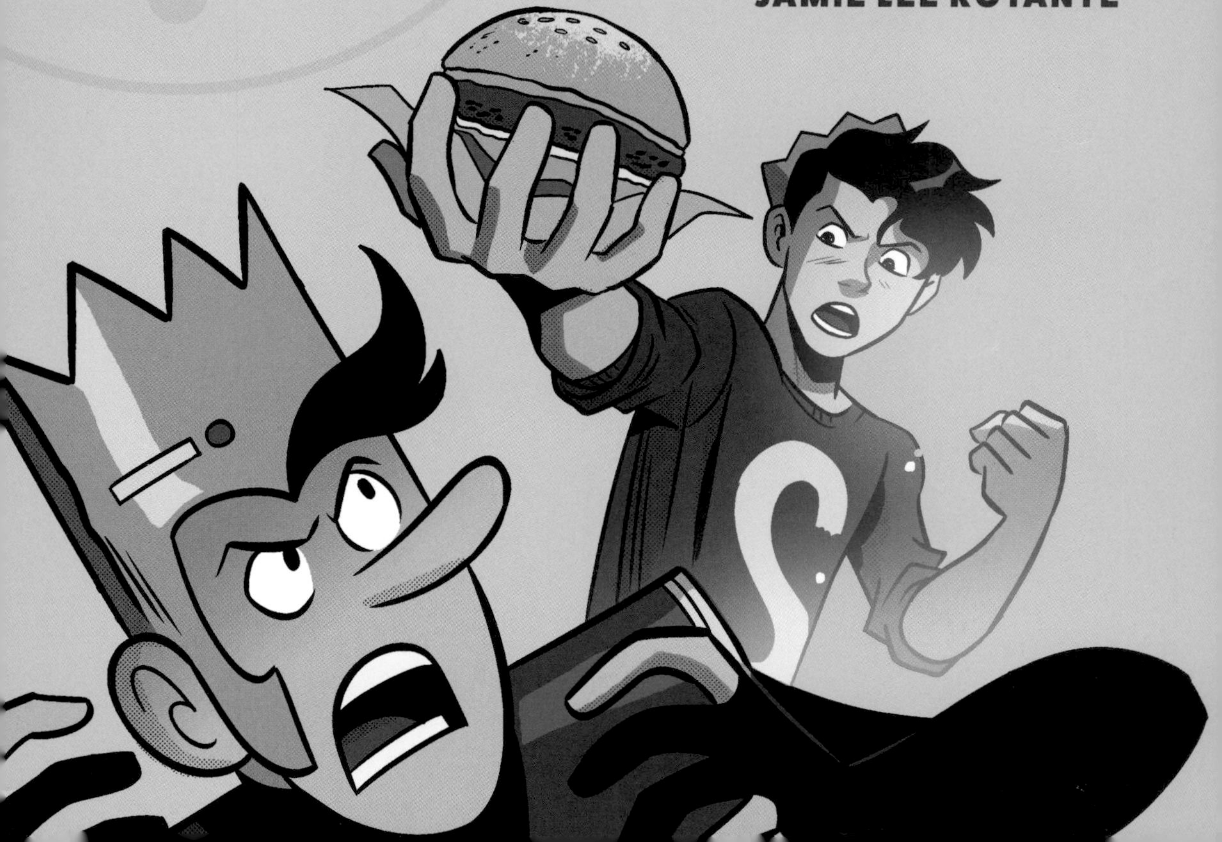

Making comics can be a lot like baking.

You need quality ingredients: characters, concept, writer, artist, colorist, letterer, editor, and production designer. You need to keep an eye on time—let one ingredient do its thing for too long and the whole project can come out overdone (Also the opposite: rush a project and it's half-baked). It takes all of these things to make a good comic. There has to be an added element to make a great comic. Much like baking, the key component is sort of a magical mystery... is it the weather? Is it something in the water? Whatever the thing is (luck, love, the spirit of a family member or Patrick Swayze guiding your hands), I feel like it's appropriate to say that *Jughead's Time Police* is an incredibly good bake.

Now, I'm not trying to brag here. Jughead Jones is a phenomenal character. Derek Charm and Matt Herms have already made oodles of magic together as an art team. Everyone involved is exceptional at their jobs. I'm merely the walnuts in this coffee walnut cake. Alex Segura is the coffee, to be sure. At any rate, I really do think we got lucky with this story. Derek had already drawn

Jughead before, and after a couple of years doing action books, he came back with a level of familiarity with the characters and a newfound passion for dynamic storytelling that really shines through. I had to tough it out being the optimistic writer in a sea of folks sending antiheroes into ultra-deep abysses, but now that "nicecore" is a thing, I was able to lean in, look at the reader and say: "You wanna see a story about friendship, music, good food, funny dogs, and have it include a bad guy who threatens the time-space continuum? Game on."

Oh, and I think Matt Herms is the sugar, 'cuz his coloring is sweeeeeet.

We got lucky with this book. All the ingredients were there, but the final bake really turned out to be a showstopper. I think we made a great story, and all worked extra hard to make sure it fits with the charm and joy of a proper Archie yarn. When it comes down to it, I also see comics—specifically Archie Comics—as similar to baking because their inherent purpose is exactly the same: to be sweet, delicious confections that leave folks fuller and happier.

Sina Grace

CHAPTER 1

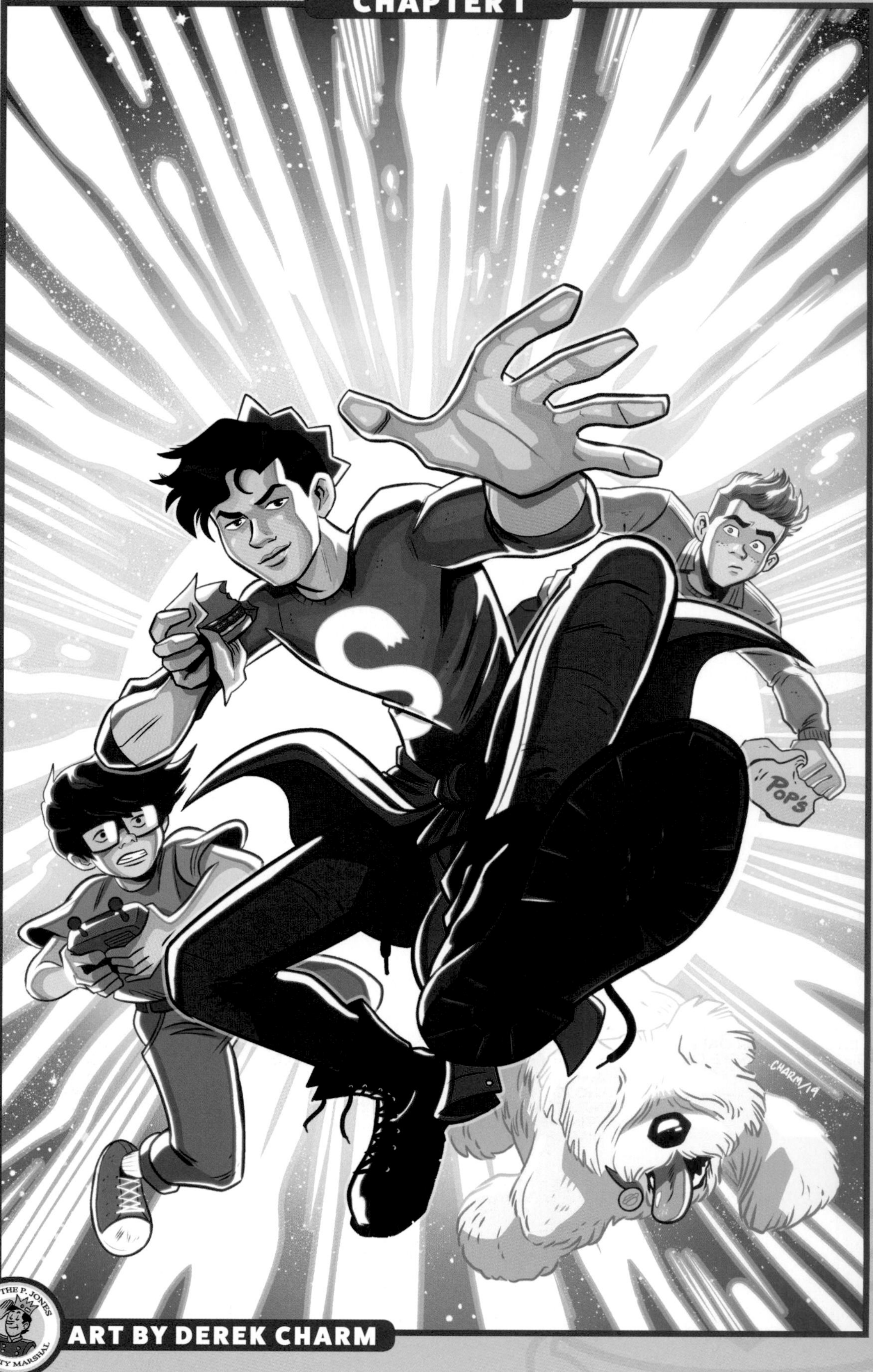
POP'S
CHARM/19

ART BY DEREK CHARM

FORSYTHE P. JONES
DEPUTY MARSHAL

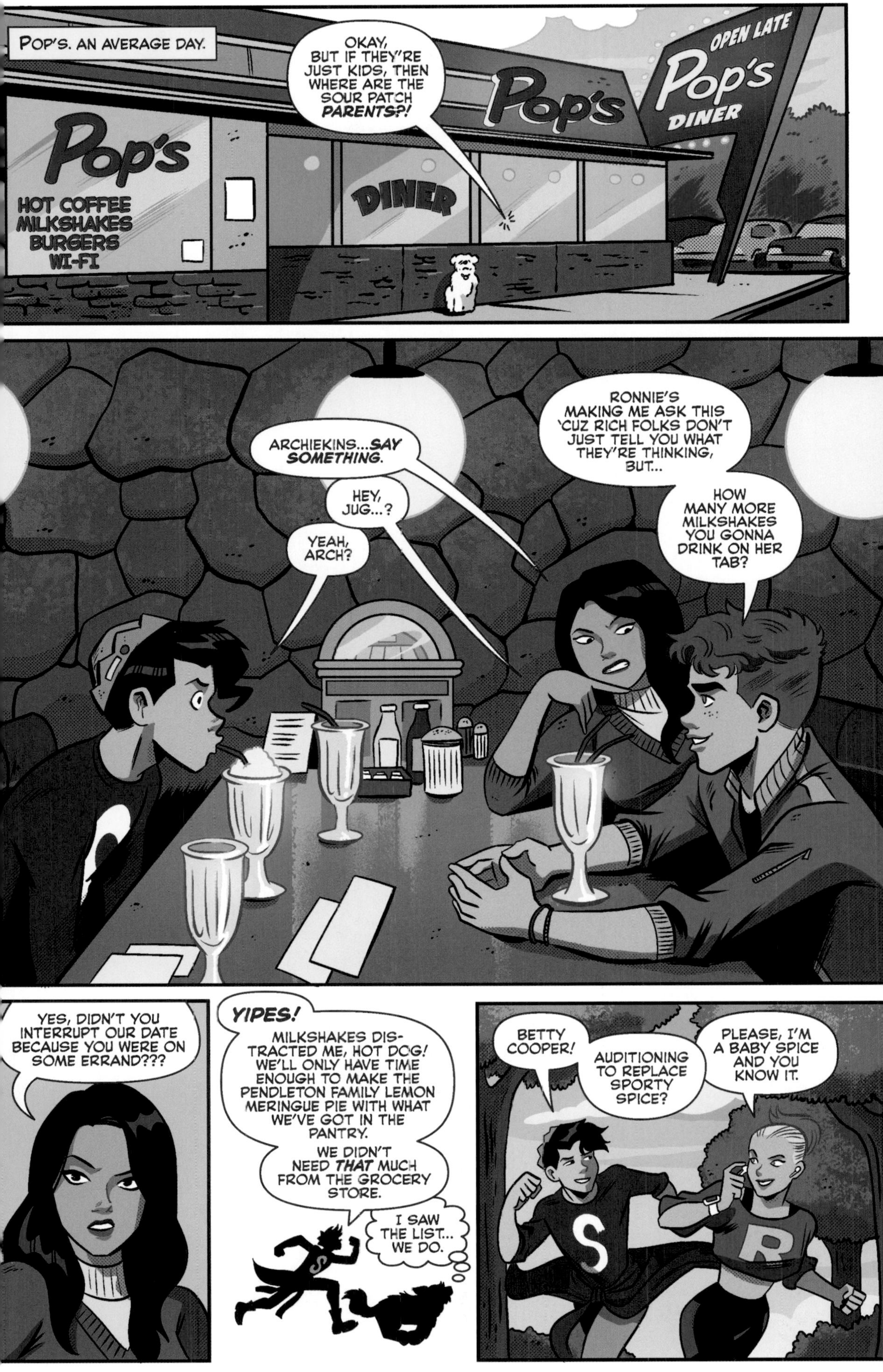
POP'S. AN AVERAGE DAY.
OKAY, BUT IF THEY'RE JUST KIDS, THEN WHERE ARE THE SOUR PATCH PARENTS?!
OPEN LATE
Pop's
DINER
Pop's
HOT COFFEE
MILKSHAKES
BURGERS
WI-FI
DINER
ARCHIEKINS...SAY SOMETHING.
HEY, JUG...?
YEAH, ARCH?
RONNIE'S MAKING ME ASK THIS 'CUZ RICH FOLKS DON'T JUST TELL YOU WHAT THEY'RE THINKING, BUT...
HOW MANY MORE MILKSHAKES YOU GONNA DRINK ON HER TAB?
YES, DIDN'T YOU INTERRUPT OUR DATE BECAUSE YOU WERE ON SOME ERRAND???
YIPES!
MILKSHAKES DIS-TRACTED ME, HOT DOG! WE'LL ONLY HAVE TIME ENOUGH TO MAKE THE PENDLETON FAMILY LEMON MERINGUE PIE WITH WHAT WE'VE GOT IN THE PANTRY.
WE DIDN'T NEED THAT MUCH FROM THE GROCERY STORE.
I SAW THE LIST... WE DO.
BETTY COOPER!
AUDITIONING TO REPLACE SPORTY SPICE?
PLEASE, I'M A BABY SPICE AND YOU KNOW IT.

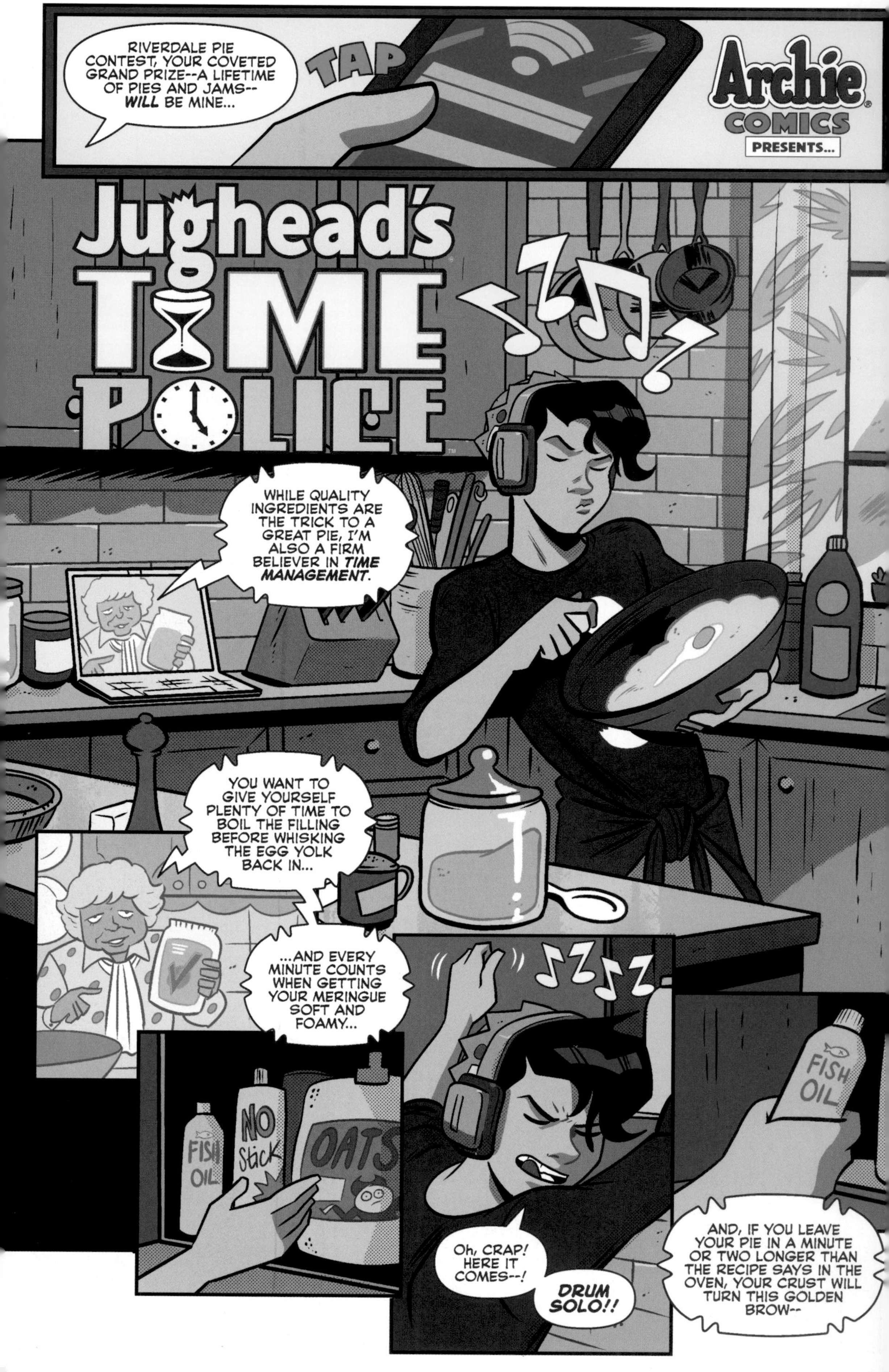
RIVERDALE PIE CONTEST, YOUR COVETED GRAND PRIZE--A LIFETIME OF PIES AND JAMS-- WILL BE MINE...
TAP
Archie COMICS PRESENTS...
Jughead's TIME POLICE
WHILE QUALITY INGREDIENTS ARE THE TRICK TO A GREAT PIE, I'M ALSO A FIRM BELIEVER IN TIME MANAGEMENT.
YOU WANT TO GIVE YOURSELF PLENTY OF TIME TO BOIL THE FILLING BEFORE WHISKING THE EGG YOLK BACK IN...
...AND EVERY MINUTE COUNTS WHEN GETTING YOUR MERINGUE SOFT AND FOAMY...
FISH OIL
NO Stick
OATS
FISH OIL
Oh, CRAP! HERE IT COMES--!
DRUM SOLO!!
AND, IF YOU LEAVE YOUR PIE IN A MINUTE OR TWO LONGER THAN THE RECIPE SAYS IN THE OVEN, YOUR CRUST WILL TURN THIS GOLDEN BROW--

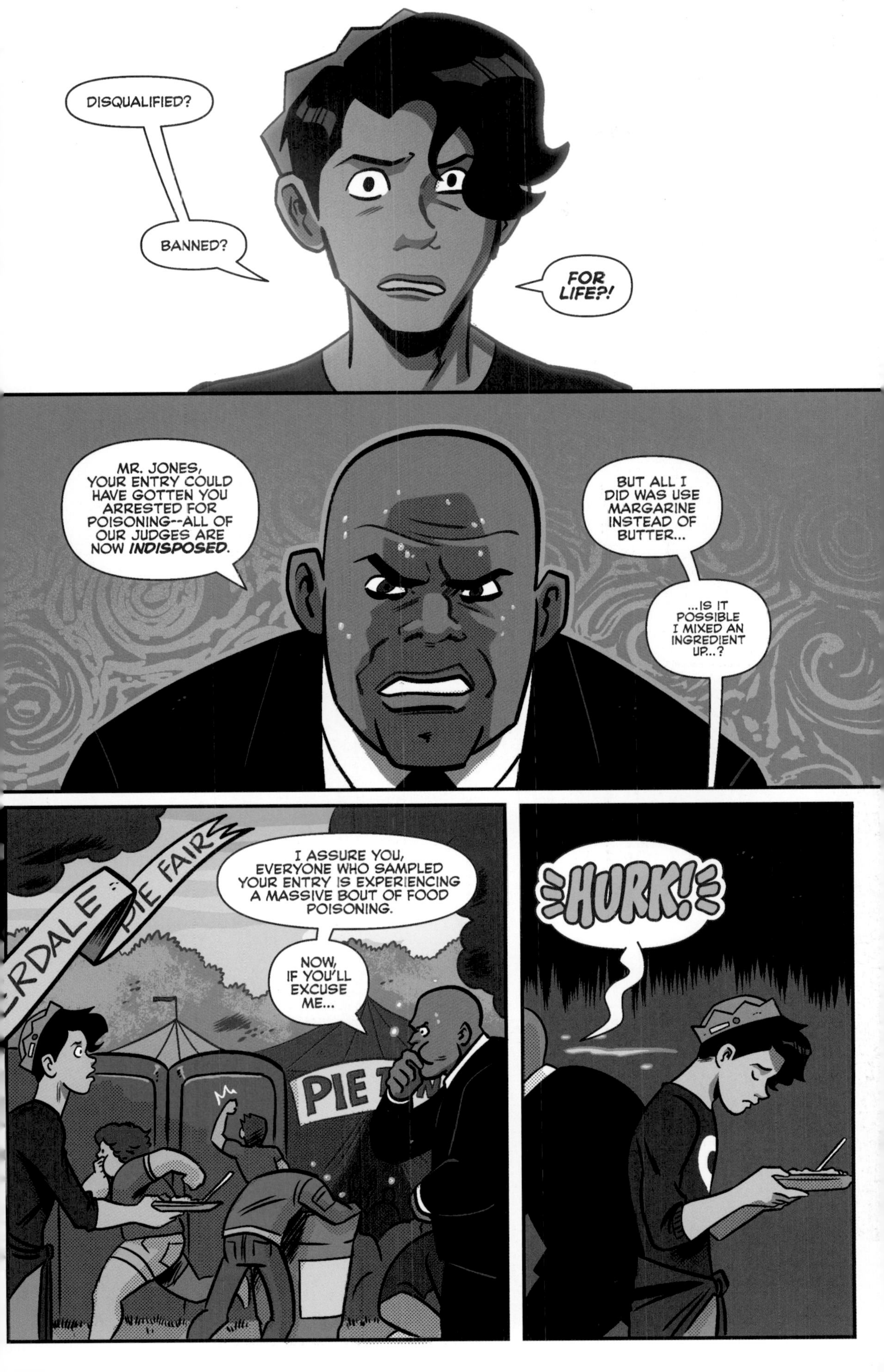
DISQUALIFIED?
BANNED?
FOR LIFE?!
MR. JONES, YOUR ENTRY COULD HAVE GOTTEN YOU ARRESTED FOR POISONING--ALL OF OUR JUDGES ARE NOW *INDISPOSED*.
BUT ALL I DID WAS USE MARGARINE INSTEAD OF BUTTER...
...IS IT POSSIBLE I MIXED AN INGREDIENT UP...?
ERDALE PIE FAIR
I ASSURE YOU, EVERYONE WHO SAMPLED YOUR ENTRY IS EXPERIENCING A MASSIVE BOUT OF FOOD POISONING.
NOW, IF YOU'LL EXCUSE ME...
PIE T
HURK!

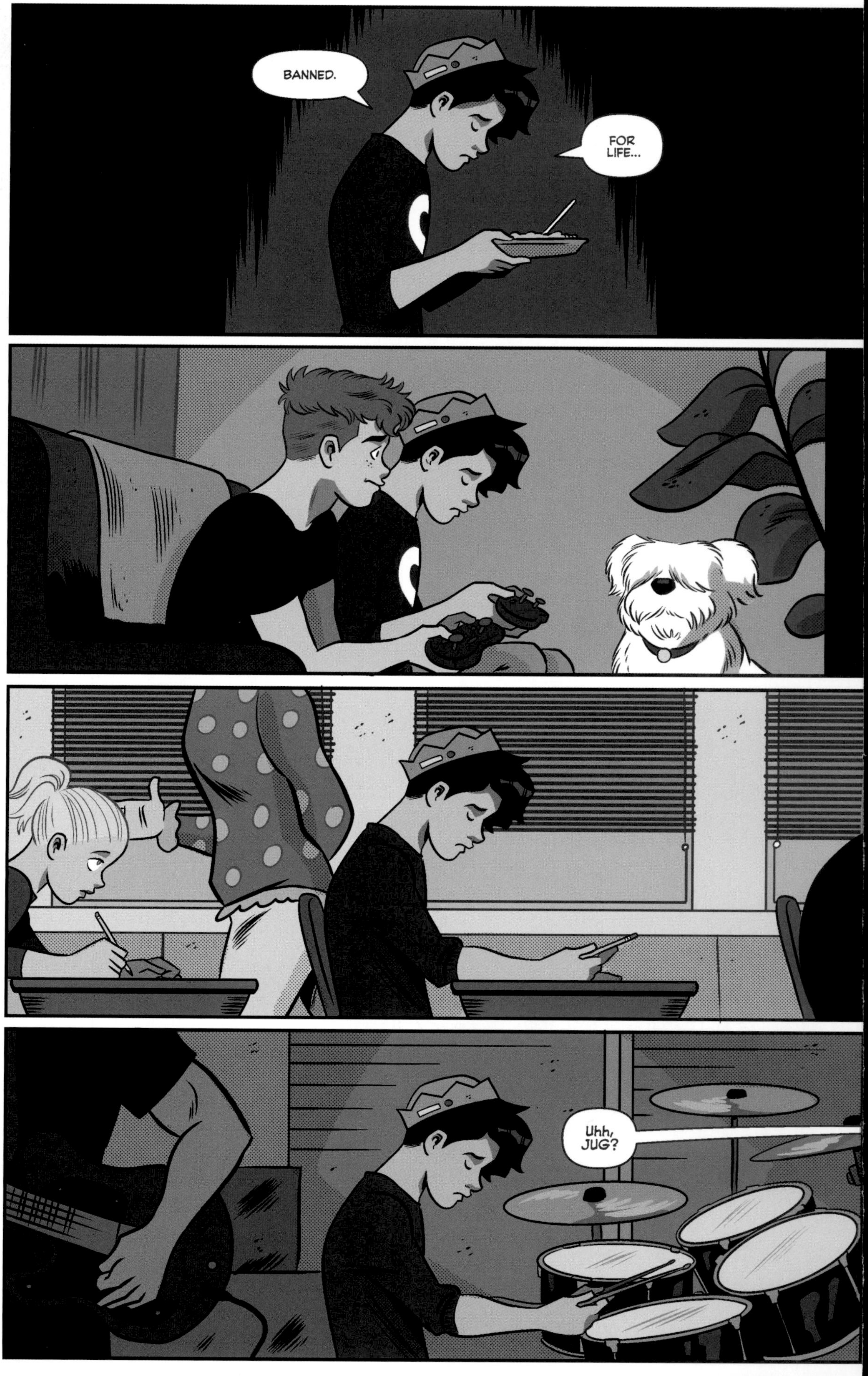
BANNED.
FOR LIFE...
Uhh, JUG?

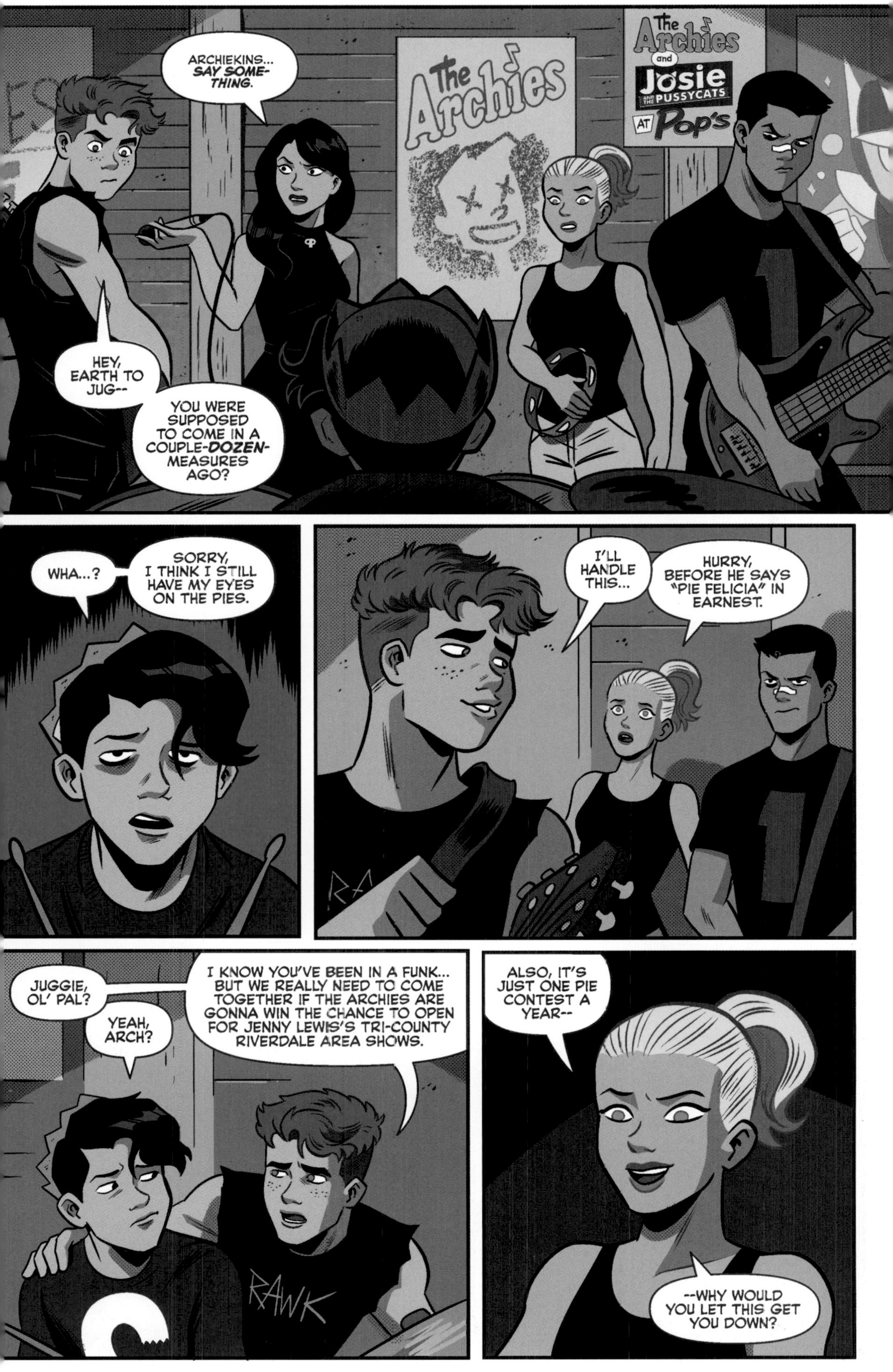

The Archies
The Archies and Josie and the Pussycats at Pop's
ARCHIEKINS... SAY SOMETHING.
HEY, EARTH TO JUG--
YOU WERE SUPPOSED TO COME IN A COUPLE-DOZEN-MEASURES AGO?
WHA...?
SORRY, I THINK I STILL HAVE MY EYES ON THE PIES.
I'LL HANDLE THIS...
HURRY, BEFORE HE SAYS "PIE FELICIA" IN EARNEST.
JUGGIE, OL' PAL?
YEAH, ARCH?
I KNOW YOU'VE BEEN IN A FUNK... BUT WE REALLY NEED TO COME TOGETHER IF THE ARCHIES ARE GONNA WIN THE CHANCE TO OPEN FOR JENNY LEWIS'S TRI-COUNTY RIVERDALE AREA SHOWS.
RAWK
ALSO, IT'S JUST ONE PIE CONTEST A YEAR--
--WHY WOULD YOU LET THIS GET YOU DOWN?

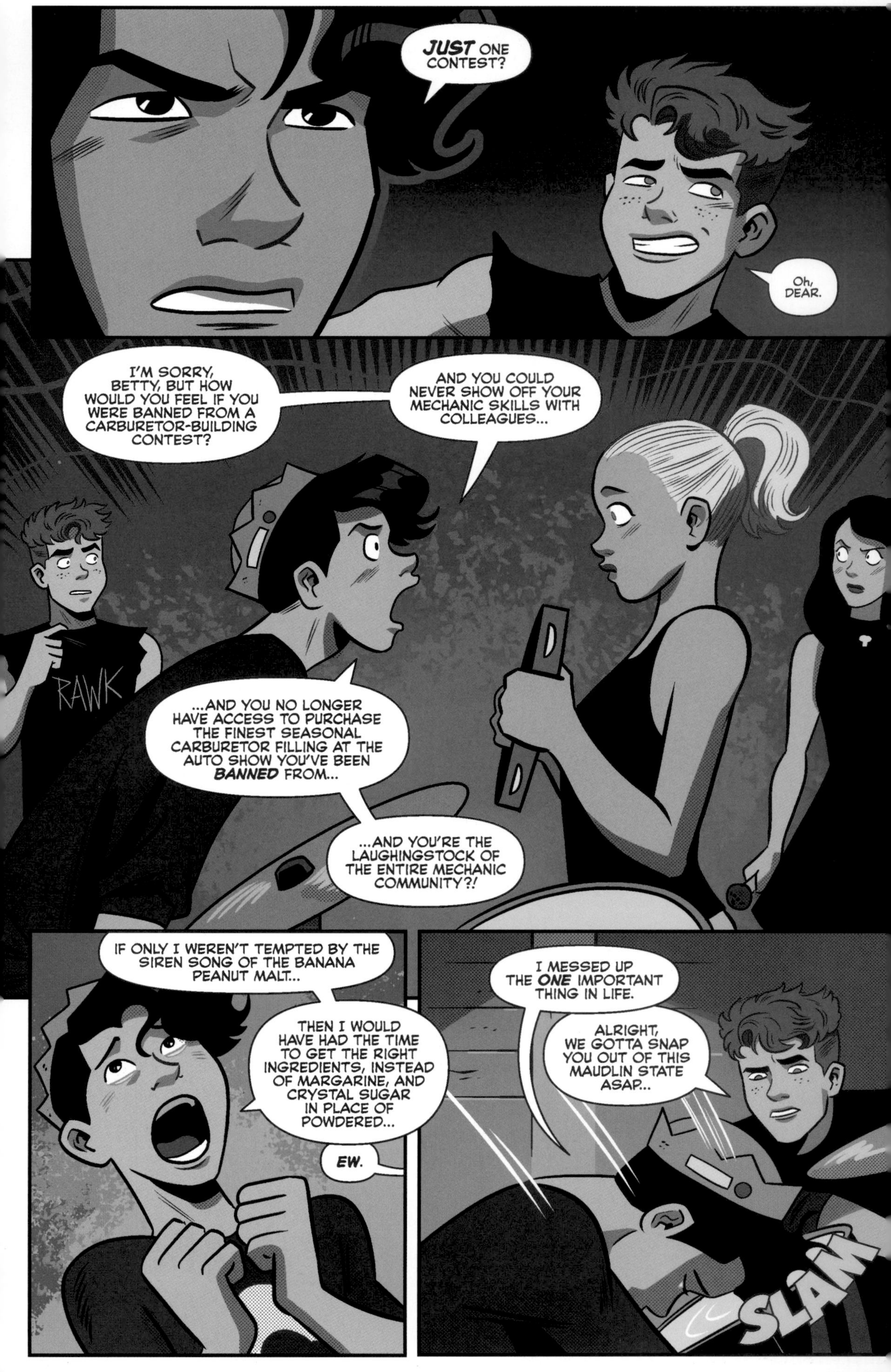

JUST ONE CONTEST?
Oh, DEAR.
I'M SORRY, BETTY, BUT HOW WOULD YOU FEEL IF YOU WERE BANNED FROM A CARBURETOR-BUILDING CONTEST?
AND YOU COULD NEVER SHOW OFF YOUR MECHANIC SKILLS WITH COLLEAGUES...
RAWK
...AND YOU NO LONGER HAVE ACCESS TO PURCHASE THE FINEST SEASONAL CARBURETOR FILLING AT THE AUTO SHOW YOU'VE BEEN BANNED FROM...
...AND YOU'RE THE LAUGHINGSTOCK OF THE ENTIRE MECHANIC COMMUNITY?!
IF ONLY I WEREN'T TEMPTED BY THE SIREN SONG OF THE BANANA PEANUT MALT...
THEN I WOULD HAVE HAD THE TIME TO GET THE RIGHT INGREDIENTS, INSTEAD OF MARGARINE, AND CRYSTAL SUGAR IN PLACE OF POWDERED...
EW.
I MESSED UP THE ONE IMPORTANT THING IN LIFE.
ALRIGHT, WE GOTTA SNAP YOU OUT OF THIS MAUDLIN STATE ASAP...
SLAM

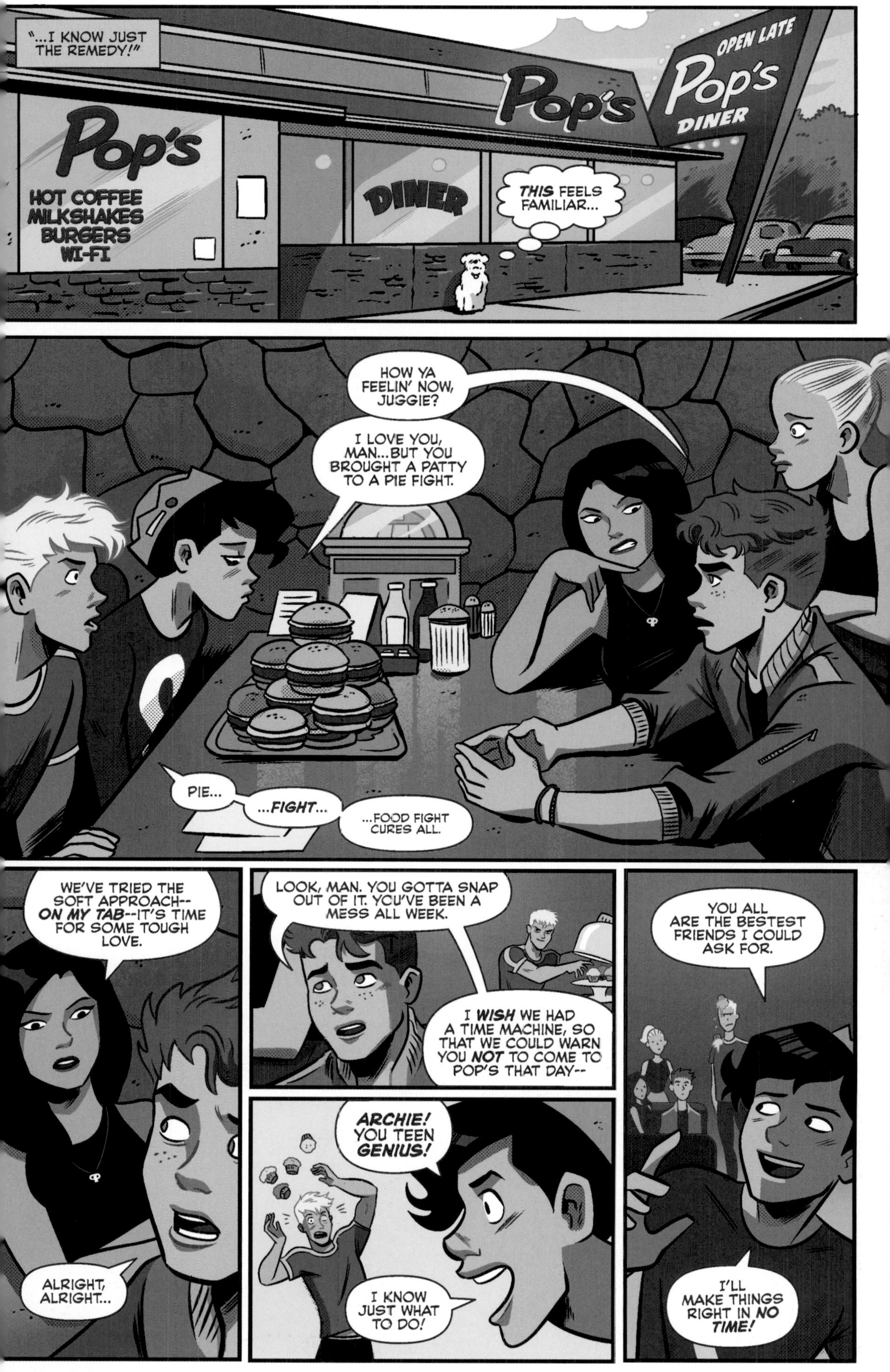
"...I KNOW JUST THE REMEDY!"
OPEN LATE
Pop's
DINER
Pop's
Pop's
HOT COFFEE
MILKSHAKES
BURGERS
WI-FI
DINER
THIS FEELS FAMILIAR...
HOW YA FEELIN' NOW, JUGGIE?
I LOVE YOU, MAN...BUT YOU BROUGHT A PATTY TO A PIE FIGHT.
PIE...
...FIGHT...
...FOOD FIGHT CURES ALL.
WE'VE TRIED THE SOFT APPROACH--ON MY TAB--IT'S TIME FOR SOME TOUGH LOVE.
ALRIGHT, ALRIGHT...
LOOK, MAN. YOU GOTTA SNAP OUT OF IT. YOU'VE BEEN A MESS ALL WEEK.
I WISH WE HAD A TIME MACHINE, SO THAT WE COULD WARN YOU NOT TO COME TO POP'S THAT DAY--
ARCHIE! YOU TEEN GENIUS!
I KNOW JUST WHAT TO DO!
YOU ALL ARE THE BESTEST FRIENDS I COULD ASK FOR.
I'LL MAKE THINGS RIGHT IN NO TIME!

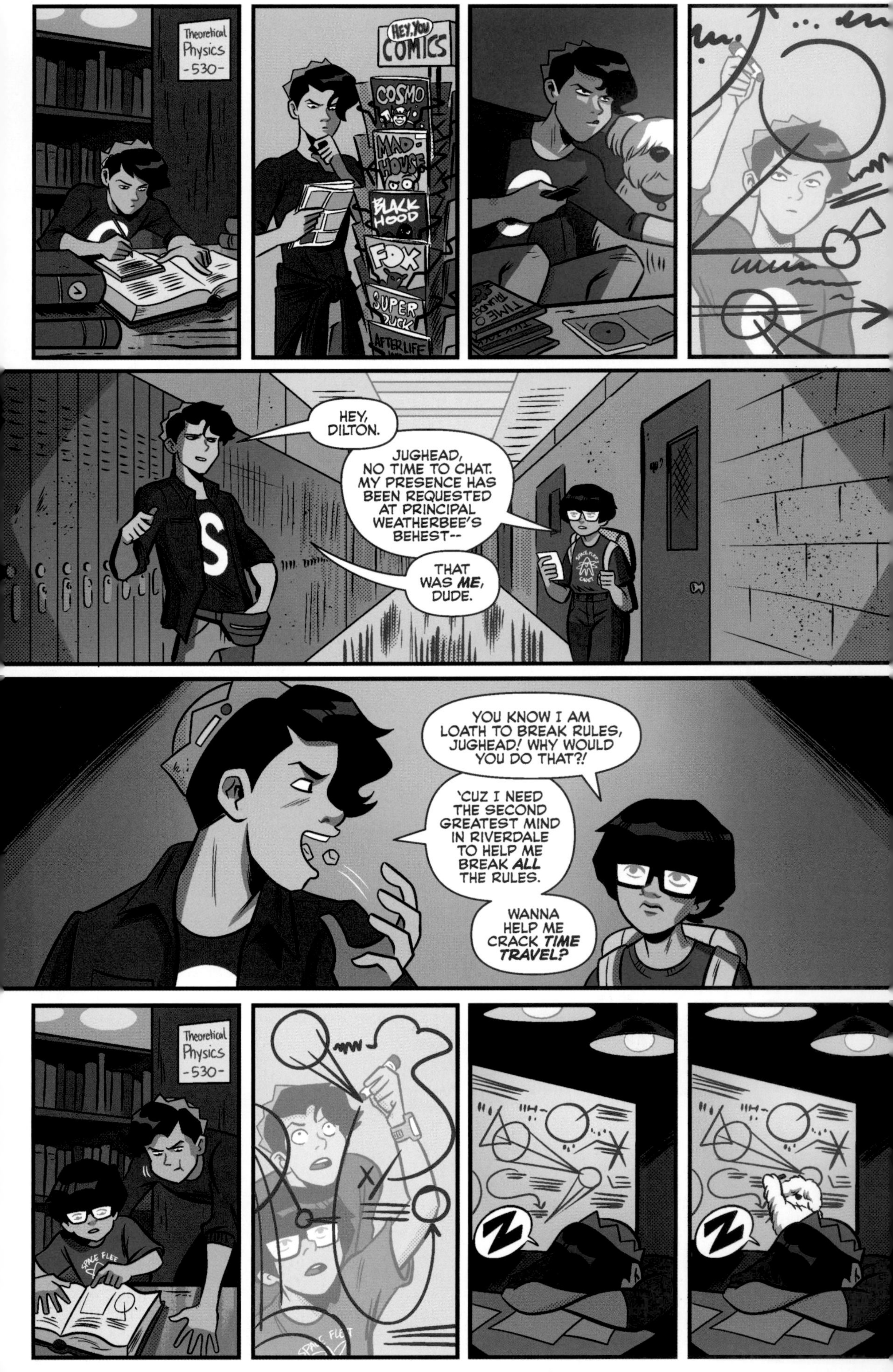
Theoretical Physics -530-
HEY, YOU COMICS
COSMO
MAD-HOUSE
BLACK HOOD
FOX
SUPER DUCK
AFTERLIFE
TIME
HEY, DILTON.
JUGHEAD, NO TIME TO CHAT. MY PRESENCE HAS BEEN REQUESTED AT PRINCIPAL WEATHERBEE'S BEHEST--
THAT WAS ME, DUDE.
YOU KNOW I AM LOATH TO BREAK RULES, JUGHEAD! WHY WOULD YOU DO THAT?!
'CUZ I NEED THE SECOND GREATEST MIND IN RIVERDALE TO HELP ME BREAK ALL THE RULES.
WANNA HELP ME CRACK TIME TRAVEL?
Theoretical Physics -530-
SPACE FLEET
Z
Z

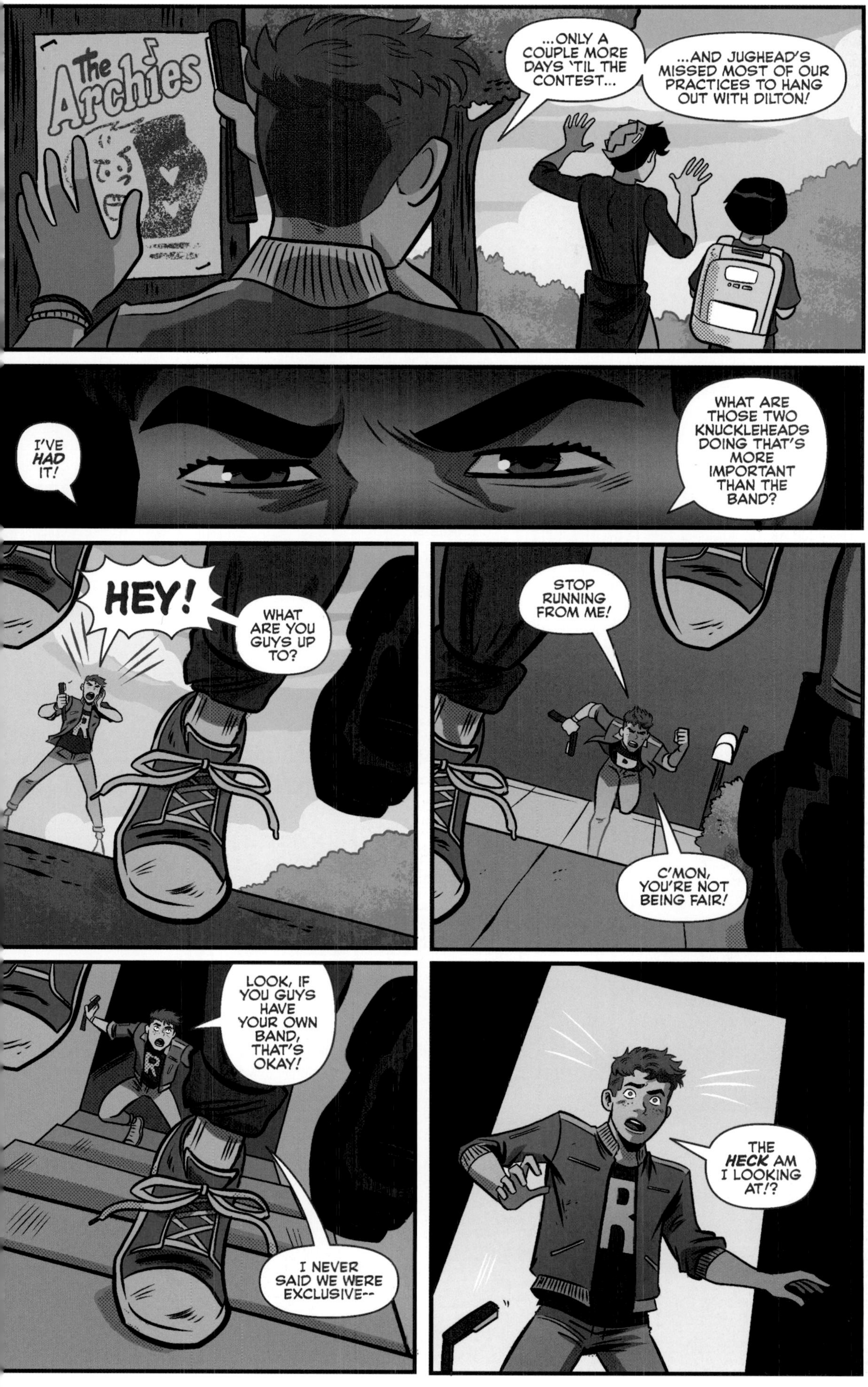
The Archies
...ONLY A COUPLE MORE DAYS 'TIL THE CONTEST...
...AND JUGHEAD'S MISSED MOST OF OUR PRACTICES TO HANG OUT WITH DILTON!
I'VE *HAD* IT!
WHAT ARE THOSE TWO KNUCKLEHEADS DOING THAT'S MORE IMPORTANT THAN THE BAND?
HEY!
WHAT ARE YOU GUYS UP TO?
STOP RUNNING FROM ME!
C'MON, YOU'RE NOT BEING FAIR!
LOOK, IF YOU GUYS HAVE YOUR OWN BAND, THAT'S OKAY!
I NEVER SAID WE WERE EXCLUSIVE--
THE *HECK* AM I LOOKING AT!?

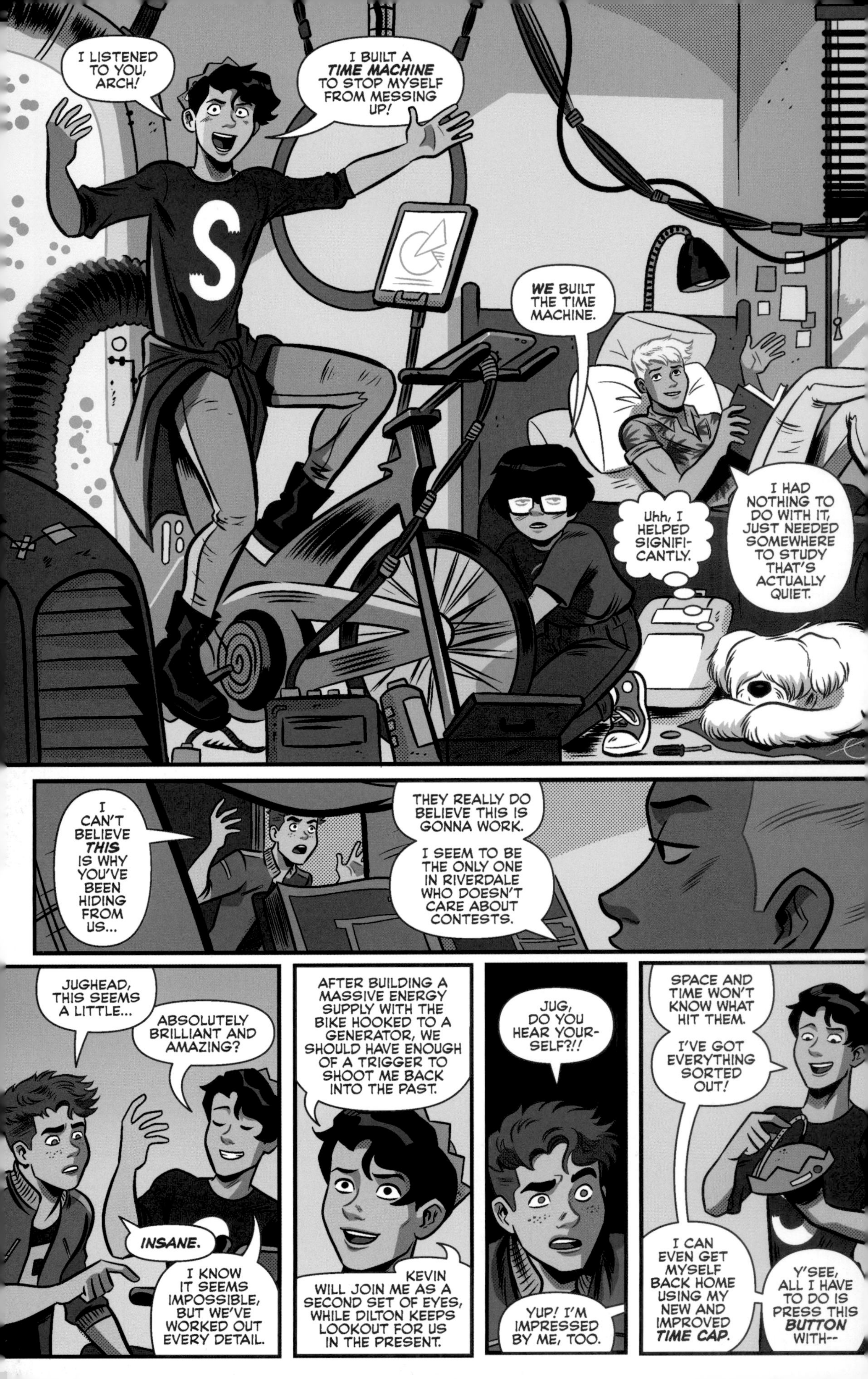
I LISTENED TO YOU, ARCH!
I BUILT A *TIME MACHINE* TO STOP MYSELF FROM MESSING UP!
WE BUILT THE TIME MACHINE.
Uhh, I HELPED SIGNIFI-CANTLY.
I HAD NOTHING TO DO WITH IT, JUST NEEDED SOMEWHERE TO STUDY THAT'S ACTUALLY QUIET.
I CAN'T BELIEVE *THIS* IS WHY YOU'VE BEEN HIDING FROM US...
THEY REALLY DO BELIEVE THIS IS GONNA WORK.
I SEEM TO BE THE ONLY ONE IN RIVERDALE WHO DOESN'T CARE ABOUT CONTESTS.
JUGHEAD, THIS SEEMS A LITTLE...
ABSOLUTELY BRILLIANT AND AMAZING?
INSANE.
I KNOW IT SEEMS IMPOSSIBLE, BUT WE'VE WORKED OUT EVERY DETAIL.
AFTER BUILDING A MASSIVE ENERGY SUPPLY WITH THE BIKE HOOKED TO A GENERATOR, WE SHOULD HAVE ENOUGH OF A TRIGGER TO SHOOT ME BACK INTO THE PAST.
KEVIN WILL JOIN ME AS A SECOND SET OF EYES, WHILE DILTON KEEPS LOOKOUT FOR US IN THE PRESENT.
JUG, DO YOU HEAR YOUR-SELF?!!
YUP! I'M IMPRESSED BY ME, TOO.
SPACE AND TIME WON'T KNOW WHAT HIT THEM.
I'VE GOT EVERYTHING SORTED OUT!
I CAN EVEN GET MYSELF BACK HOME USING MY NEW AND IMPROVED *TIME CAP*.
Y'SEE, ALL I HAVE TO DO IS PRESS THIS *BUTTON* WITH--

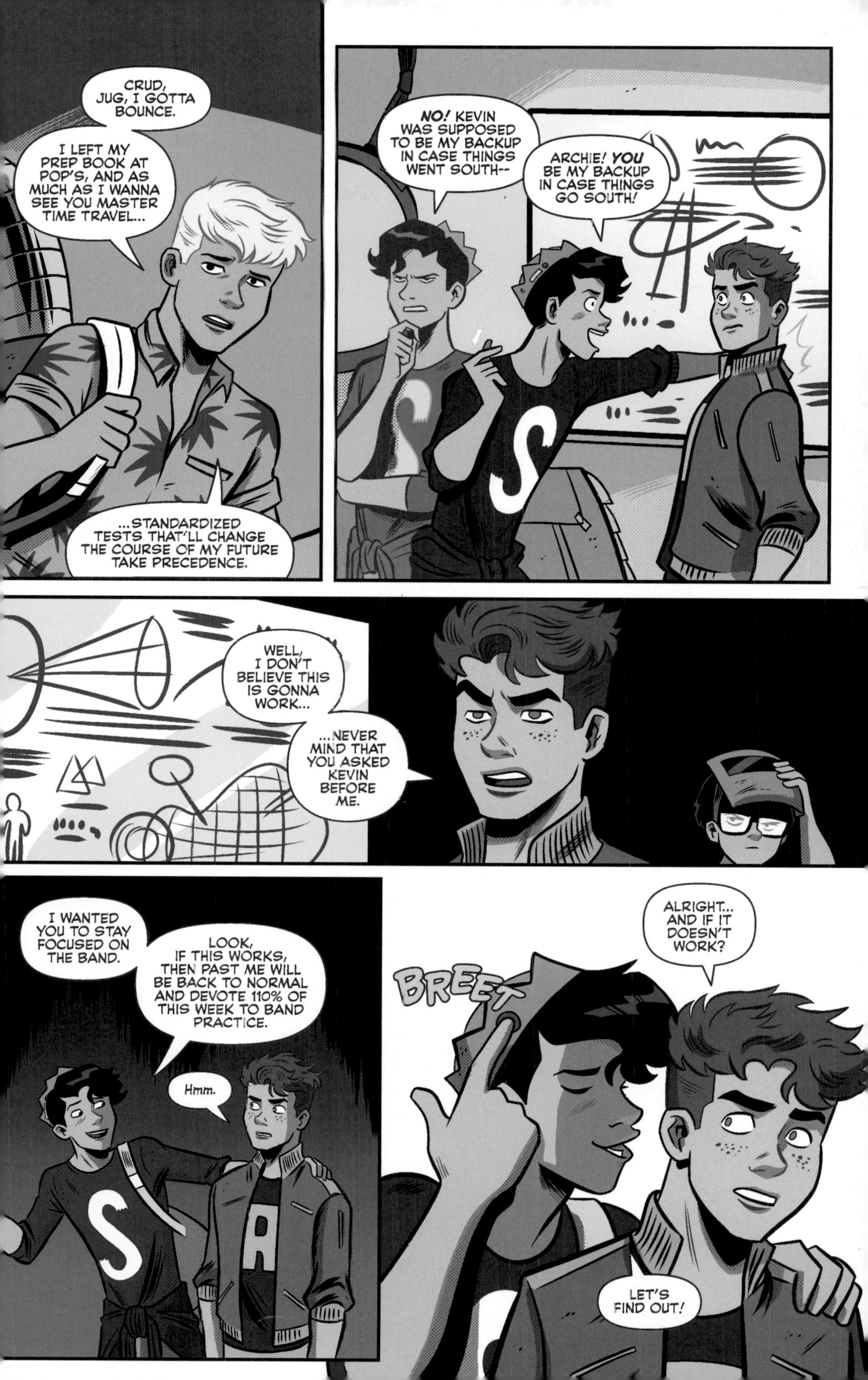
CRUD, JUG, I GOTTA BOUNCE.
I LEFT MY PREP BOOK AT POP'S, AND AS MUCH AS I WANNA SEE YOU MASTER TIME TRAVEL...
...STANDARDIZED TESTS THAT'LL CHANGE THE COURSE OF MY FUTURE TAKE PRECEDENCE.
NO! KEVIN WAS SUPPOSED TO BE MY BACKUP IN CASE THINGS WENT SOUTH--
ARCHIE! YOU BE MY BACKUP IN CASE THINGS GO SOUTH!
WELL, I DON'T BELIEVE THIS IS GONNA WORK...
...NEVER MIND THAT YOU ASKED KEVIN BEFORE ME.
I WANTED YOU TO STAY FOCUSED ON THE BAND.
LOOK, IF THIS WORKS, THEN PAST ME WILL BE BACK TO NORMAL AND DEVOTE 110% OF THIS WEEK TO BAND PRACTICE.
Hmm.
ALRIGHT... AND IF IT DOESN'T WORK?
BREEET
LET'S FIND OUT!

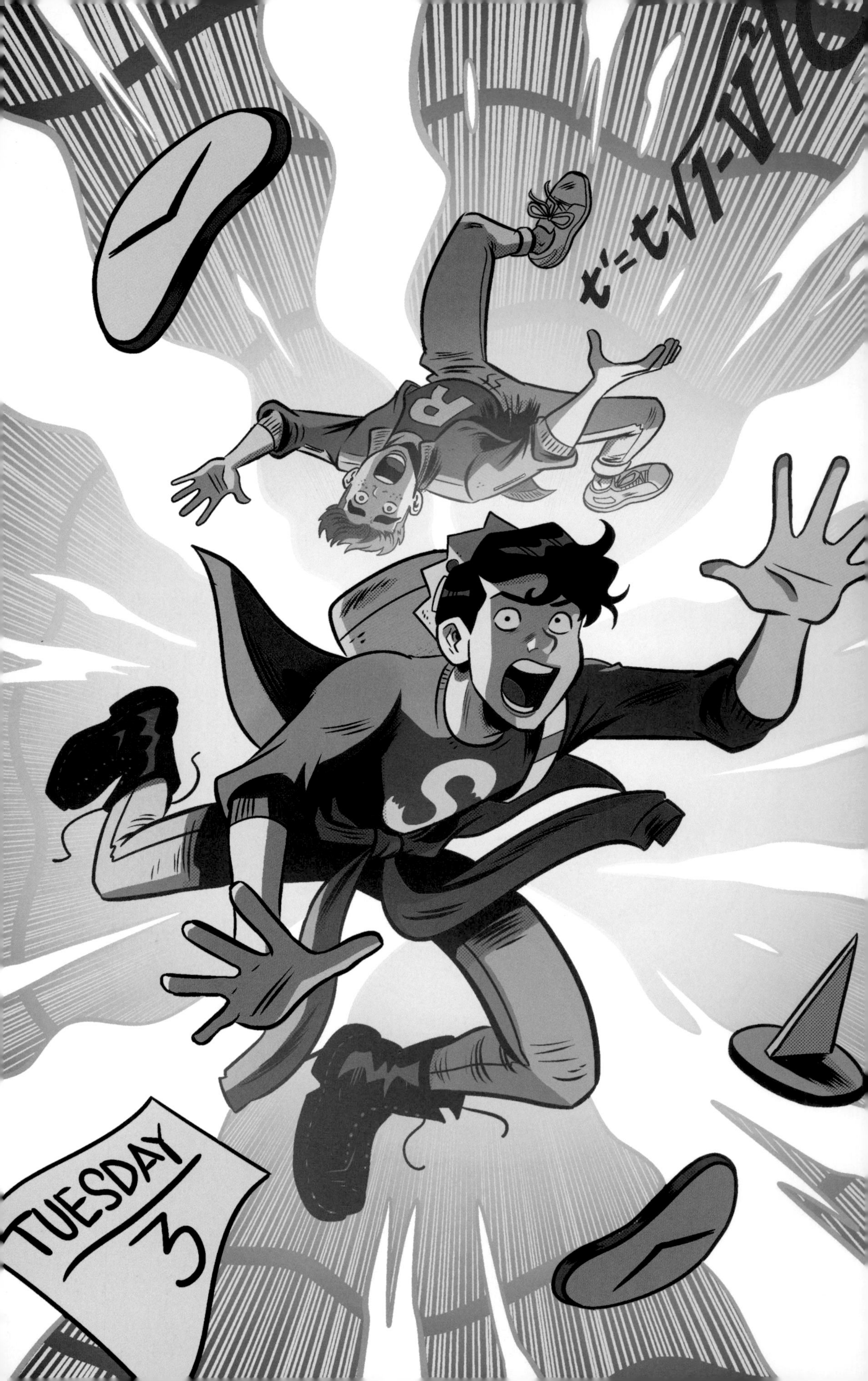
TUESDAY
3

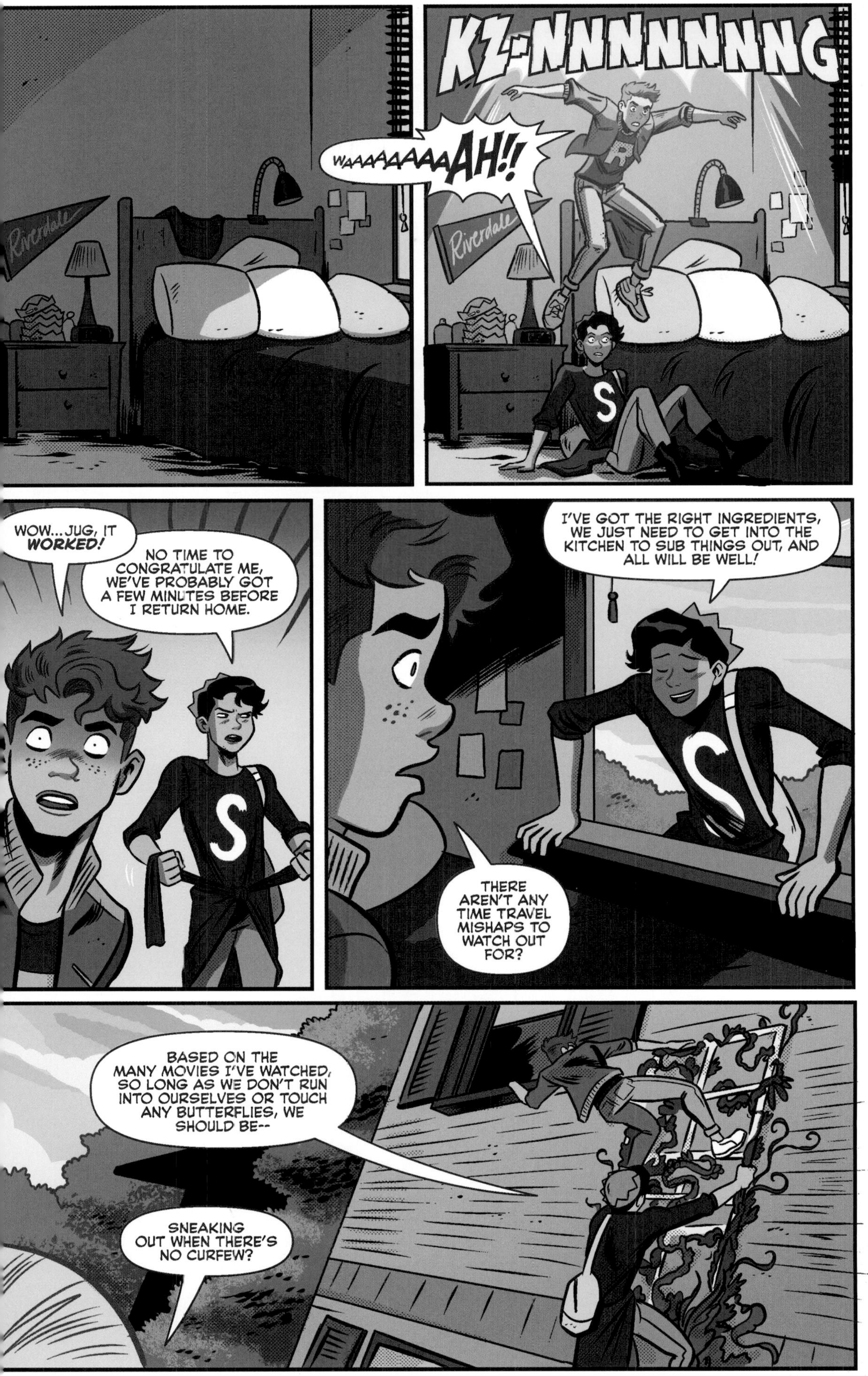

Riverdale
KZ-NNNNNNNG
WAAAAAAAAAH!!
Riverdale
WOW...JUG, IT WORKED!
NO TIME TO CONGRATULATE ME, WE'VE PROBABLY GOT A FEW MINUTES BEFORE I RETURN HOME.
I'VE GOT THE RIGHT INGREDIENTS, WE JUST NEED TO GET INTO THE KITCHEN TO SUB THINGS OUT, AND ALL WILL BE WELL!
THERE AREN'T ANY TIME TRAVEL MISHAPS TO WATCH OUT FOR?
BASED ON THE MANY MOVIES I'VE WATCHED, SO LONG AS WE DON'T RUN INTO OURSELVES OR TOUCH ANY BUTTERFLIES, WE SHOULD BE--
SNEAKING OUT WHEN THERE'S NO CURFEW?

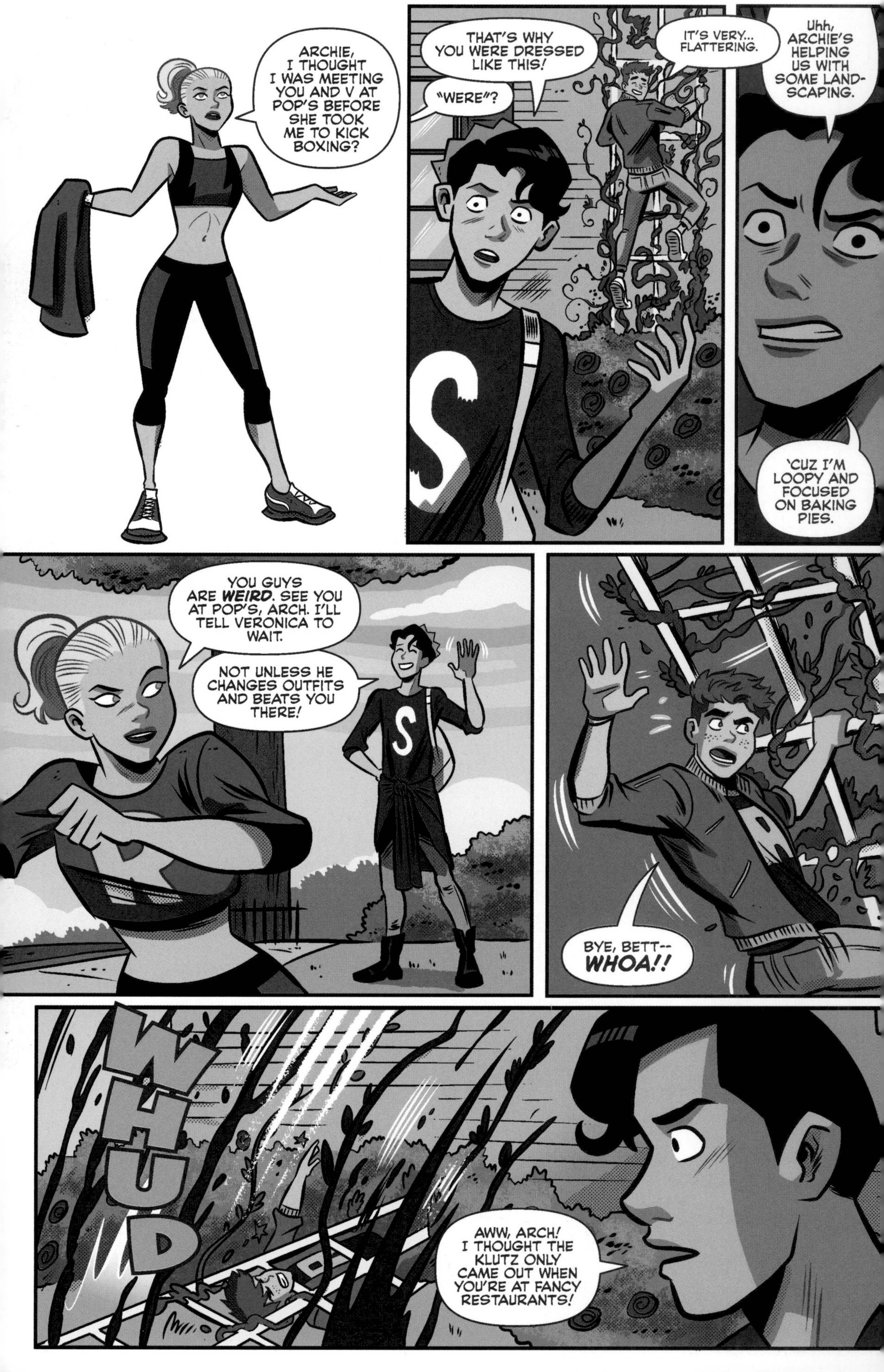
ARCHIE, I THOUGHT I WAS MEETING YOU AND V AT POP'S BEFORE SHE TOOK ME TO KICK BOXING?
THAT'S WHY YOU WERE DRESSED LIKE THIS!
"WERE"?
IT'S VERY... FLATTERING.
Uhh, ARCHIE'S HELPING US WITH SOME LAND-SCAPING.
'CUZ I'M LOOPY AND FOCUSED ON BAKING PIES.
YOU GUYS ARE *WEIRD*. SEE YOU AT POP'S, ARCH. I'LL TELL VERONICA TO WAIT.
NOT UNLESS HE CHANGES OUTFITS AND BEATS YOU THERE!
BYE, BETT-- **WHOA!!**
WHUD
AWW, ARCH! I THOUGHT THE KLUTZ ONLY CAME OUT WHEN YOU'RE AT FANCY RESTAURANTS!

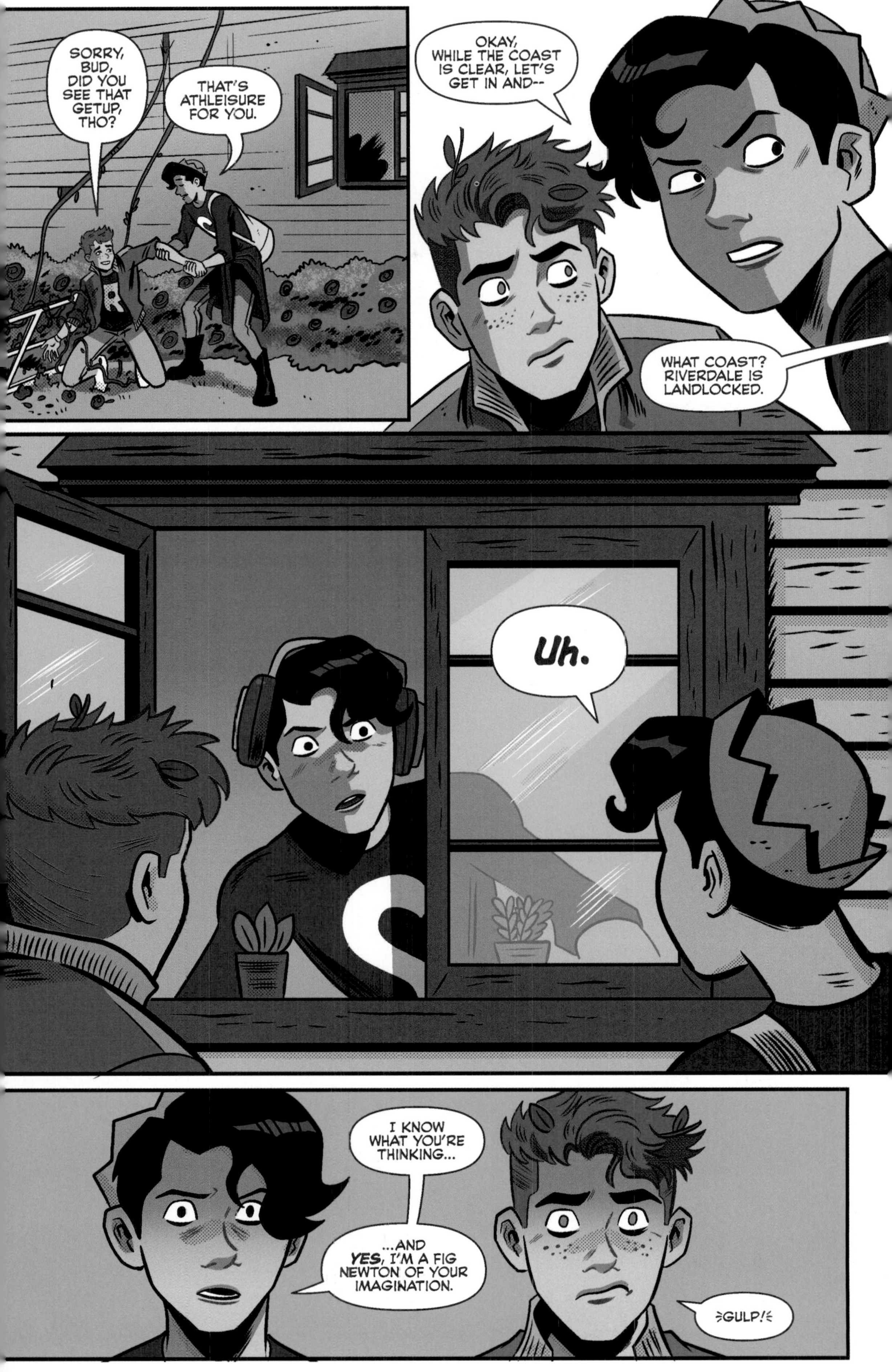
SORRY, BUD, DID YOU SEE THAT GETUP, THO?
THAT'S ATHLEISURE FOR YOU.
OKAY, WHILE THE COAST IS CLEAR, LET'S GET IN AND--
WHAT COAST? RIVERDALE IS LANDLOCKED.
Uh.
I KNOW WHAT YOU'RE THINKING...
...AND *YES*, I'M A FIG NEWTON OF YOUR IMAGINATION.
GULP!

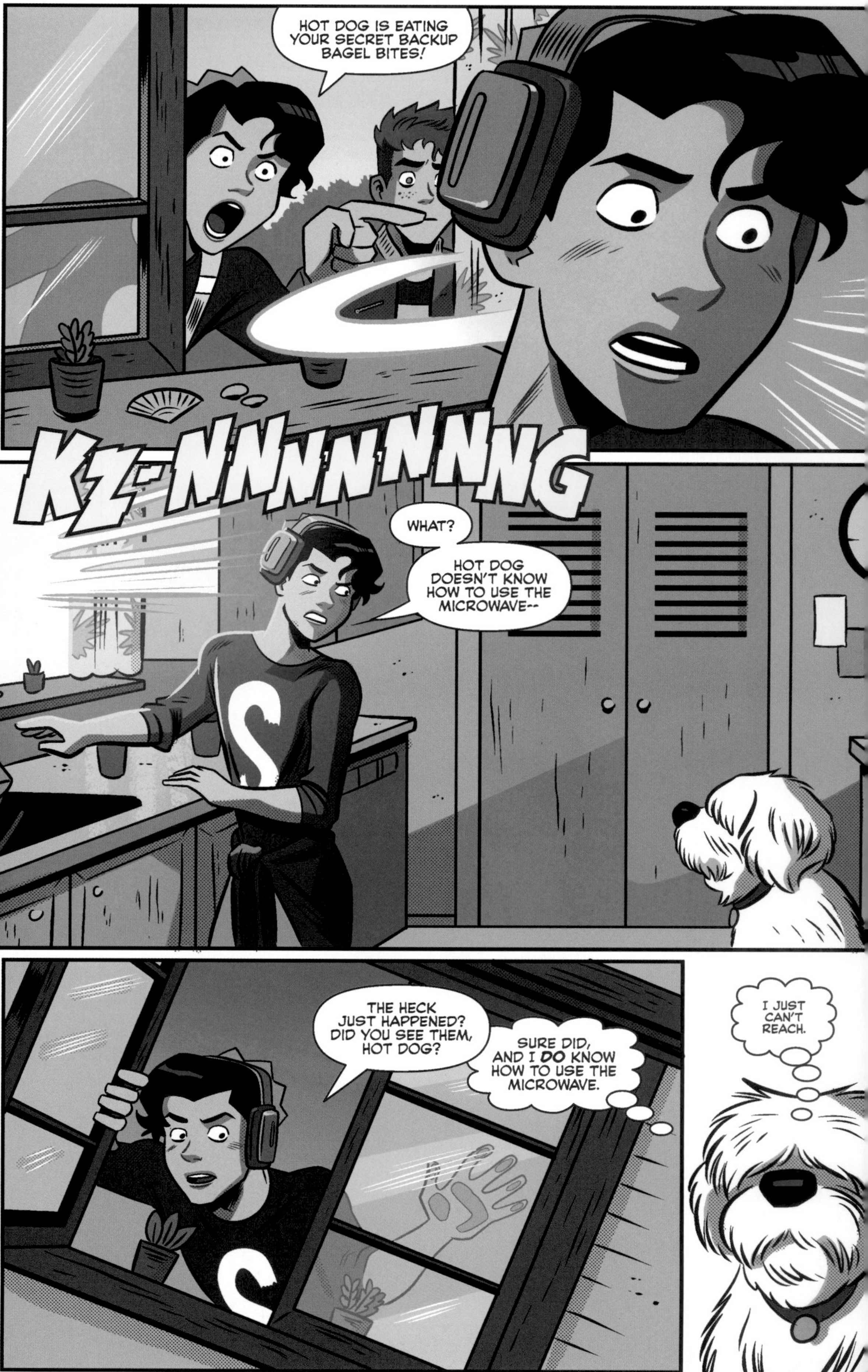
HOT DOG IS EATING YOUR SECRET BACKUP BAGEL BITES!
KZ-NNNNNNNG
WHAT?
HOT DOG DOESN'T KNOW HOW TO USE THE MICROWAVE--
THE HECK JUST HAPPENED? DID YOU SEE THEM, HOT DOG?
SURE DID, AND I DO KNOW HOW TO USE THE MICROWAVE.
I JUST CAN'T REACH.

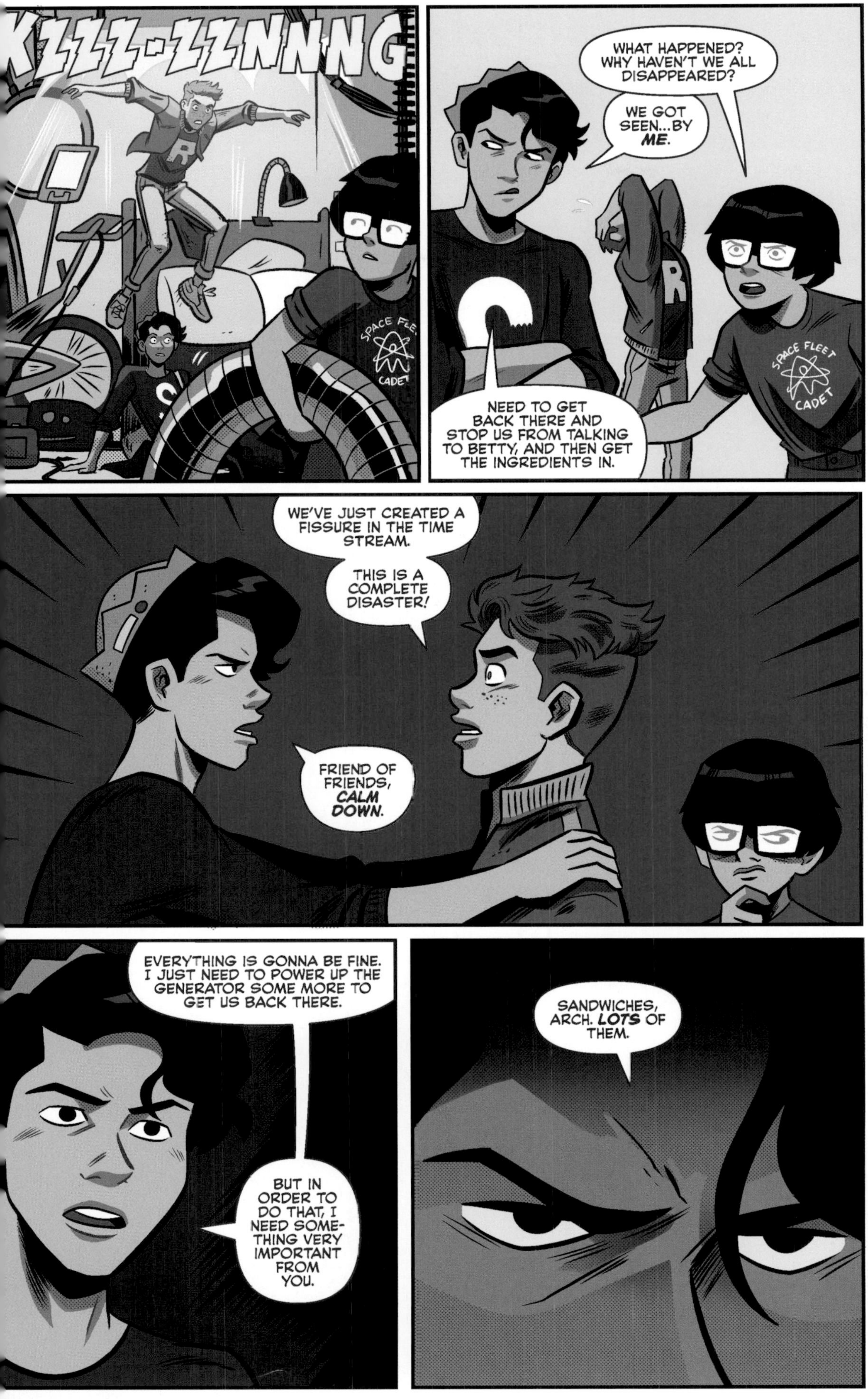
KZZZ-ZZNNNG
SPACE FLEET CADET
WHAT HAPPENED? WHY HAVEN'T WE ALL DISAPPEARED?
WE GOT SEEN...BY ME.
NEED TO GET BACK THERE AND STOP US FROM TALKING TO BETTY, AND THEN GET THE INGREDIENTS IN.
SPACE FLEET CADET
WE'VE JUST CREATED A FISSURE IN THE TIME STREAM.
THIS IS A COMPLETE DISASTER!
FRIEND OF FRIENDS, CALM DOWN.
EVERYTHING IS GONNA BE FINE. I JUST NEED TO POWER UP THE GENERATOR SOME MORE TO GET US BACK THERE.
BUT IN ORDER TO DO THAT, I NEED SOME-THING VERY IMPORTANT FROM YOU.
SANDWICHES, ARCH. LOTS OF THEM.

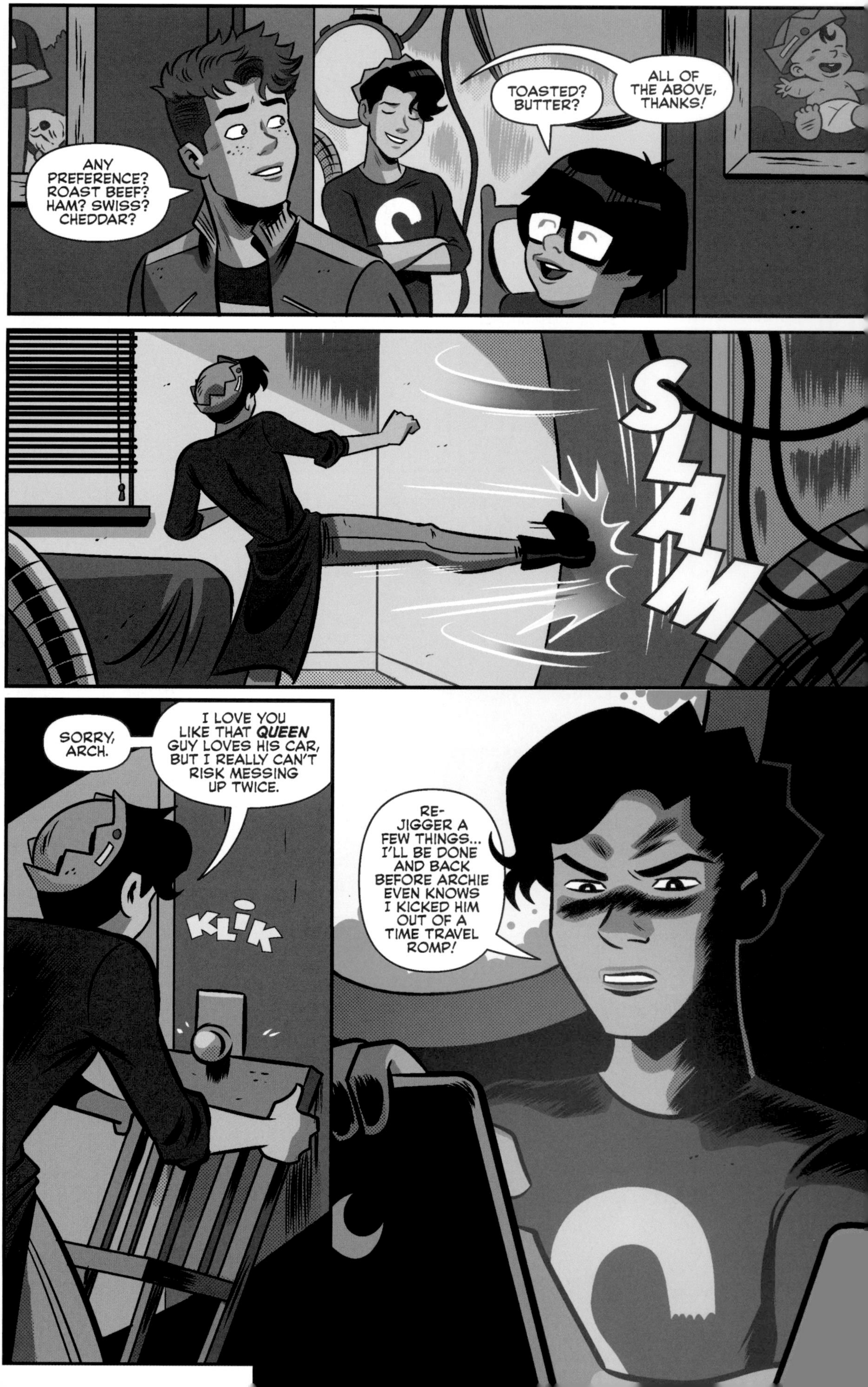
ANY PREFERENCE? ROAST BEEF? HAM? SWISS? CHEDDAR?
TOASTED? BUTTER?
ALL OF THE ABOVE, THANKS!
SLAM
SORRY, ARCH.
I LOVE YOU LIKE THAT **QUEEN** GUY LOVES HIS CAR, BUT I REALLY CAN'T RISK MESSING UP TWICE.
KLIK
RE-JIGGER A FEW THINGS... I'LL BE DONE AND BACK BEFORE ARCHIE EVEN KNOWS I KICKED HIM OUT OF A TIME TRAVEL ROMP!

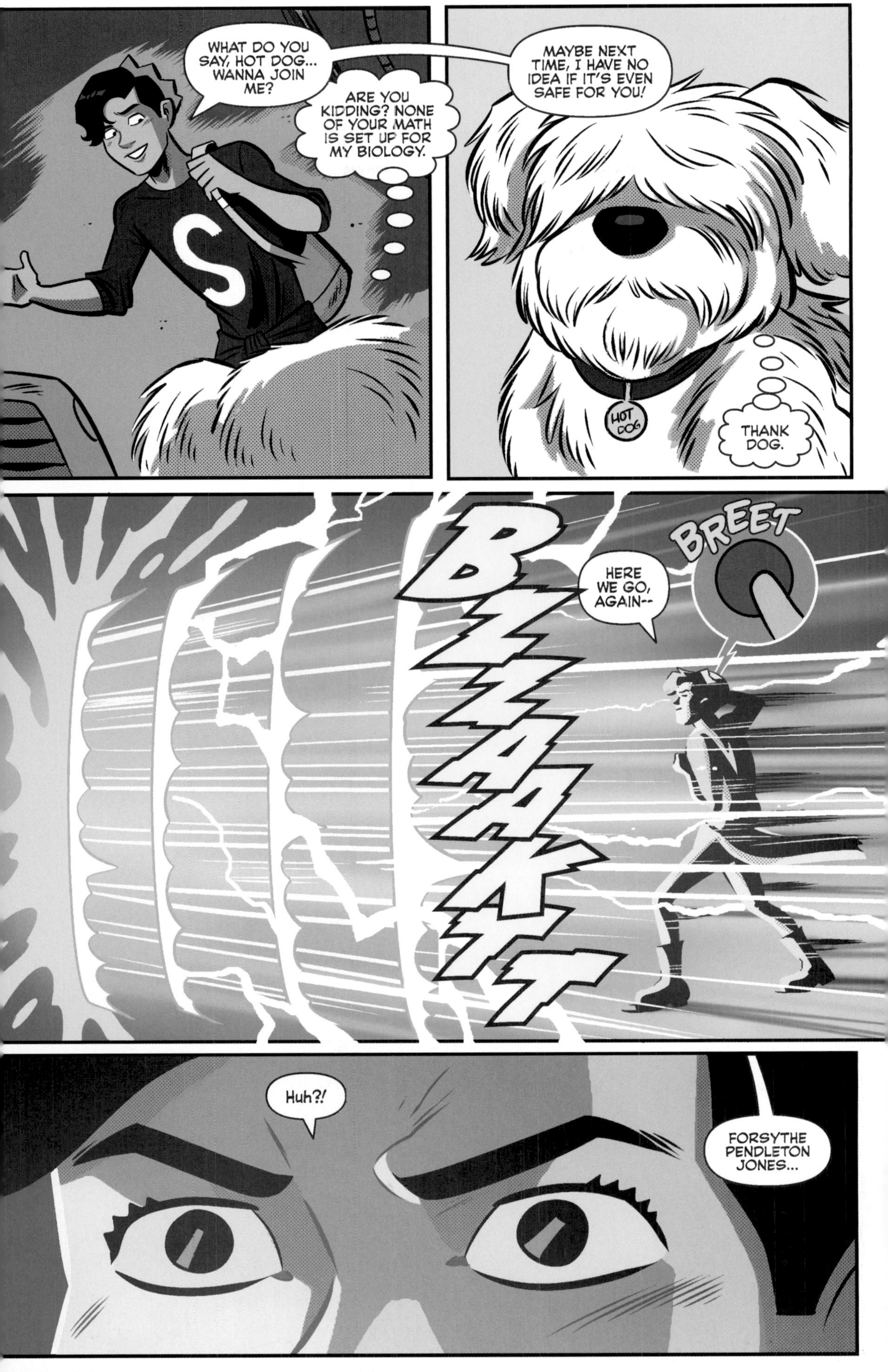
WHAT DO YOU SAY, HOT DOG... WANNA JOIN ME?
ARE YOU KIDDING? NONE OF YOUR MATH IS SET UP FOR MY BIOLOGY.
MAYBE NEXT TIME, I HAVE NO IDEA IF IT'S EVEN SAFE FOR YOU!
HOT DOG
THANK DOG.
BZZZAKTT
BREET
HERE WE GO, AGAIN--
Huh?!
FORSYTHE PENDLETON JONES...

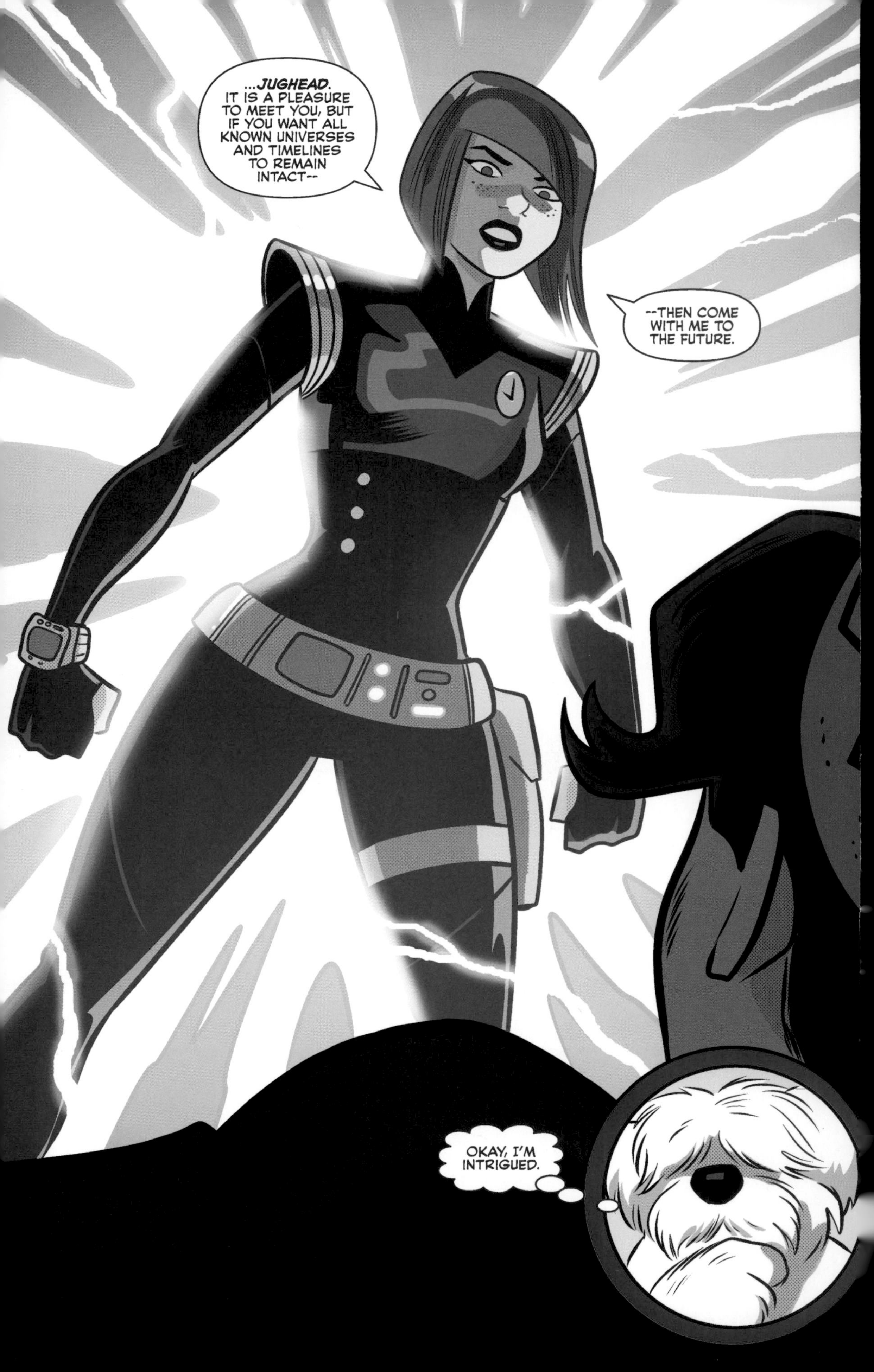
...JUGHEAD. IT IS A PLEASURE TO MEET YOU, BUT IF YOU WANT ALL KNOWN UNIVERSES AND TIMELINES TO REMAIN INTACT--
--THEN COME WITH ME TO THE FUTURE.
OKAY, I'M INTRIGUED.

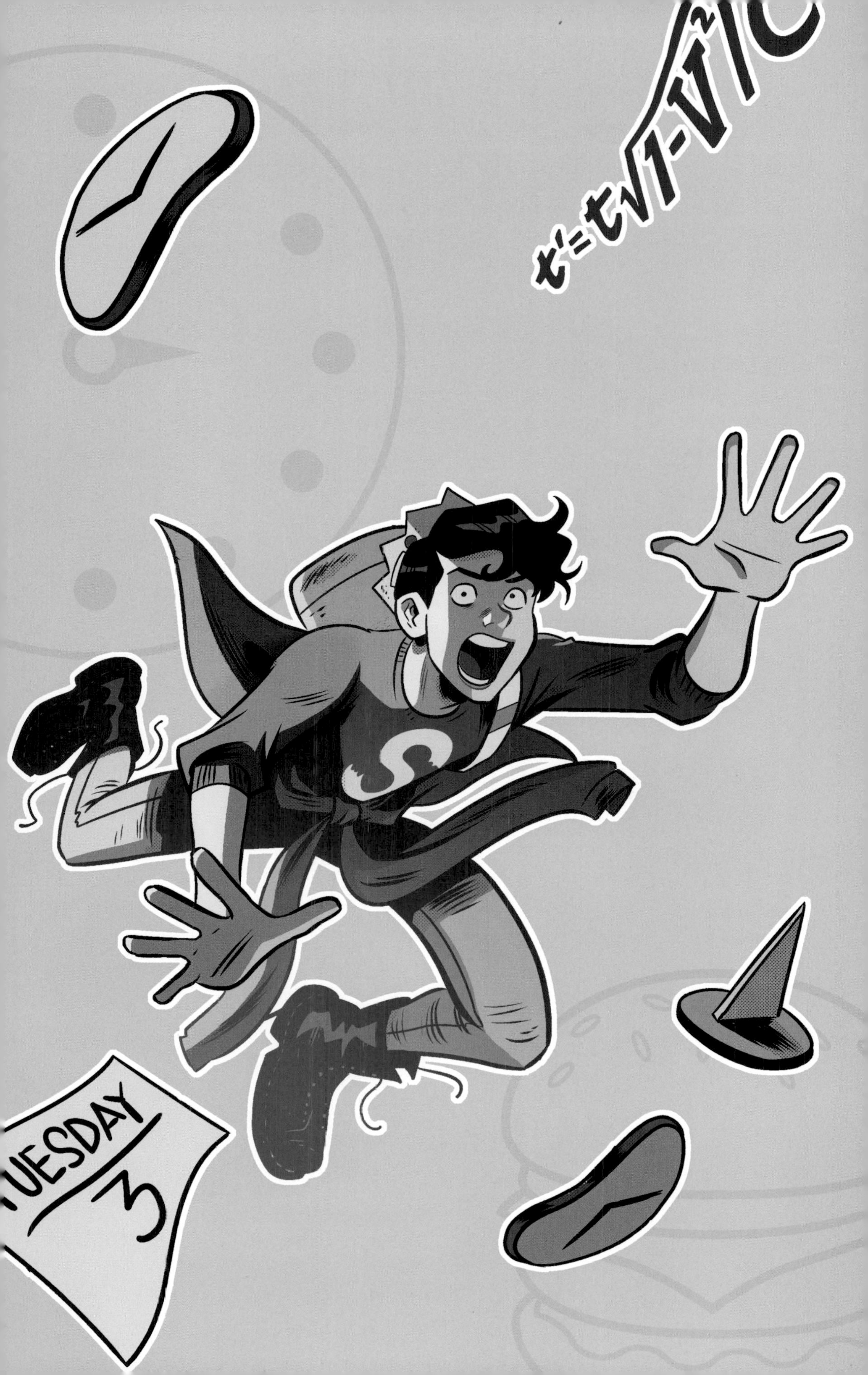

TUESDAY
3

CHAPTER 2

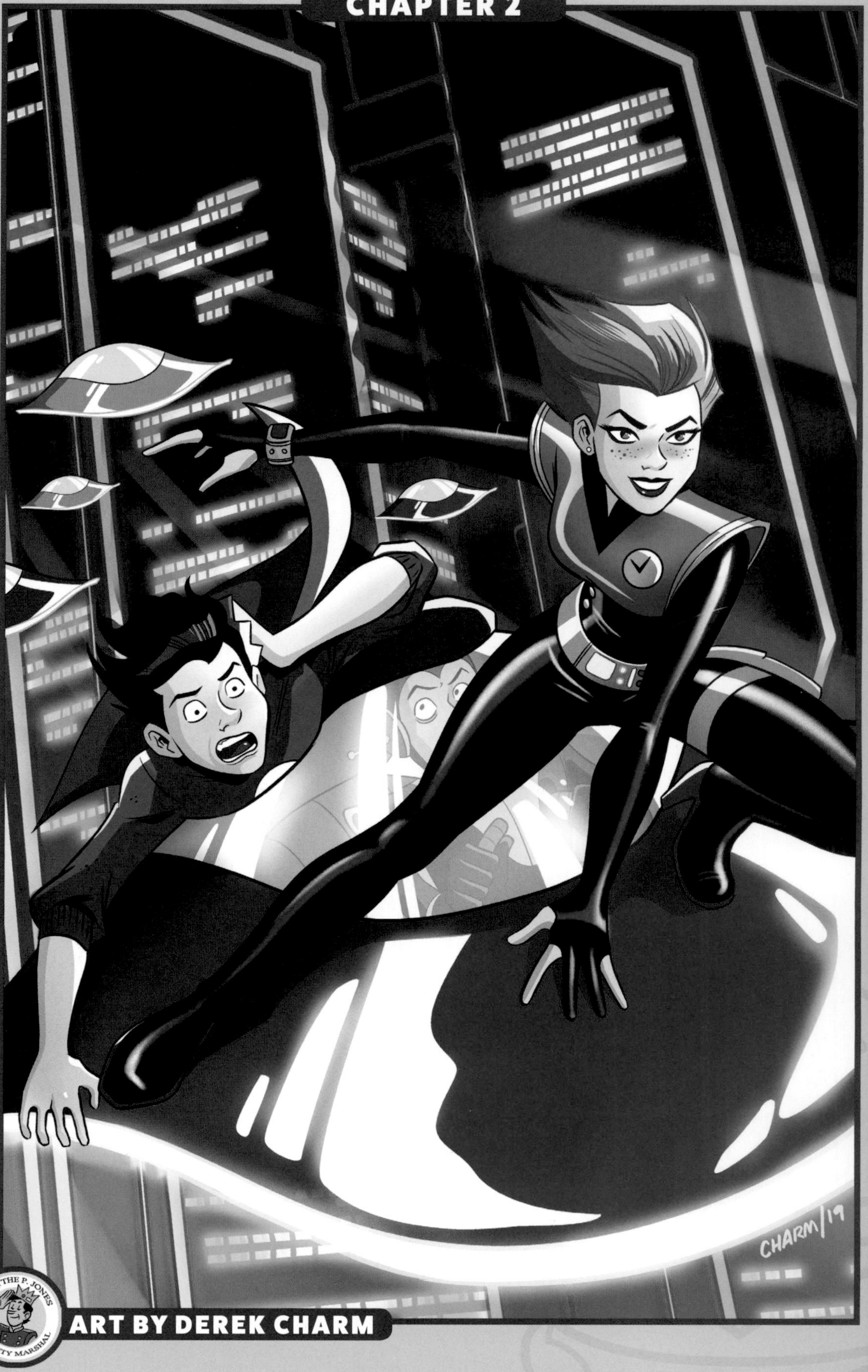
CHARM/19

ART BY DEREK CHARM

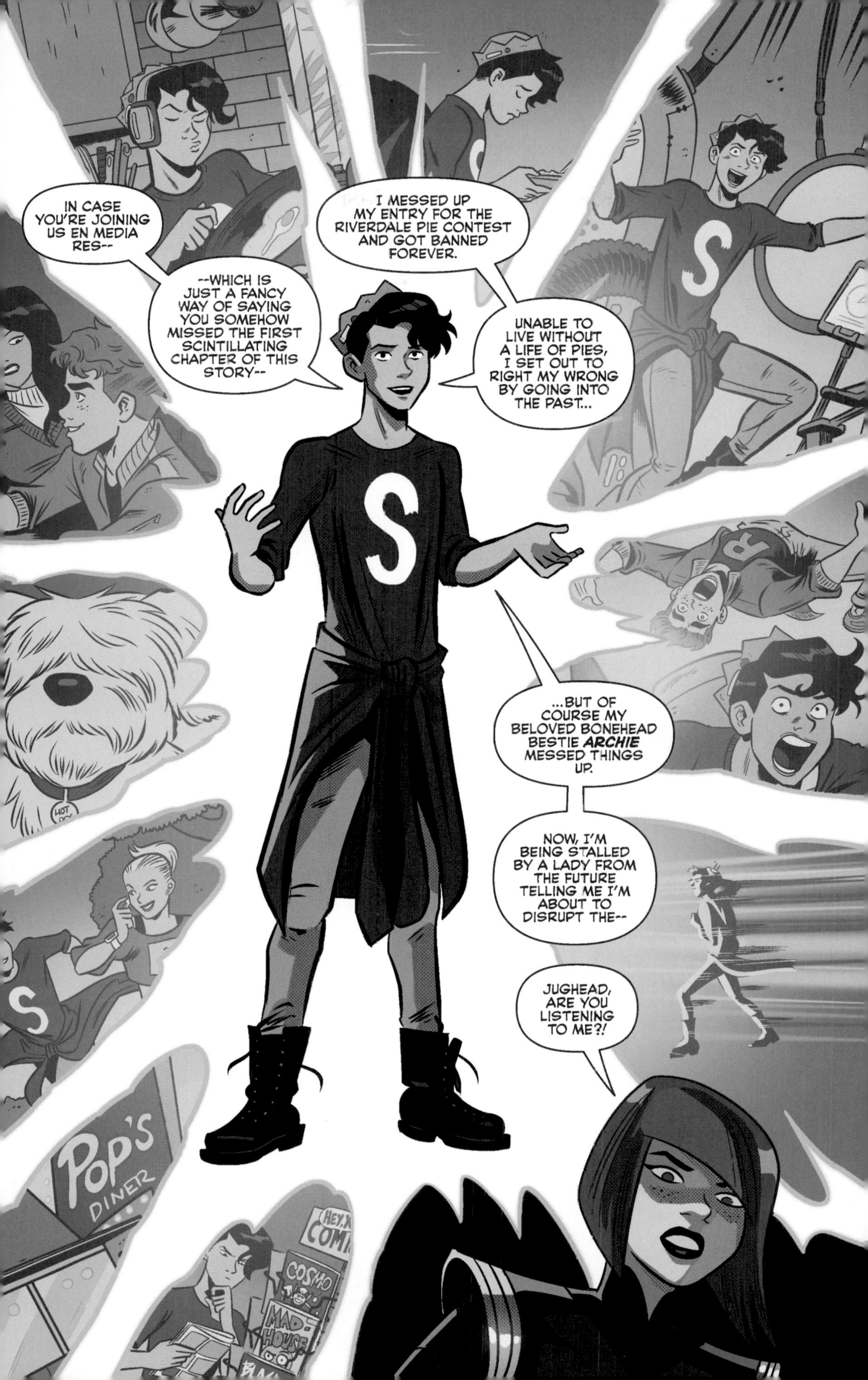
IN CASE YOU'RE JOINING US EN MEDIA RES--
--WHICH IS JUST A FANCY WAY OF SAYING YOU SOMEHOW MISSED THE FIRST SCINTILLATING CHAPTER OF THIS STORY--
I MESSED UP MY ENTRY FOR THE RIVERDALE PIE CONTEST AND GOT BANNED FOREVER.
UNABLE TO LIVE WITHOUT A LIFE OF PIES, I SET OUT TO RIGHT MY WRONG BY GOING INTO THE PAST...
...BUT OF COURSE MY BELOVED BONEHEAD BESTIE ***ARCHIE*** MESSED THINGS UP.
NOW, I'M BEING STALLED BY A LADY FROM THE FUTURE TELLING ME I'M ABOUT TO DISRUPT THE--
JUGHEAD, ARE YOU LISTENING TO ME?!
POP'S DINER
COSMO
MAD-HOUSE

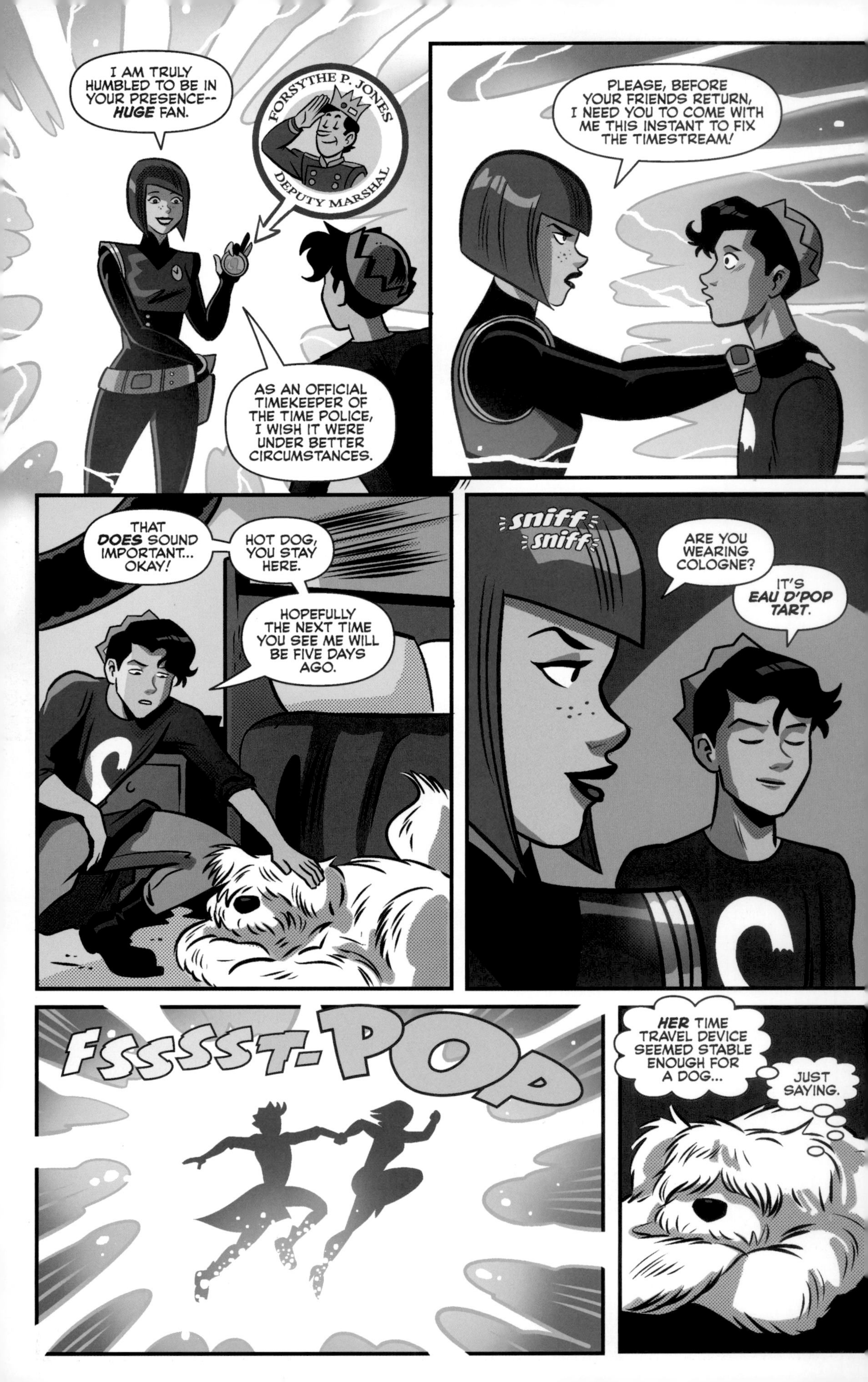
I AM TRULY HUMBLED TO BE IN YOUR PRESENCE-- *HUGE* FAN.
FORSYTHE P. JONES
DEPUTY MARSHAL
AS AN OFFICIAL TIMEKEEPER OF THE TIME POLICE, I WISH IT WERE UNDER BETTER CIRCUMSTANCES.
PLEASE, BEFORE YOUR FRIENDS RETURN, I NEED YOU TO COME WITH ME THIS INSTANT TO FIX THE TIMESTREAM!
THAT *DOES* SOUND IMPORTANT... OKAY!
HOT DOG, YOU STAY HERE.
HOPEFULLY THE NEXT TIME YOU SEE ME WILL BE FIVE DAYS AGO.
sniff sniff
ARE YOU WEARING COLOGNE?
IT'S *EAU D'POP TART*.
FSSSST-POP
HER TIME TRAVEL DEVICE SEEMED STABLE ENOUGH FOR A DOG...
JUST SAYING.

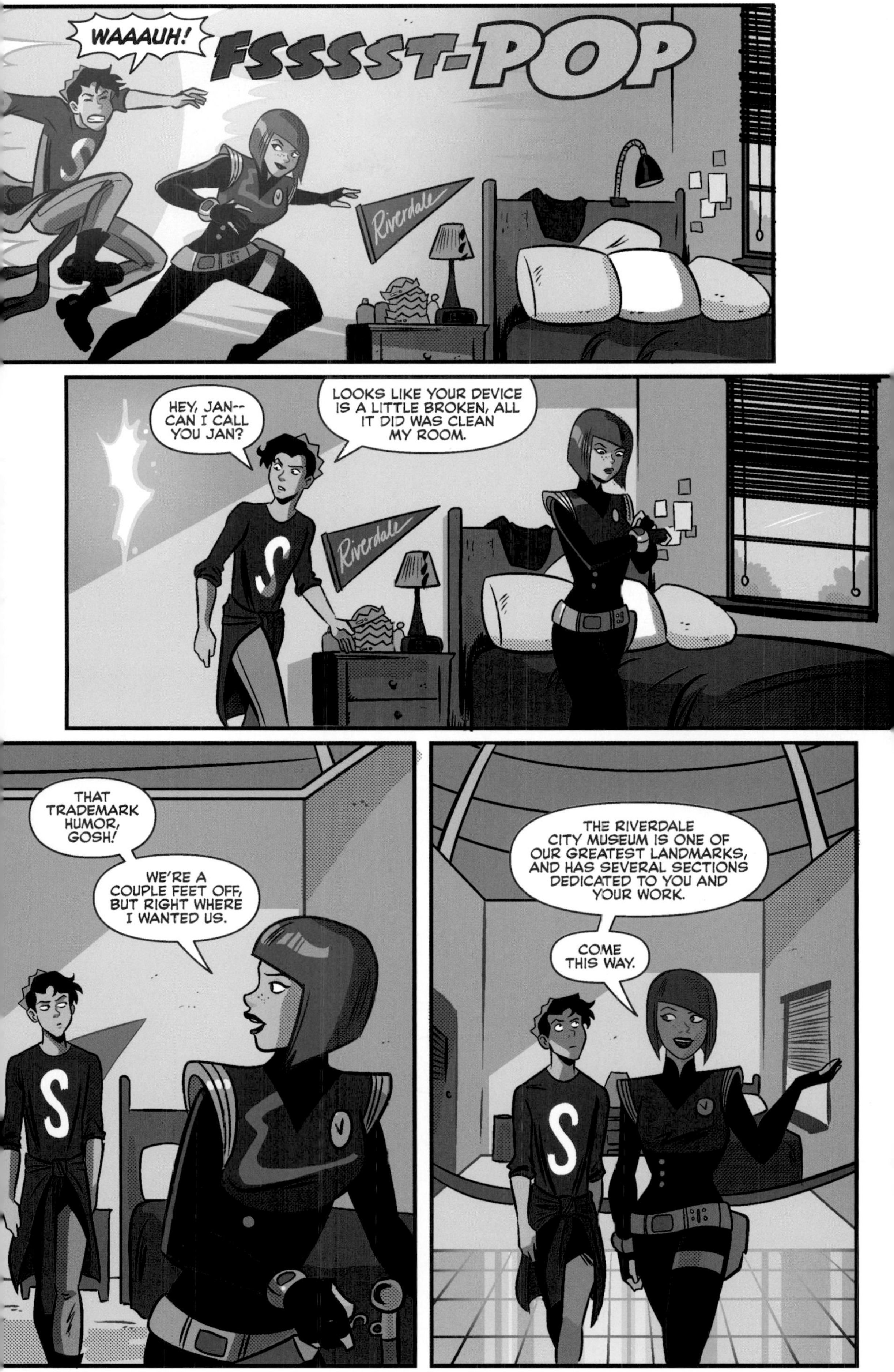
WAAAUH!
FSSSST-POP
Riverdale
HEY, JAN-- CAN I CALL YOU JAN?
LOOKS LIKE YOUR DEVICE IS A LITTLE BROKEN, ALL IT DID WAS CLEAN MY ROOM.
Riverdale
THAT TRADEMARK HUMOR, GOSH!
WE'RE A COUPLE FEET OFF, BUT RIGHT WHERE I WANTED US.
THE RIVERDALE CITY MUSEUM IS ONE OF OUR GREATEST LANDMARKS, AND HAS SEVERAL SECTIONS DEDICATED TO YOU AND YOUR WORK.
COME THIS WAY.

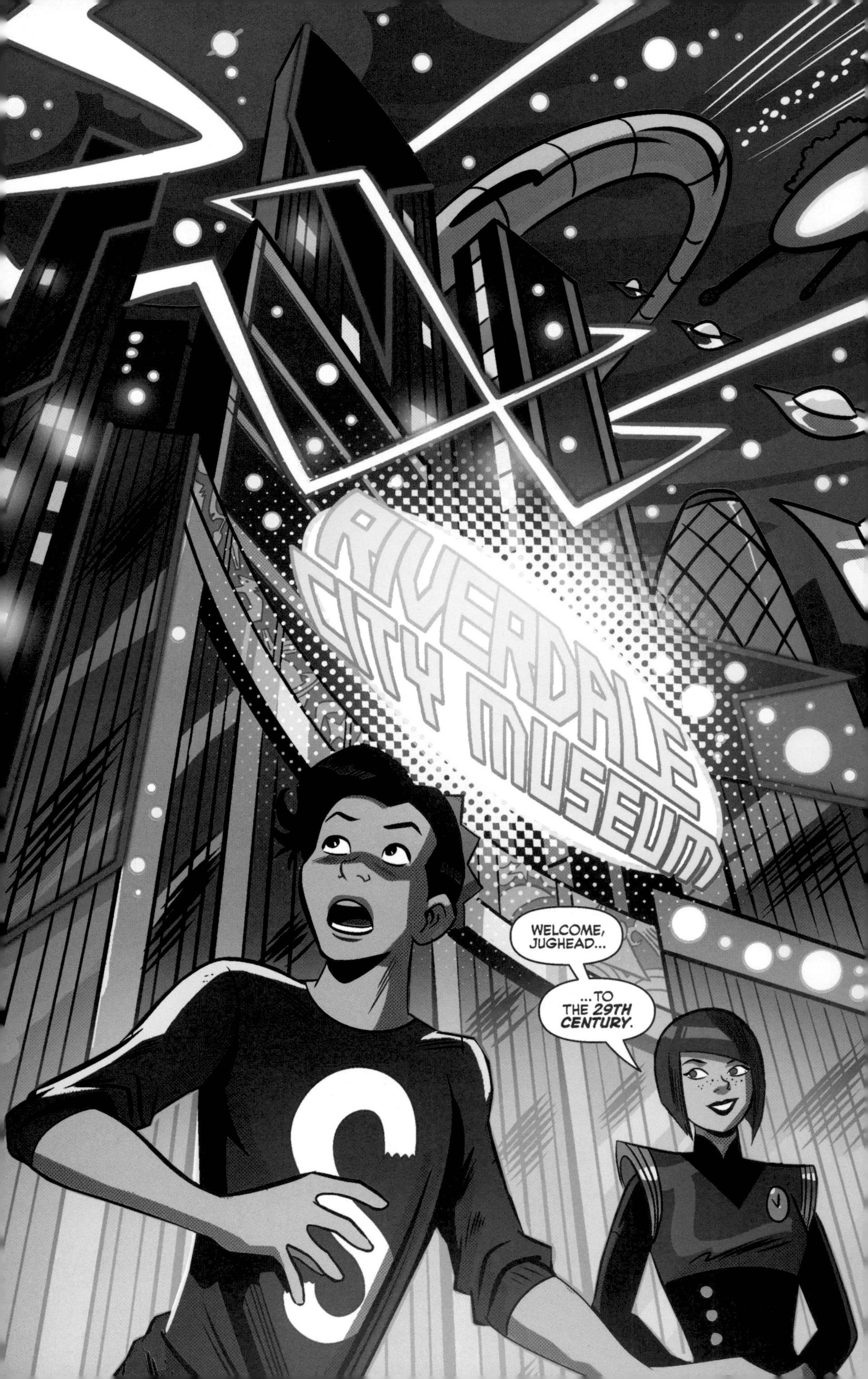
RIVERDALE CITY MUSEUM
WELCOME, JUGHEAD...
...TO THE 29TH CENTURY.

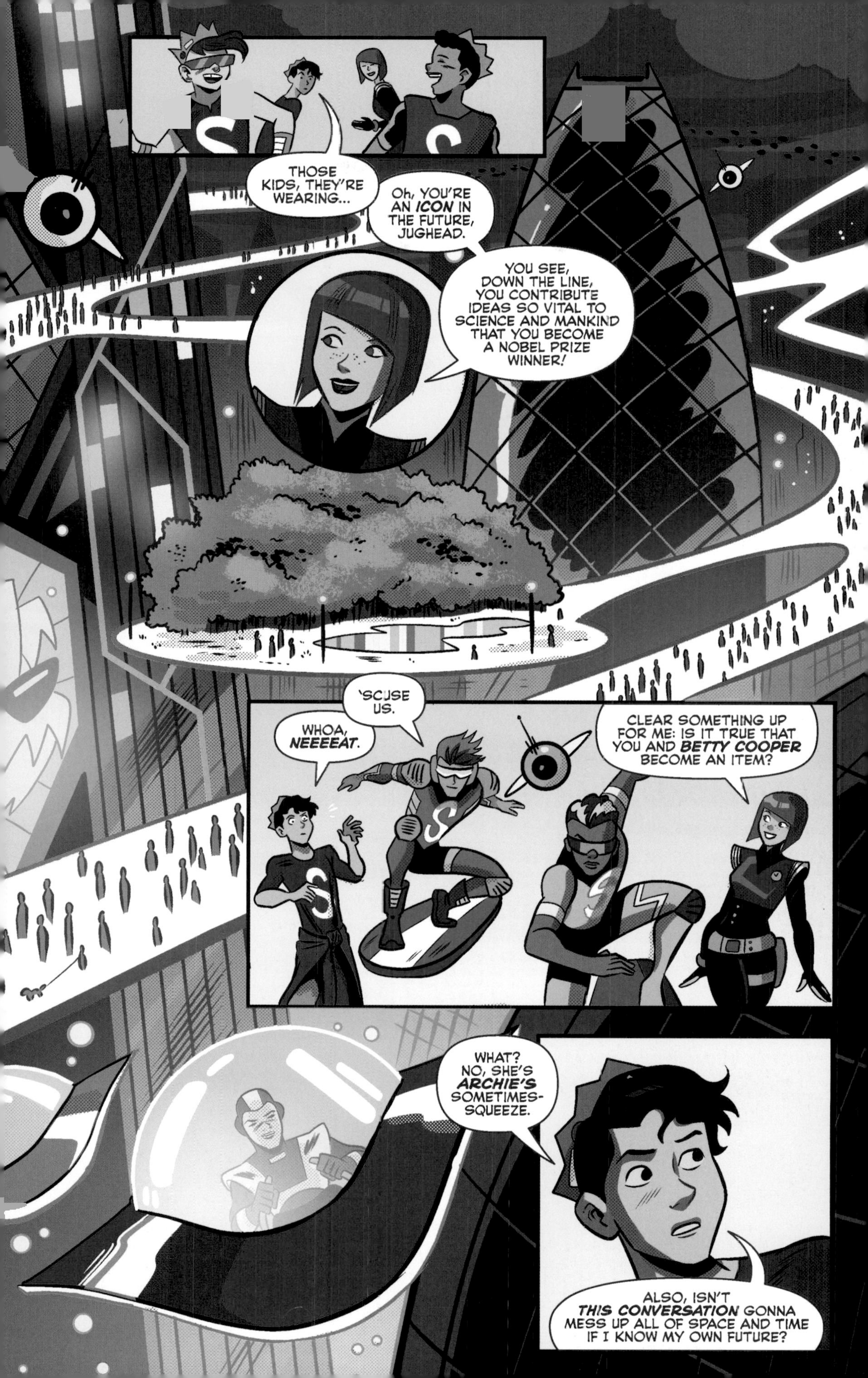
THOSE KIDS, THEY'RE WEARING...
Oh, YOU'RE AN ICON IN THE FUTURE, JUGHEAD.
YOU SEE, DOWN THE LINE, YOU CONTRIBUTE IDEAS SO VITAL TO SCIENCE AND MANKIND THAT YOU BECOME A NOBEL PRIZE WINNER!
'SCUSE US.
WHOA, NEEEEAT.
CLEAR SOMETHING UP FOR ME: IS IT TRUE THAT YOU AND BETTY COOPER BECOME AN ITEM?
WHAT? NO, SHE'S ARCHIE'S SOMETIMES-SQUEEZE.
ALSO, ISN'T THIS CONVERSATION GONNA MESS UP ALL OF SPACE AND TIME IF I KNOW MY OWN FUTURE?

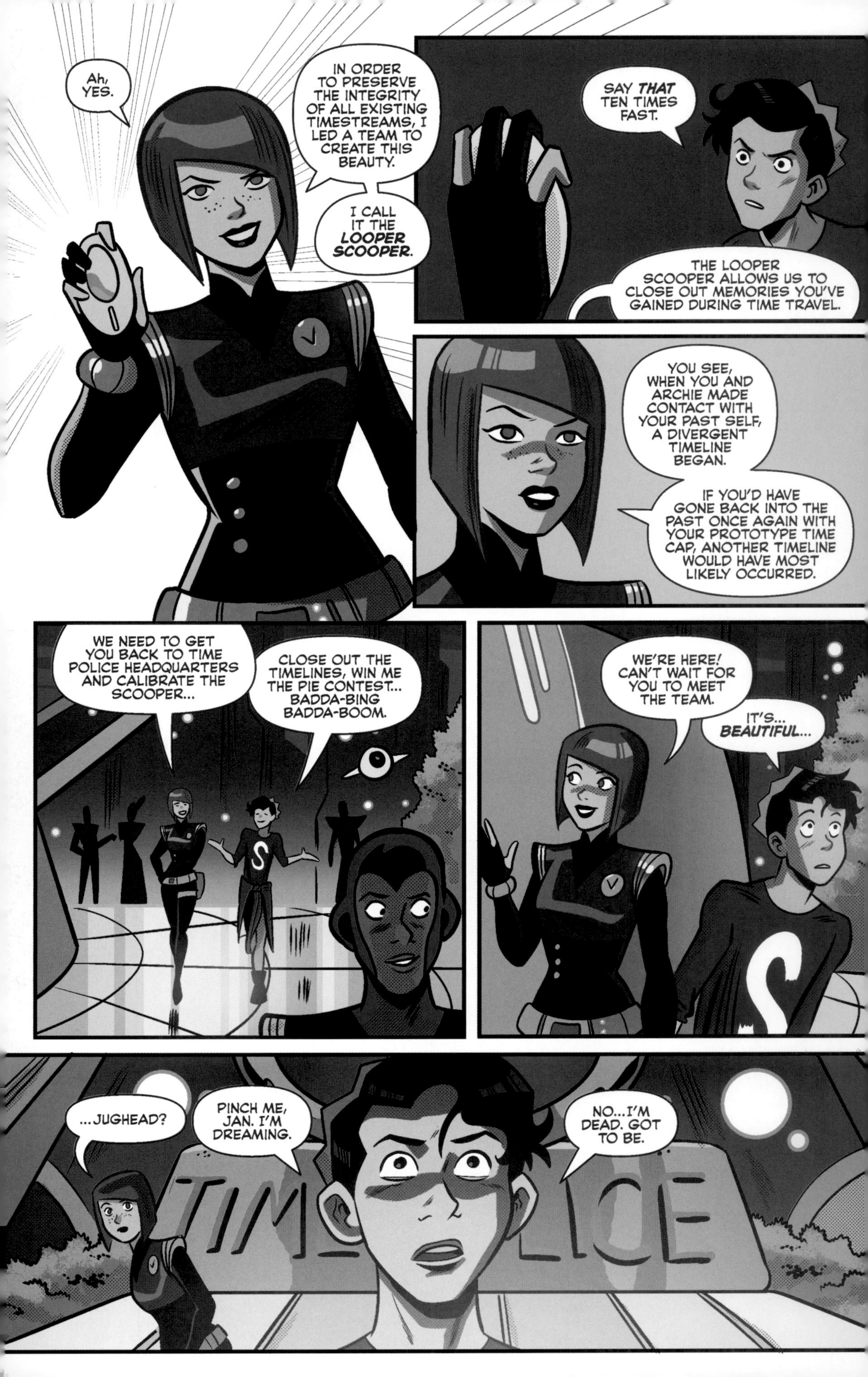

Ah, YES.
IN ORDER TO PRESERVE THE INTEGRITY OF ALL EXISTING TIMESTREAMS, I LED A TEAM TO CREATE THIS BEAUTY.
I CALL IT THE LOOPER SCOOPER.
SAY THAT TEN TIMES FAST.
THE LOOPER SCOOPER ALLOWS US TO CLOSE OUT MEMORIES YOU'VE GAINED DURING TIME TRAVEL.
YOU SEE, WHEN YOU AND ARCHIE MADE CONTACT WITH YOUR PAST SELF, A DIVERGENT TIMELINE BEGAN.
IF YOU'D HAVE GONE BACK INTO THE PAST ONCE AGAIN WITH YOUR PROTOTYPE TIME CAP, ANOTHER TIMELINE WOULD HAVE MOST LIKELY OCCURRED.
WE NEED TO GET YOU BACK TO TIME POLICE HEADQUARTERS AND CALIBRATE THE SCOOPER...
CLOSE OUT THE TIMELINES, WIN ME THE PIE CONTEST... BADDA-BING BADDA-BOOM.
WE'RE HERE! CAN'T WAIT FOR YOU TO MEET THE TEAM.
IT'S... BEAUTIFUL...
...JUGHEAD?
PINCH ME, JAN. I'M DREAMING.
NO...I'M DEAD. GOT TO BE.

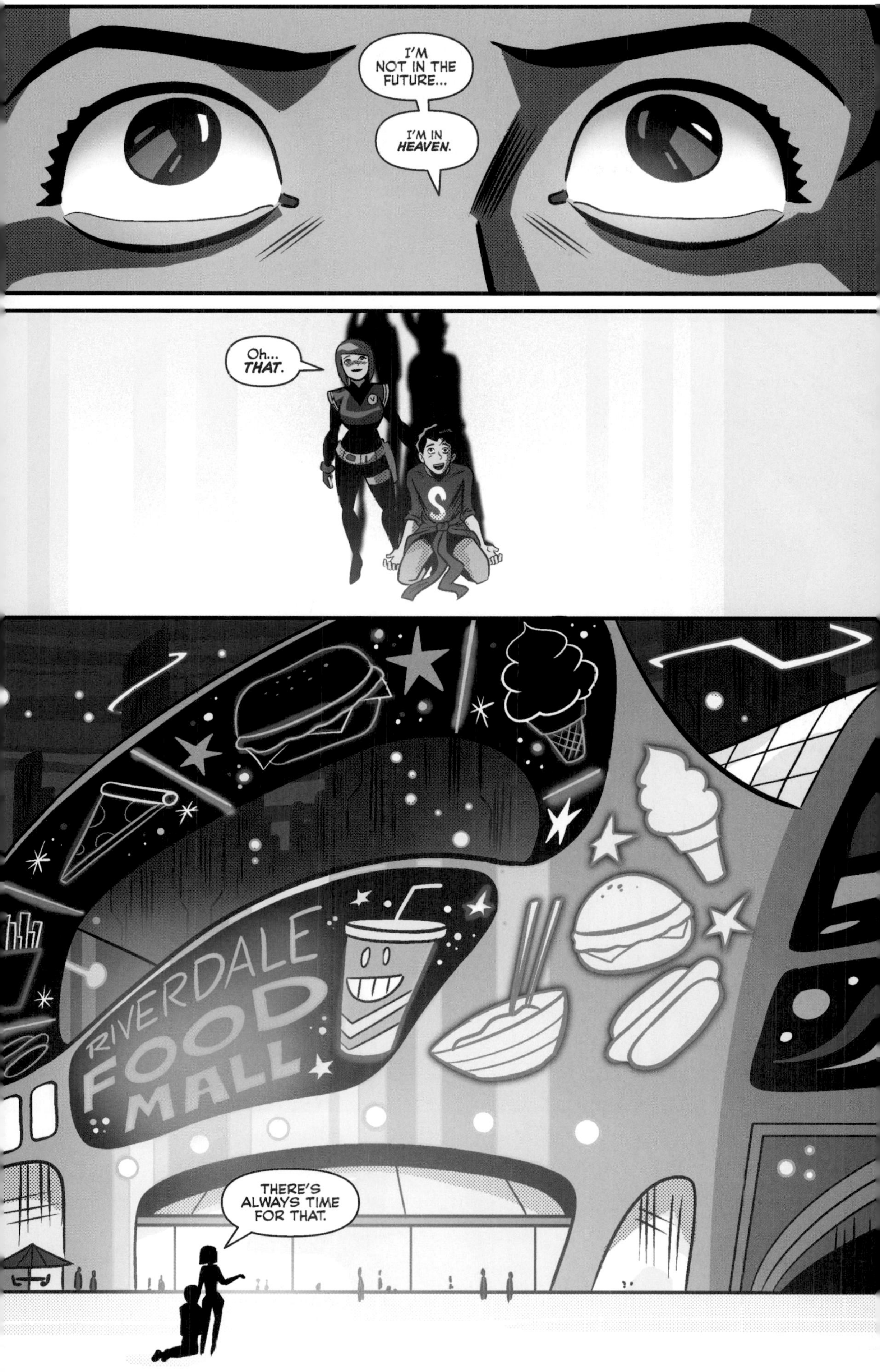
I'M NOT IN THE FUTURE...
I'M IN HEAVEN.
Oh... THAT.
RIVERDALE FOOD MALL
THERE'S ALWAYS TIME FOR THAT.

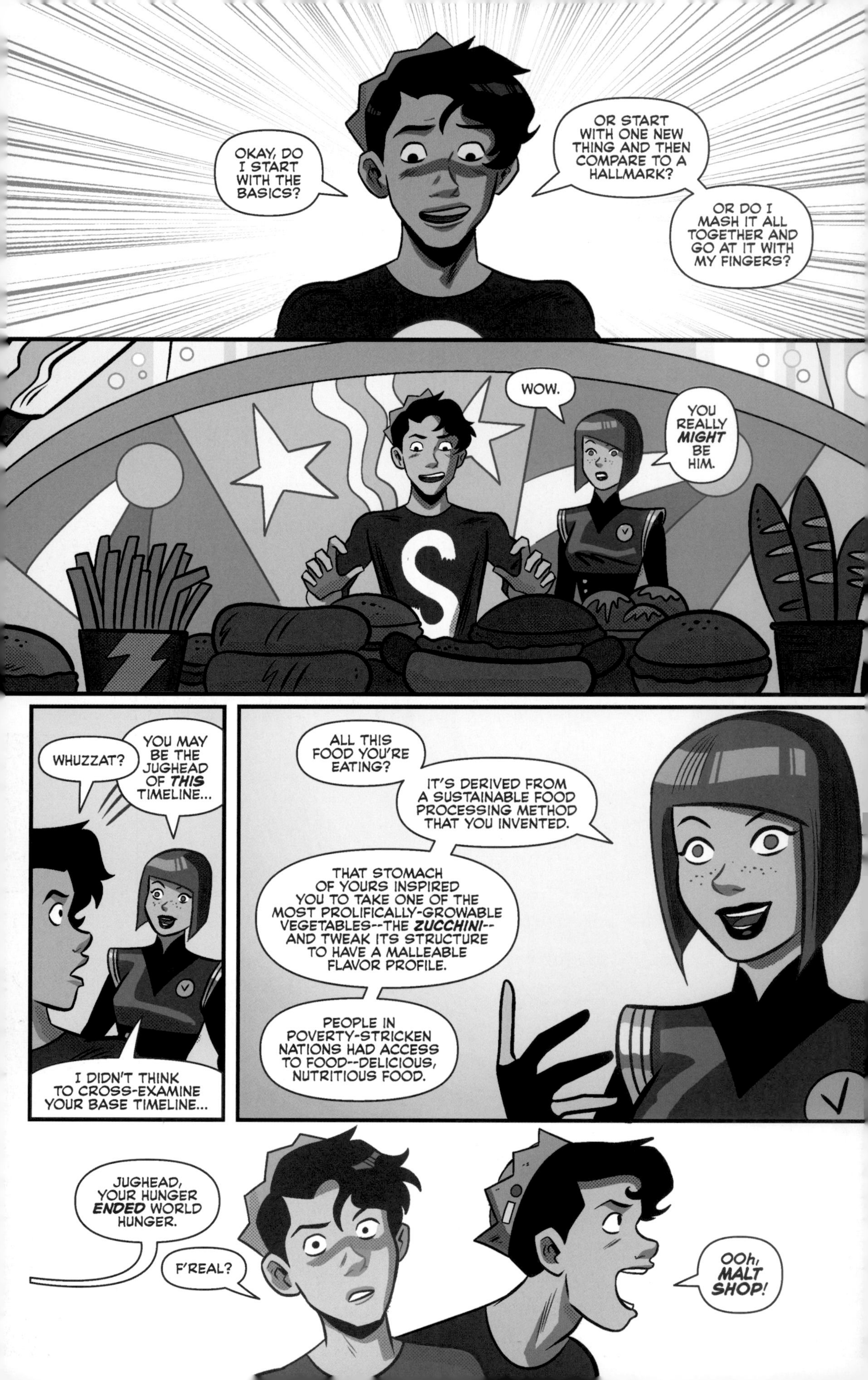
OKAY, DO I START WITH THE BASICS?
OR START WITH ONE NEW THING AND THEN COMPARE TO A HALLMARK?
OR DO I MASH IT ALL TOGETHER AND GO AT IT WITH MY FINGERS?
WOW.
YOU REALLY ***MIGHT*** BE HIM.
WHUZZAT?
YOU MAY BE THE JUGHEAD OF ***THIS*** TIMELINE...
I DIDN'T THINK TO CROSS-EXAMINE YOUR BASE TIMELINE...
ALL THIS FOOD YOU'RE EATING?
IT'S DERIVED FROM A SUSTAINABLE FOOD PROCESSING METHOD THAT YOU INVENTED.
THAT STOMACH OF YOURS INSPIRED YOU TO TAKE ONE OF THE MOST PROLIFICALLY-GROWABLE VEGETABLES--THE ***ZUCCHINI***--AND TWEAK ITS STRUCTURE TO HAVE A MALLEABLE FLAVOR PROFILE.
PEOPLE IN POVERTY-STRICKEN NATIONS HAD ACCESS TO FOOD--DELICIOUS, NUTRITIOUS FOOD.
JUGHEAD, YOUR HUNGER ***ENDED*** WORLD HUNGER.
F'REAL?
*OOh, **MALT SHOP!***

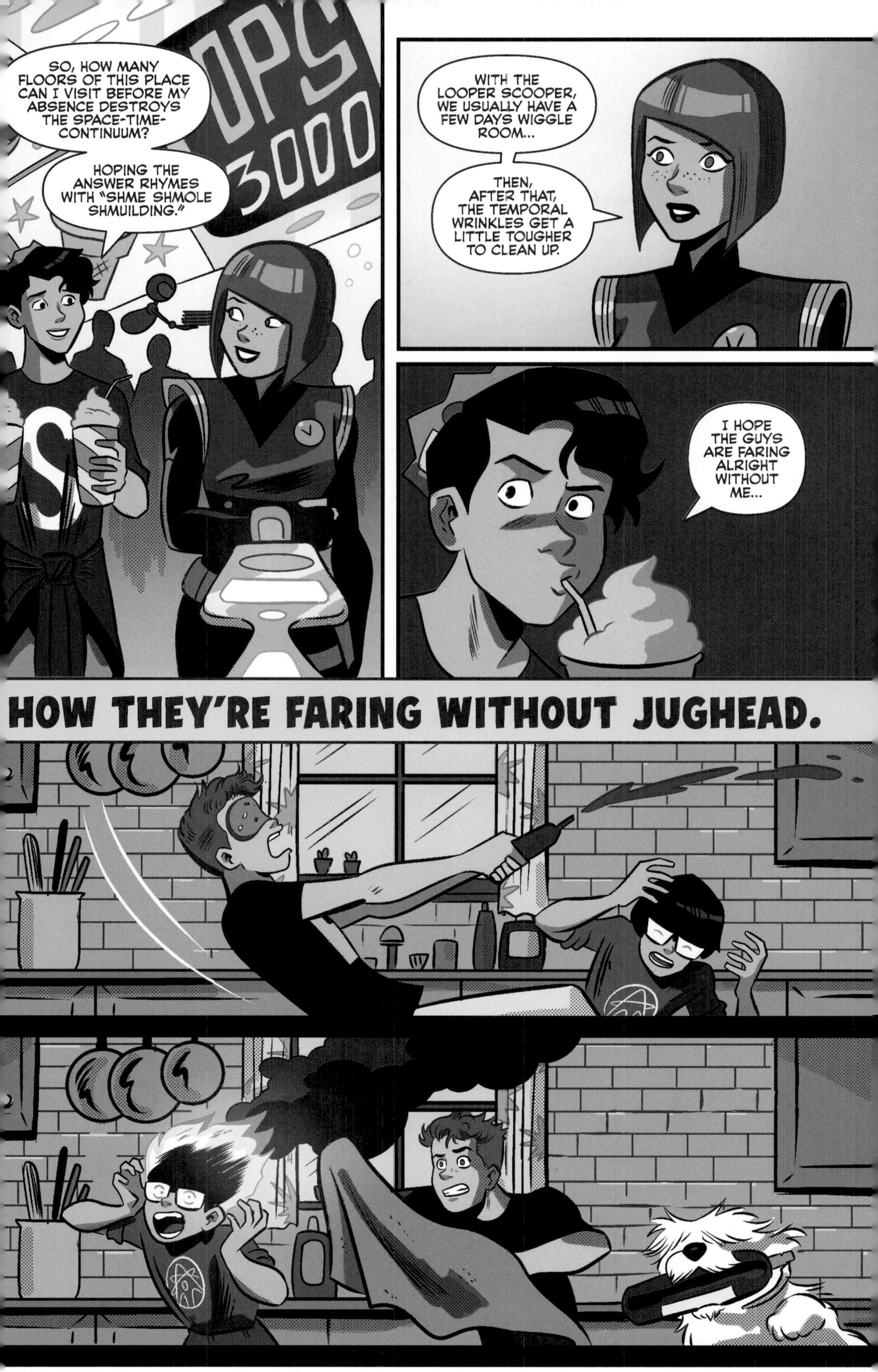
SO, HOW MANY FLOORS OF THIS PLACE CAN I VISIT BEFORE MY ABSENCE DESTROYS THE SPACE-TIME-CONTINUUM?
HOPING THE ANSWER RHYMES WITH "SHME SHMOLE SHMUILDING."
WITH THE LOOPER SCOOPER, WE USUALLY HAVE A FEW DAYS WIGGLE ROOM...
THEN, AFTER THAT, THE TEMPORAL WRINKLES GET A LITTLE TOUGHER TO CLEAN UP.
I HOPE THE GUYS ARE FARING ALRIGHT WITHOUT ME...
HOW THEY'RE FARING WITHOUT JUGHEAD.

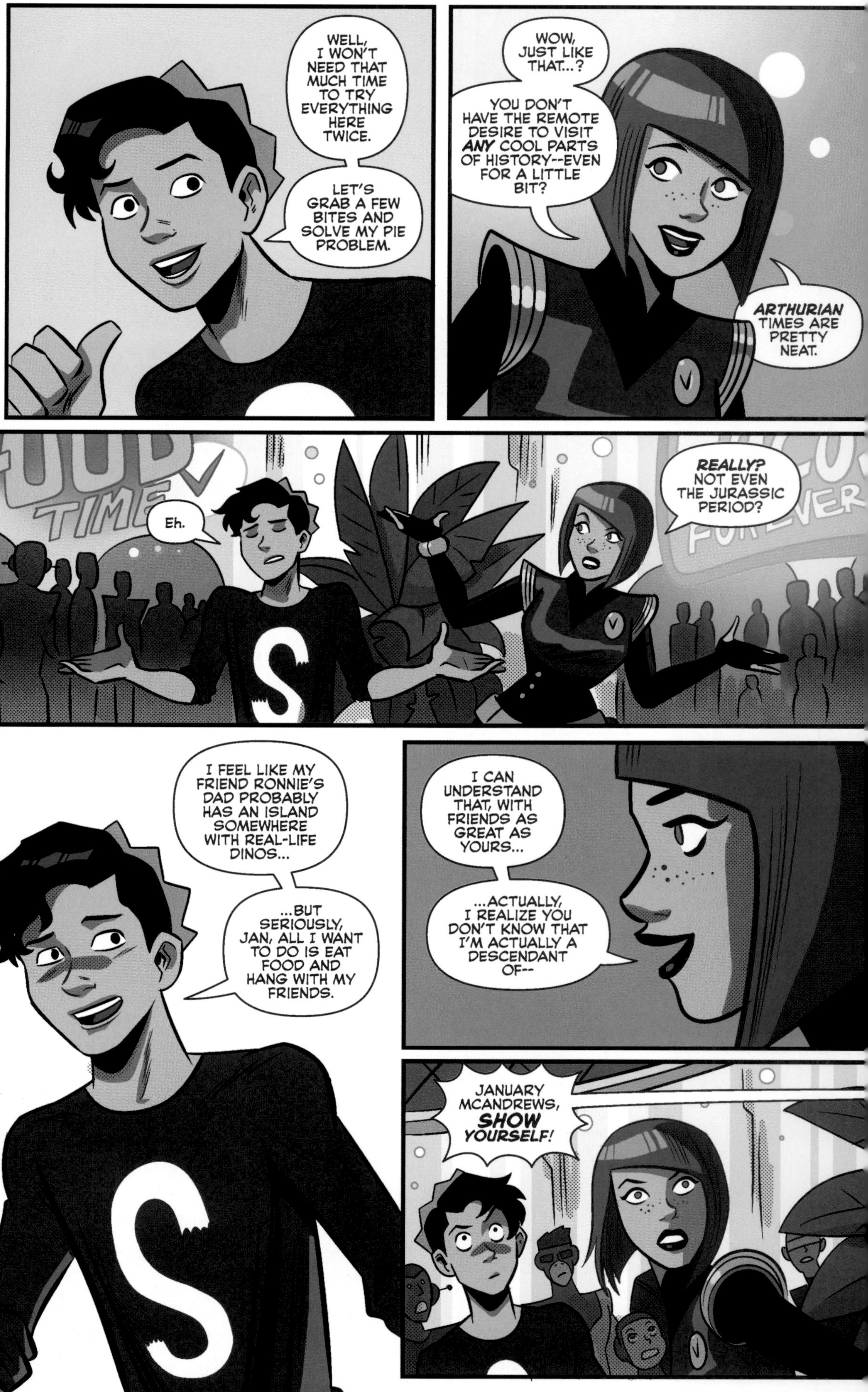
WELL, I WON'T NEED THAT MUCH TIME TO TRY EVERYTHING HERE TWICE.
LET'S GRAB A FEW BITES AND SOLVE MY PIE PROBLEM.
WOW, JUST LIKE THAT...?
YOU DON'T HAVE THE REMOTE DESIRE TO VISIT ANY COOL PARTS OF HISTORY--EVEN FOR A LITTLE BIT?
ARTHURIAN TIMES ARE PRETTY NEAT.
FOOD TIME
Eh.
REALLY? NOT EVEN THE JURASSIC PERIOD?
FOREVER
I FEEL LIKE MY FRIEND RONNIE'S DAD PROBABLY HAS AN ISLAND SOMEWHERE WITH REAL-LIFE DINOS...
...BUT SERIOUSLY, JAN, ALL I WANT TO DO IS EAT FOOD AND HANG WITH MY FRIENDS.
I CAN UNDERSTAND THAT, WITH FRIENDS AS GREAT AS YOURS...
...ACTUALLY, I REALIZE YOU DON'T KNOW THAT I'M ACTUALLY A DESCENDANT OF--
JANUARY MCANDREWS, SHOW YOURSELF!

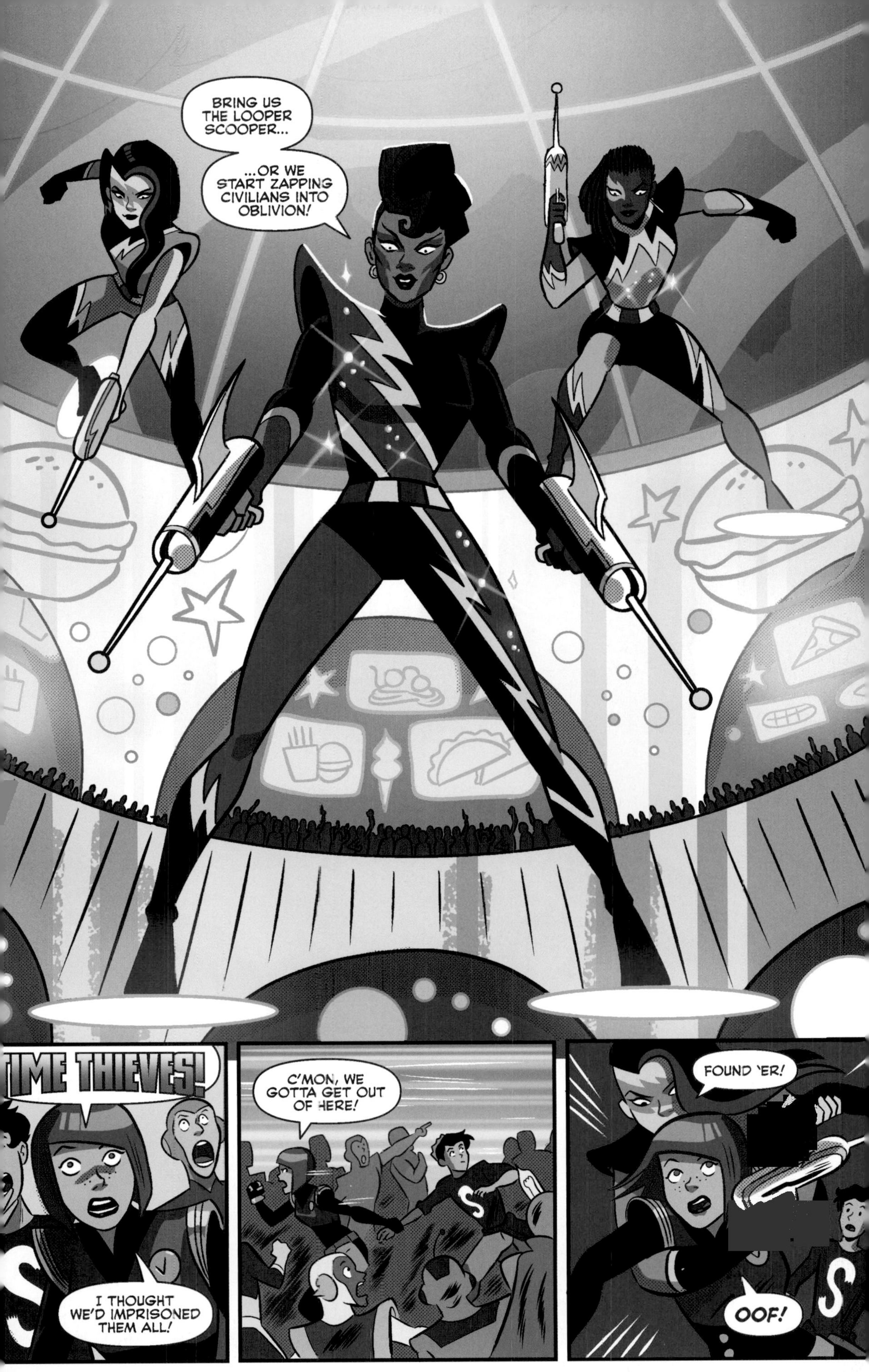
BRING US THE LOOPER SCOOPER...
...OR WE START ZAPPING CIVILIANS INTO OBLIVION!
TIME THIEVES!
I THOUGHT WE'D IMPRISONED THEM ALL!
C'MON, WE GOTTA GET OUT OF HERE!
FOUND 'ER!
OOF!

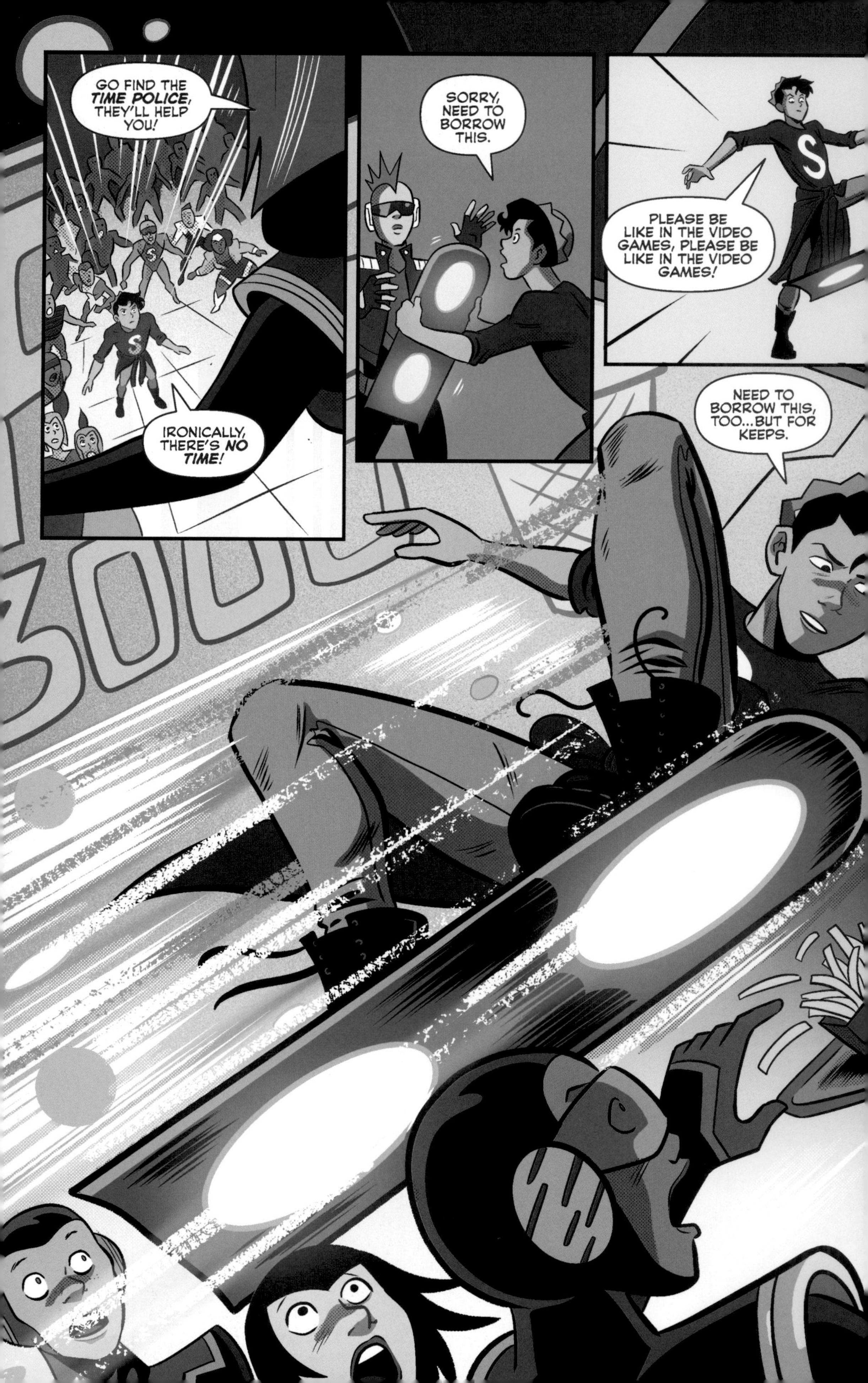
GO FIND THE TIME POLICE, THEY'LL HELP YOU!
IRONICALLY, THERE'S NO TIME!
SORRY, NEED TO BORROW THIS.
PLEASE BE LIKE IN THE VIDEO GAMES, PLEASE BE LIKE IN THE VIDEO GAMES!
NEED TO BORROW THIS, TOO...BUT FOR KEEPS.

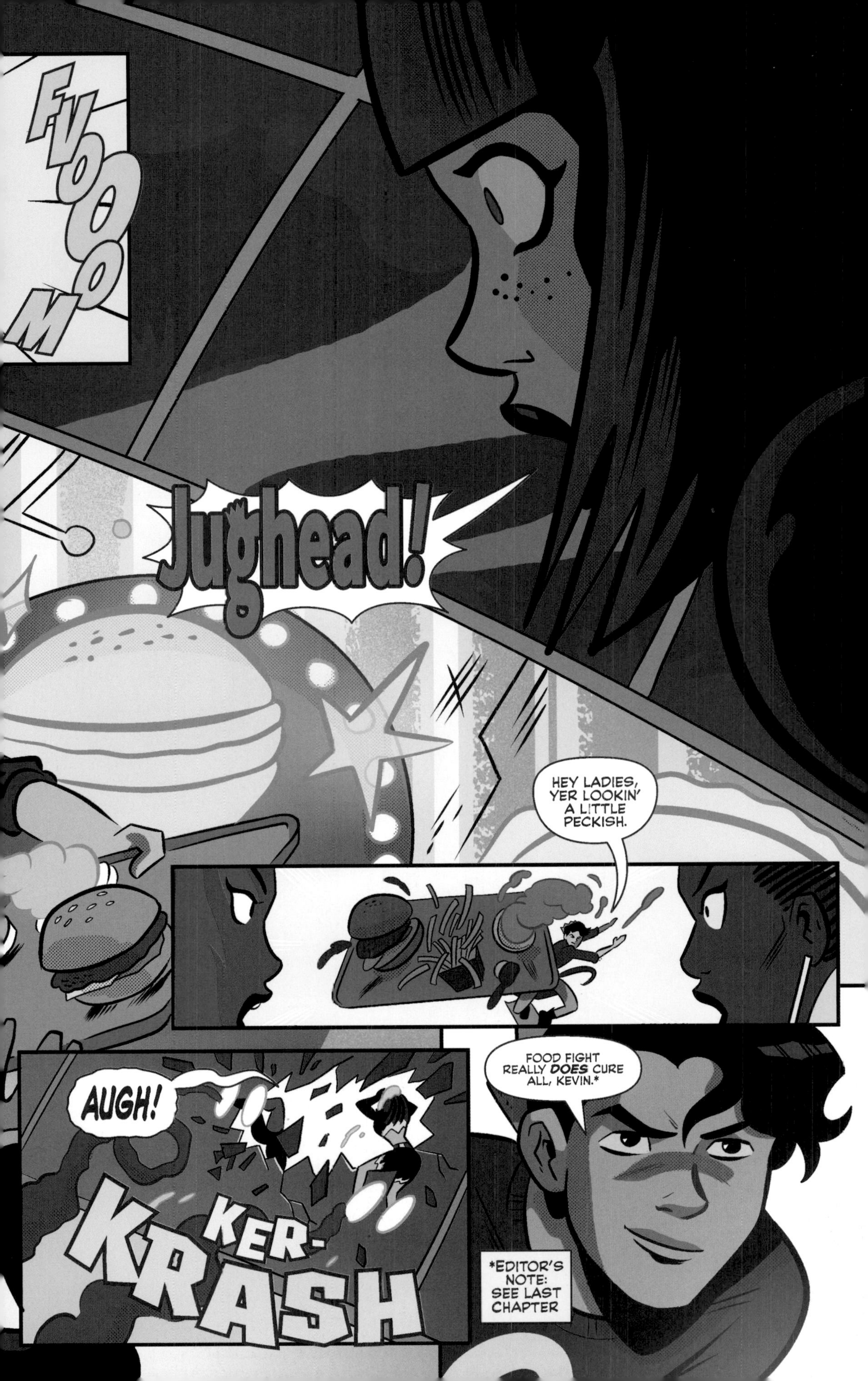
FVOOOOM
Jughead!
HEY LADIES, YER LOOKIN' A LITTLE PECKISH.
AUGH!
KER-KRASH
FOOD FIGHT REALLY **DOES** CURE ALL, KEVIN.*
*EDITOR'S NOTE: SEE LAST CHAPTER

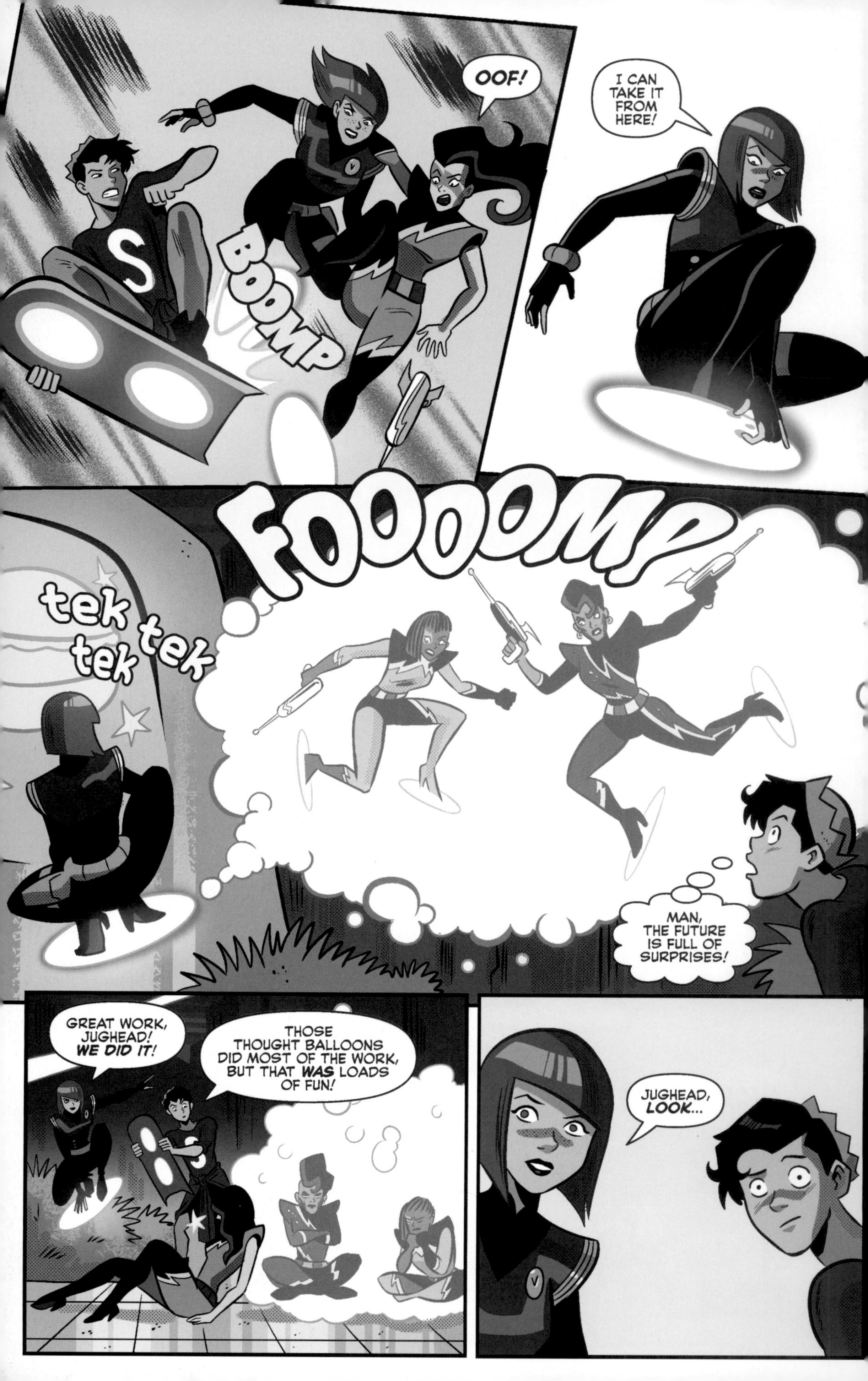
OOF!
BOOOMP
I CAN TAKE IT FROM HERE!
FOOOOMP
tek tek tek
MAN, THE FUTURE IS FULL OF SURPRISES!
GREAT WORK, JUGHEAD! WE DID IT!
THOSE THOUGHT BALLOONS DID MOST OF THE WORK, BUT THAT WAS LOADS OF FUN!
JUGHEAD, LOOK...

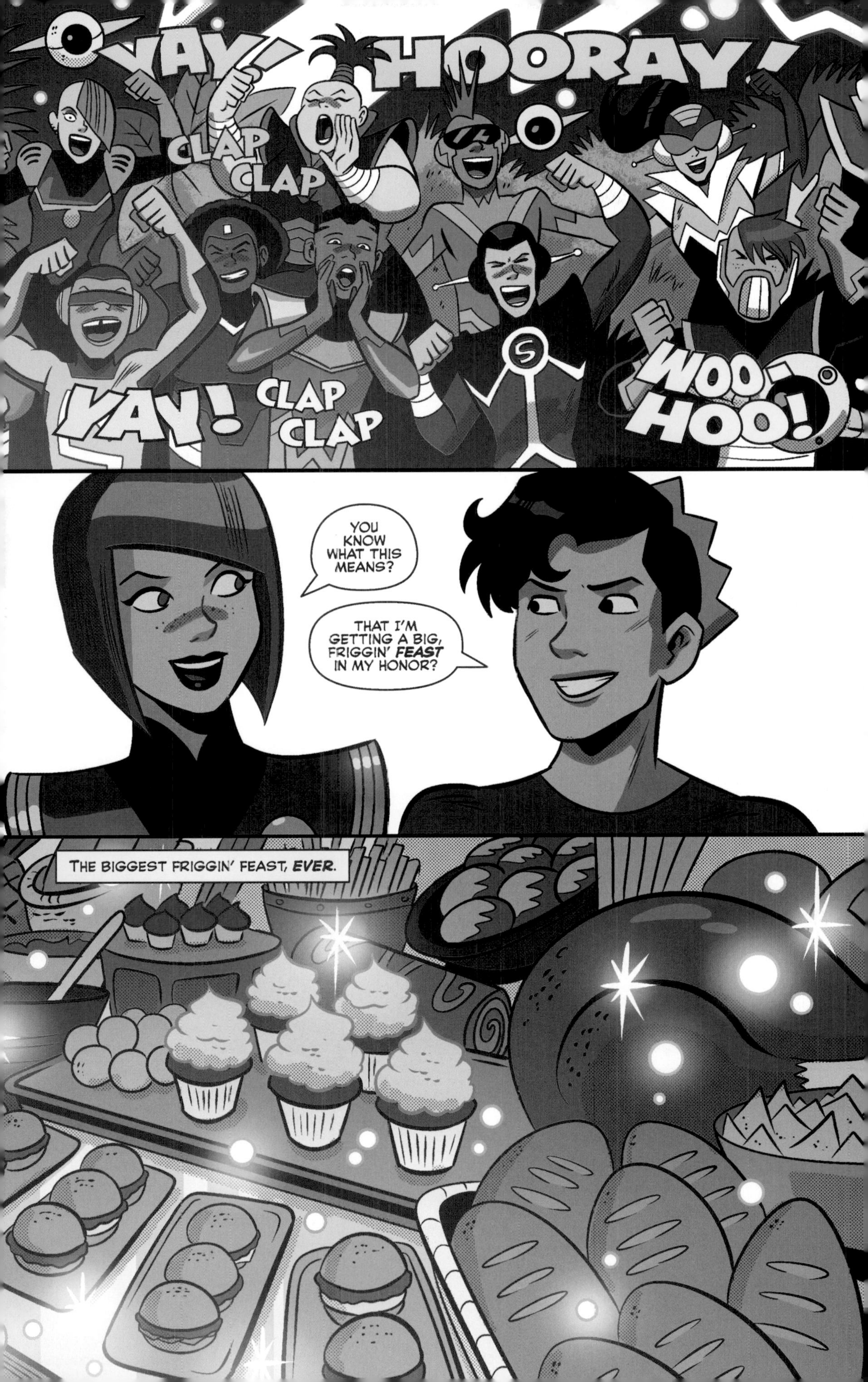
YAY!
HOORAY!
CLAP CLAP
YAY!
CLAP CLAP
WOO-HOO!
YOU KNOW WHAT THIS MEANS?
THAT I'M GETTING A BIG, FRIGGIN' *FEAST* IN MY HONOR?
THE BIGGEST FRIGGIN' FEAST, *EVER*.

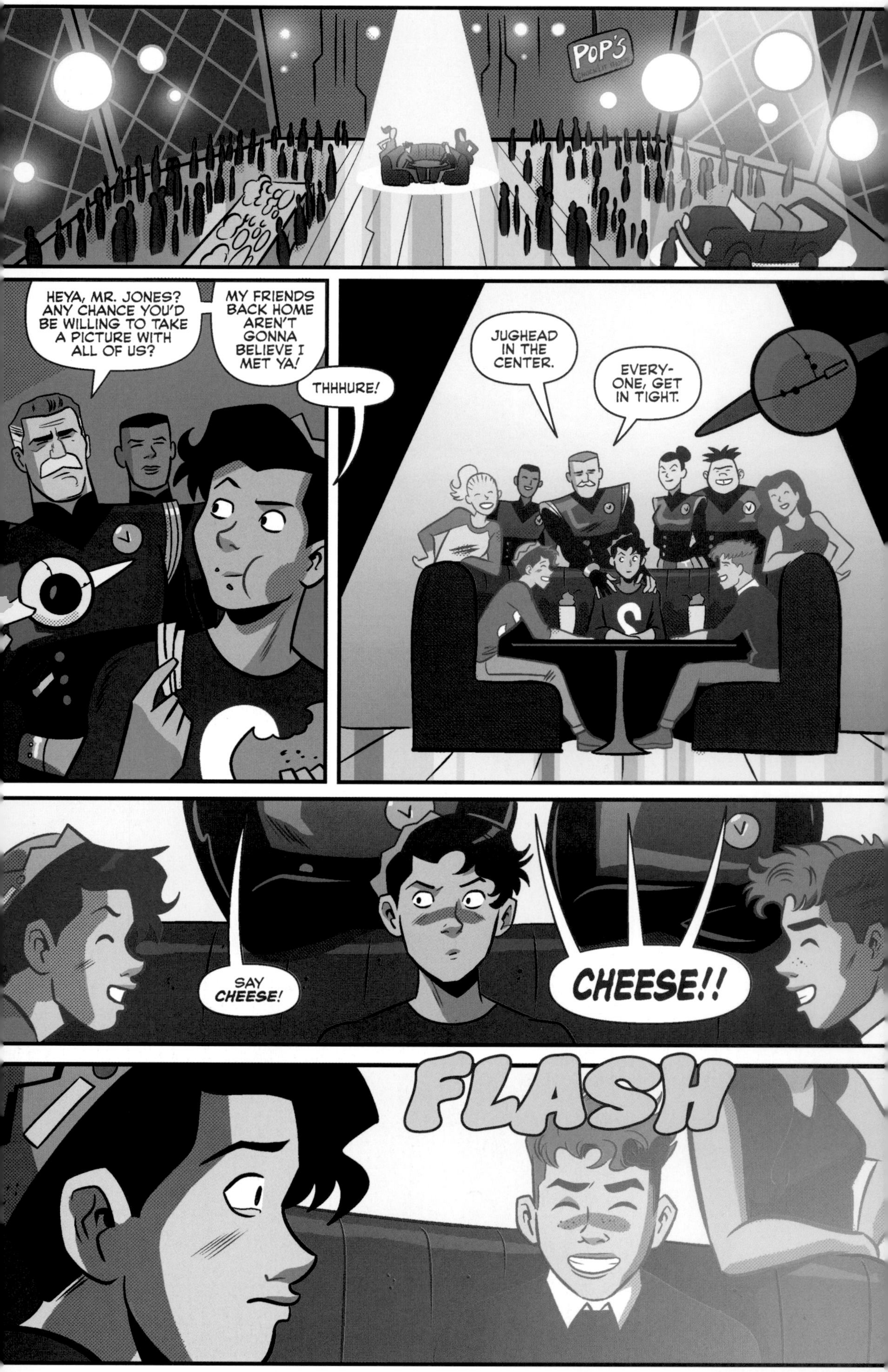
POP'S
HEYA, MR. JONES? ANY CHANCE YOU'D BE WILLING TO TAKE A PICTURE WITH ALL OF US?
MY FRIENDS BACK HOME AREN'T GONNA BELIEVE I MET YA!
THHHURE!
JUGHEAD IN THE CENTER.
EVERY-ONE, GET IN TIGHT.
SAY CHEESE!
CHEESE!!
FLASH

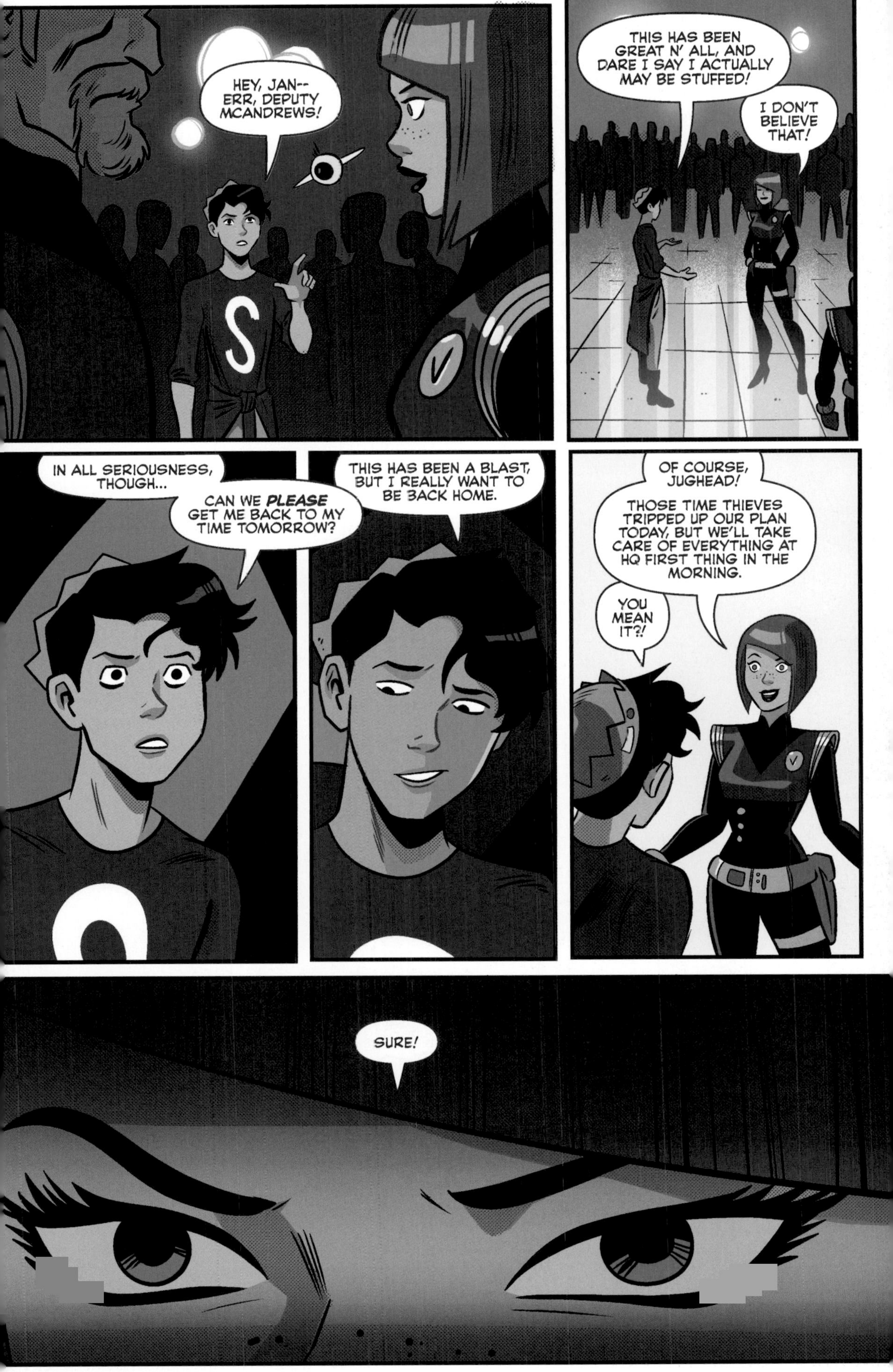
HEY, JAN-- ERR, DEPUTY MCANDREWS!
THIS HAS BEEN GREAT N' ALL, AND DARE I SAY I ACTUALLY MAY BE STUFFED!
I DON'T BELIEVE THAT!
IN ALL SERIOUSNESS, THOUGH...
CAN WE PLEASE GET ME BACK TO MY TIME TOMORROW?
THIS HAS BEEN A BLAST, BUT I REALLY WANT TO BE BACK HOME.
OF COURSE, JUGHEAD!
THOSE TIME THIEVES TRIPPED UP OUR PLAN TODAY, BUT WE'LL TAKE CARE OF EVERYTHING AT HQ FIRST THING IN THE MORNING.
YOU MEAN IT?!
SURE!

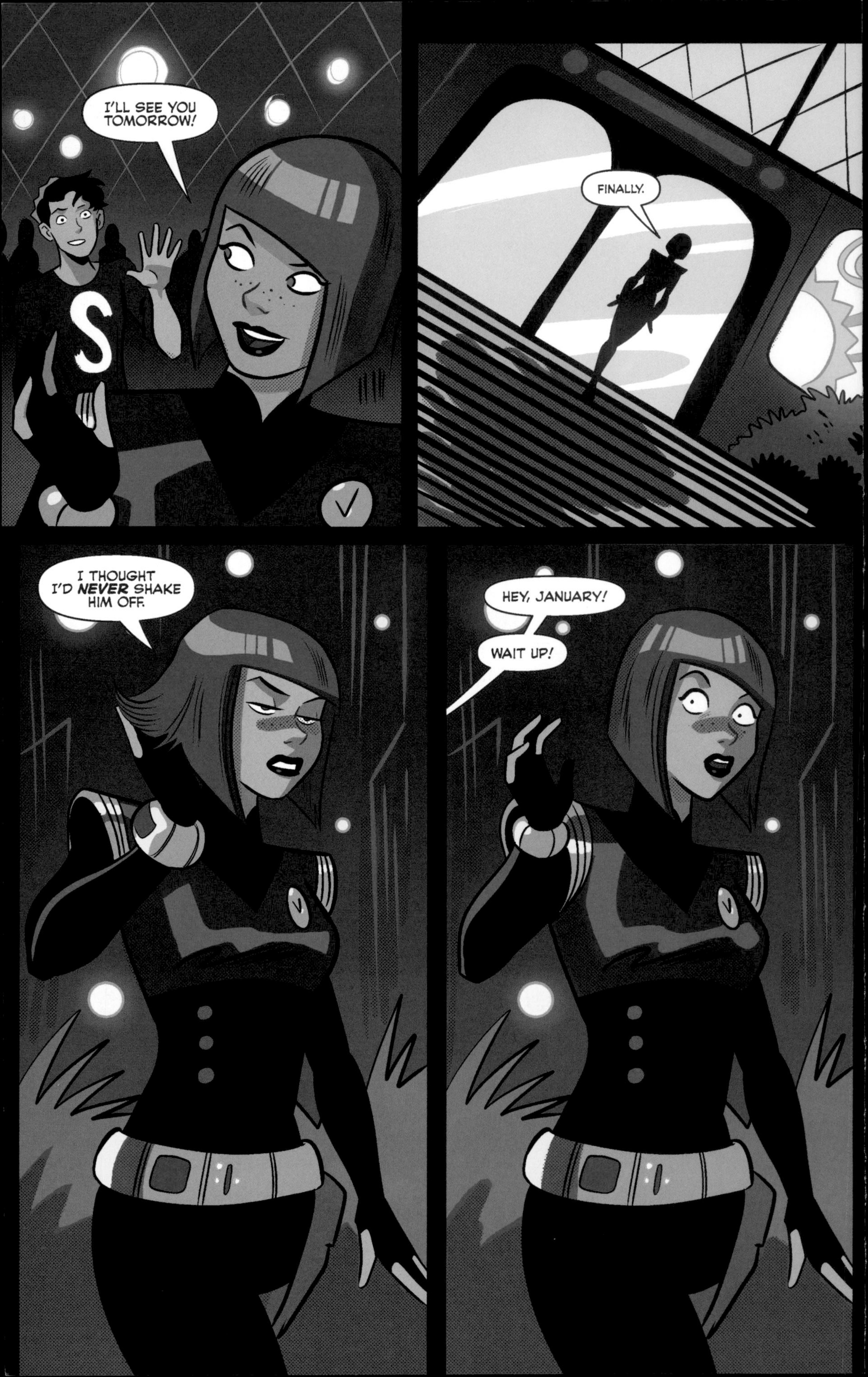
I'LL SEE YOU TOMORROW!
FINALLY.
I THOUGHT I'D NEVER SHAKE HIM OFF.
HEY, JANUARY!
WAIT UP!

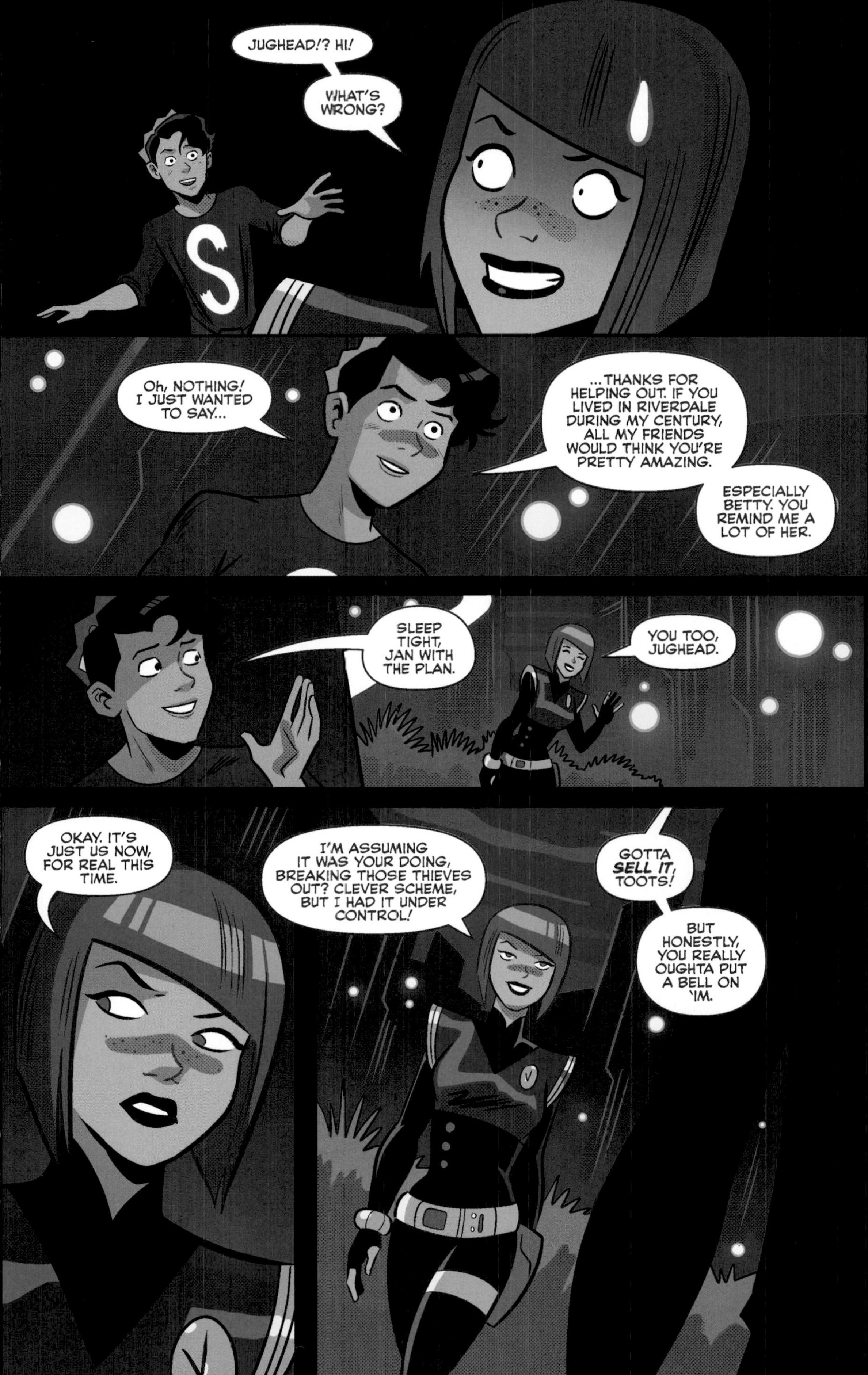
JUGHEAD!? HI!
WHAT'S WRONG?
Oh, NOTHING! I JUST WANTED TO SAY...
...THANKS FOR HELPING OUT. IF YOU LIVED IN RIVERDALE DURING MY CENTURY, ALL MY FRIENDS WOULD THINK YOU'RE PRETTY AMAZING.
ESPECIALLY BETTY. YOU REMIND ME A LOT OF HER.
SLEEP TIGHT, JAN WITH THE PLAN.
YOU TOO, JUGHEAD.
OKAY. IT'S JUST US NOW, FOR REAL THIS TIME.
I'M ASSUMING IT WAS YOUR DOING, BREAKING THOSE THIEVES OUT? CLEVER SCHEME, BUT I HAD IT UNDER CONTROL!
GOTTA SELL IT, TOOTS!
BUT HONESTLY, YOU REALLY OUGHTA PUT A BELL ON 'IM.

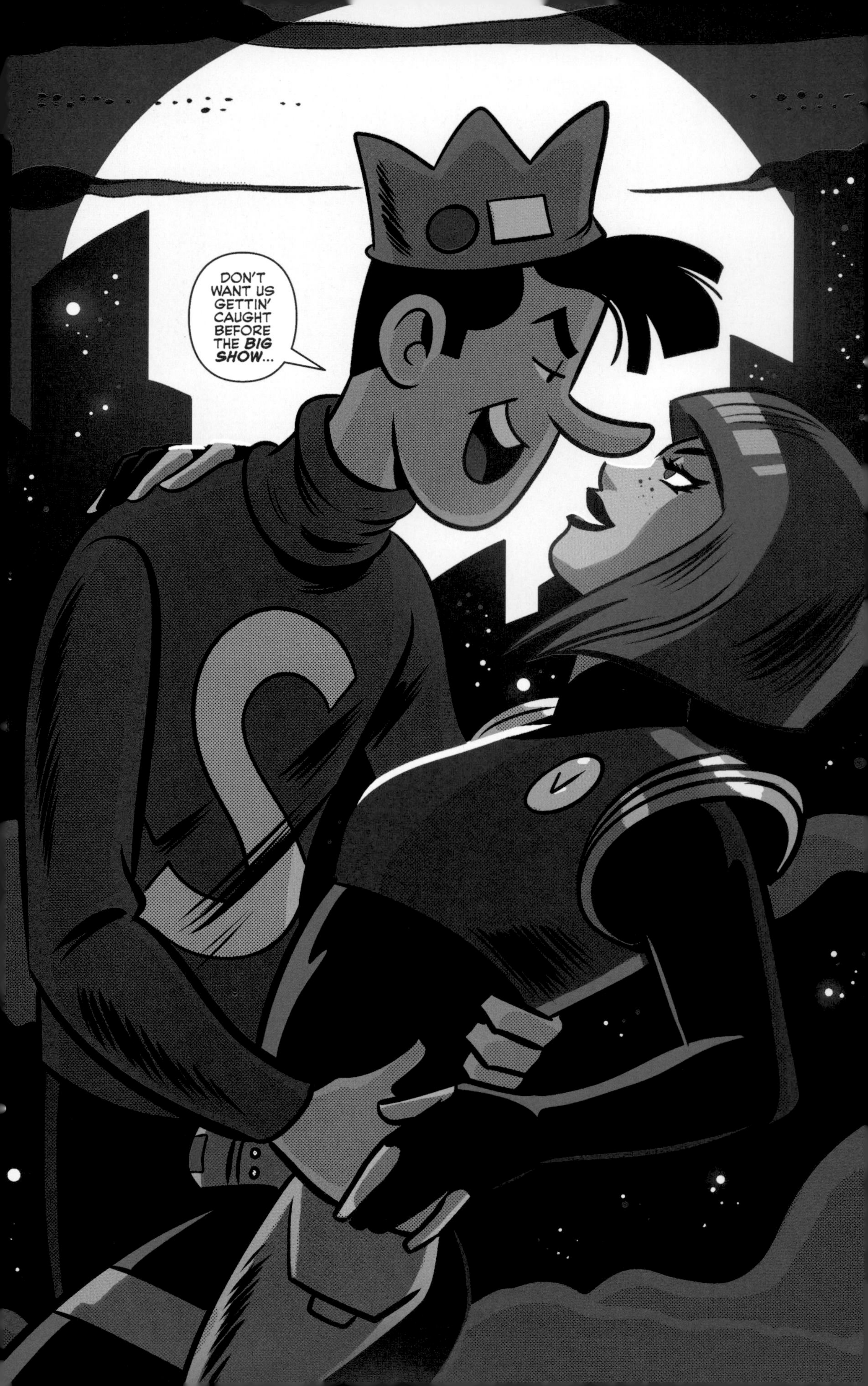
DON'T WANT US GETTIN' CAUGHT BEFORE THE **BIG SHOW**...

CHAPTER 3

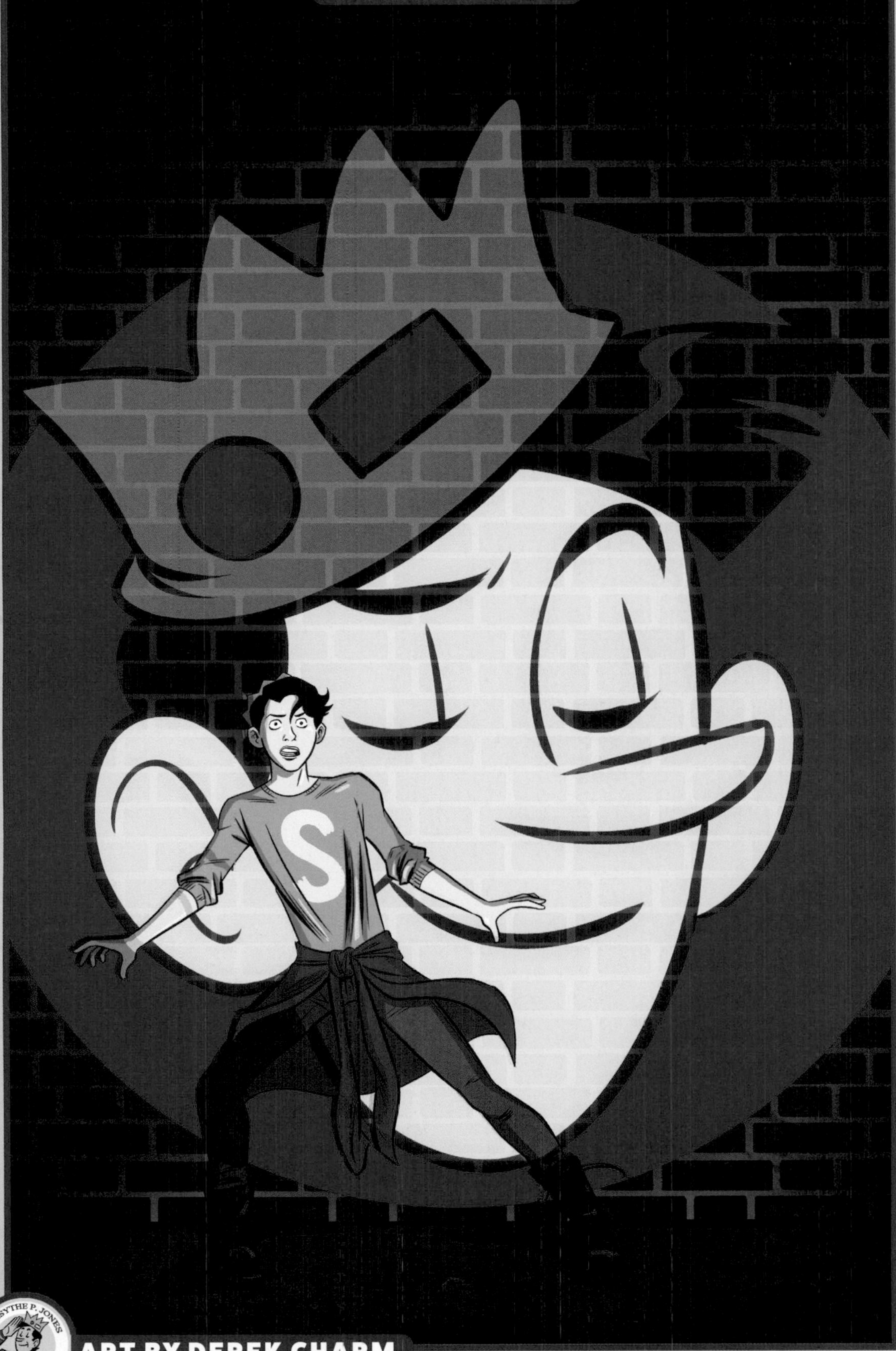

ART BY DEREK CHARM

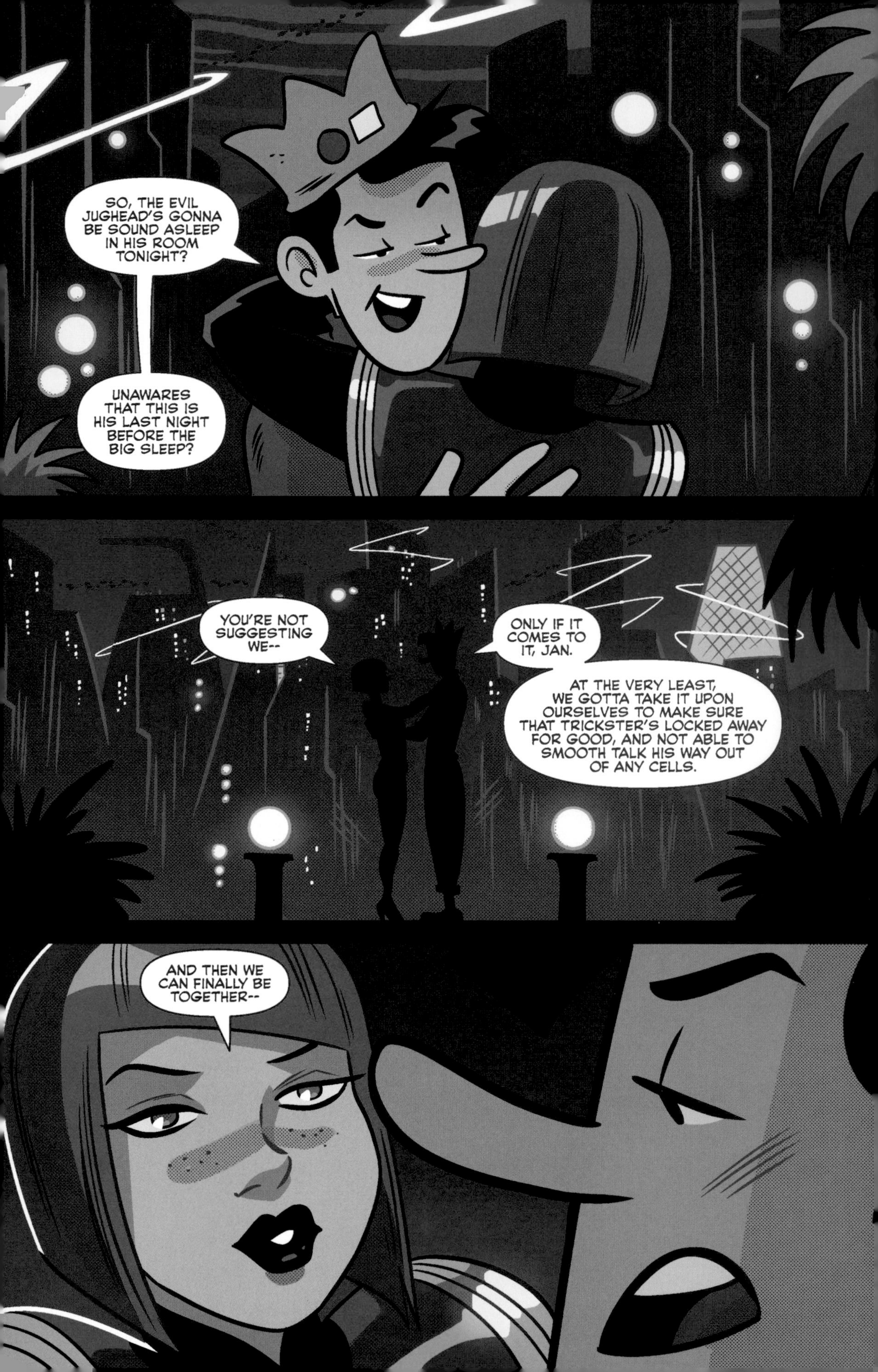
SO, THE EVIL JUGHEAD'S GONNA BE SOUND ASLEEP IN HIS ROOM TONIGHT?
UNAWARES THAT THIS IS HIS LAST NIGHT BEFORE THE BIG SLEEP?
YOU'RE NOT SUGGESTING WE--
ONLY IF IT COMES TO IT, JAN.
AT THE VERY LEAST, WE GOTTA TAKE IT UPON OURSELVES TO MAKE SURE THAT TRICKSTER'S LOCKED AWAY FOR GOOD, AND NOT ABLE TO SMOOTH TALK HIS WAY OUT OF ANY CELLS.
AND THEN WE CAN FINALLY BE TOGETHER--

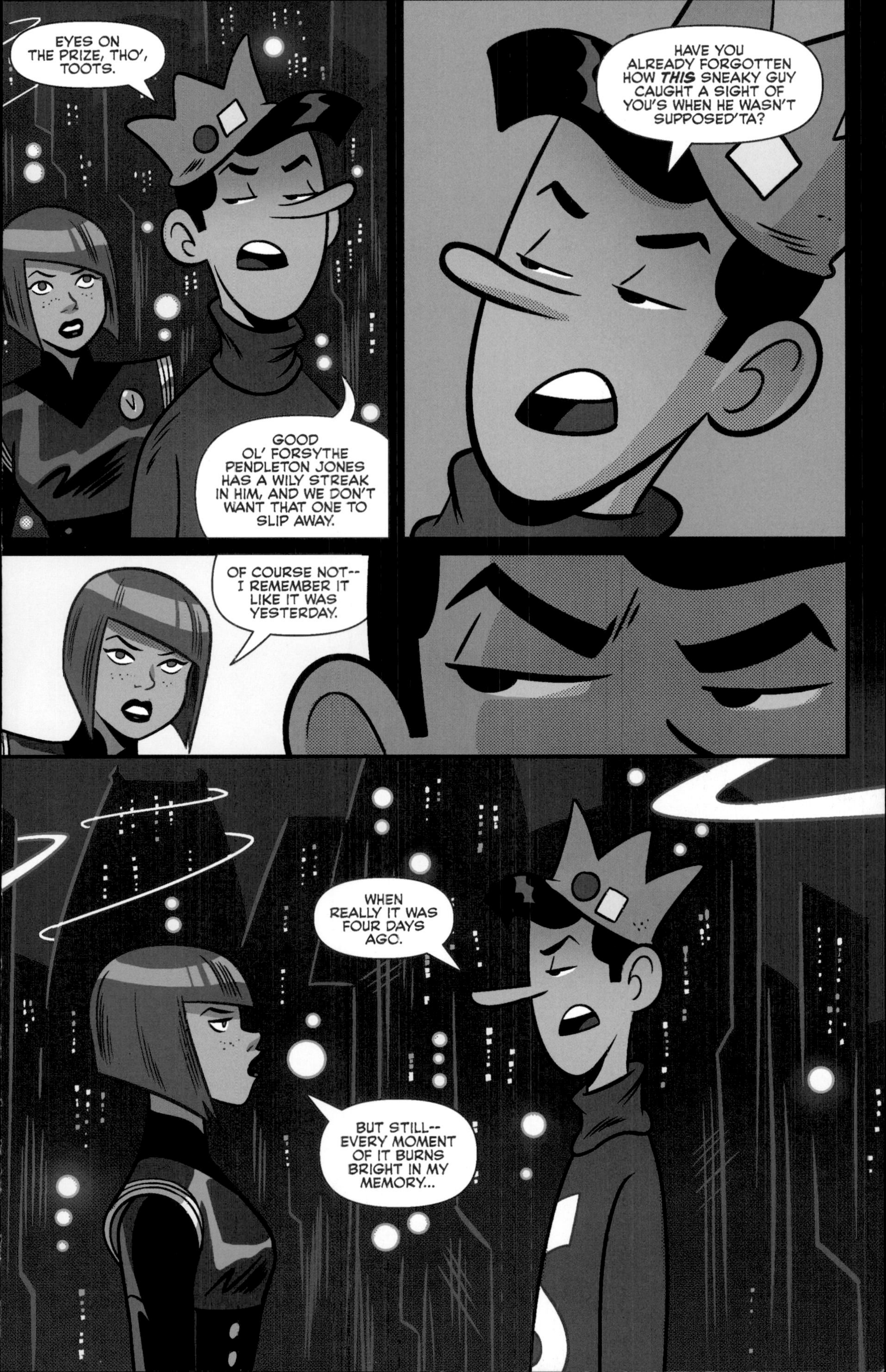
EYES ON THE PRIZE, THO', TOOTS.
GOOD OL' FORSYTHE PENDLETON JONES HAS A WILY STREAK IN HIM, AND WE DON'T WANT THAT ONE TO SLIP AWAY.
HAVE YOU ALREADY FORGOTTEN HOW *THIS* SNEAKY GUY CAUGHT A SIGHT OF YOU'S WHEN HE WASN'T SUPPOSED'TA?
OF COURSE NOT-- I REMEMBER IT LIKE IT WAS YESTERDAY.
WHEN REALLY IT WAS FOUR DAYS AGO.
BUT STILL-- EVERY MOMENT OF IT BURNS BRIGHT IN MY MEMORY...

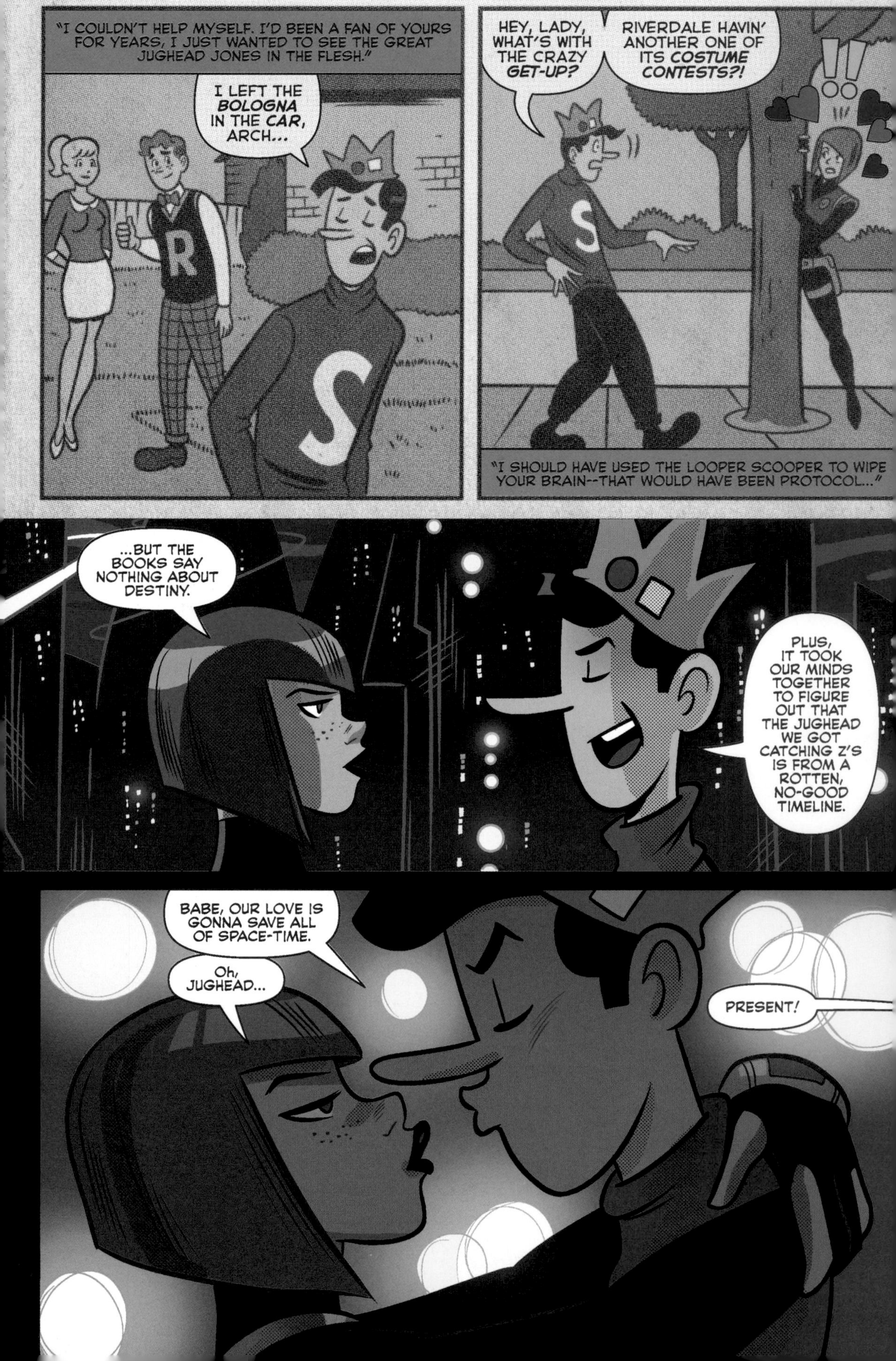
"I COULDN'T HELP MYSELF. I'D BEEN A FAN OF YOURS FOR YEARS, I JUST WANTED TO SEE THE GREAT JUGHEAD JONES IN THE FLESH."
I LEFT THE *BOLOGNA* IN THE *CAR*, ARCH...
HEY, LADY, WHAT'S WITH THE CRAZY *GET-UP?*
RIVERDALE HAVIN' ANOTHER ONE OF ITS *COSTUME CONTESTS?!*
"I SHOULD HAVE USED THE LOOPER SCOOPER TO WIPE YOUR BRAIN--THAT WOULD HAVE BEEN PROTOCOL..."
...BUT THE BOOKS SAY NOTHING ABOUT DESTINY.
PLUS, IT TOOK OUR MINDS TOGETHER TO FIGURE OUT THAT THE JUGHEAD WE GOT CATCHING Z'S IS FROM A ROTTEN, NO-GOOD TIMELINE.
BABE, OUR LOVE IS GONNA SAVE ALL OF SPACE-TIME.
Oh, JUGHEAD...
PRESENT!

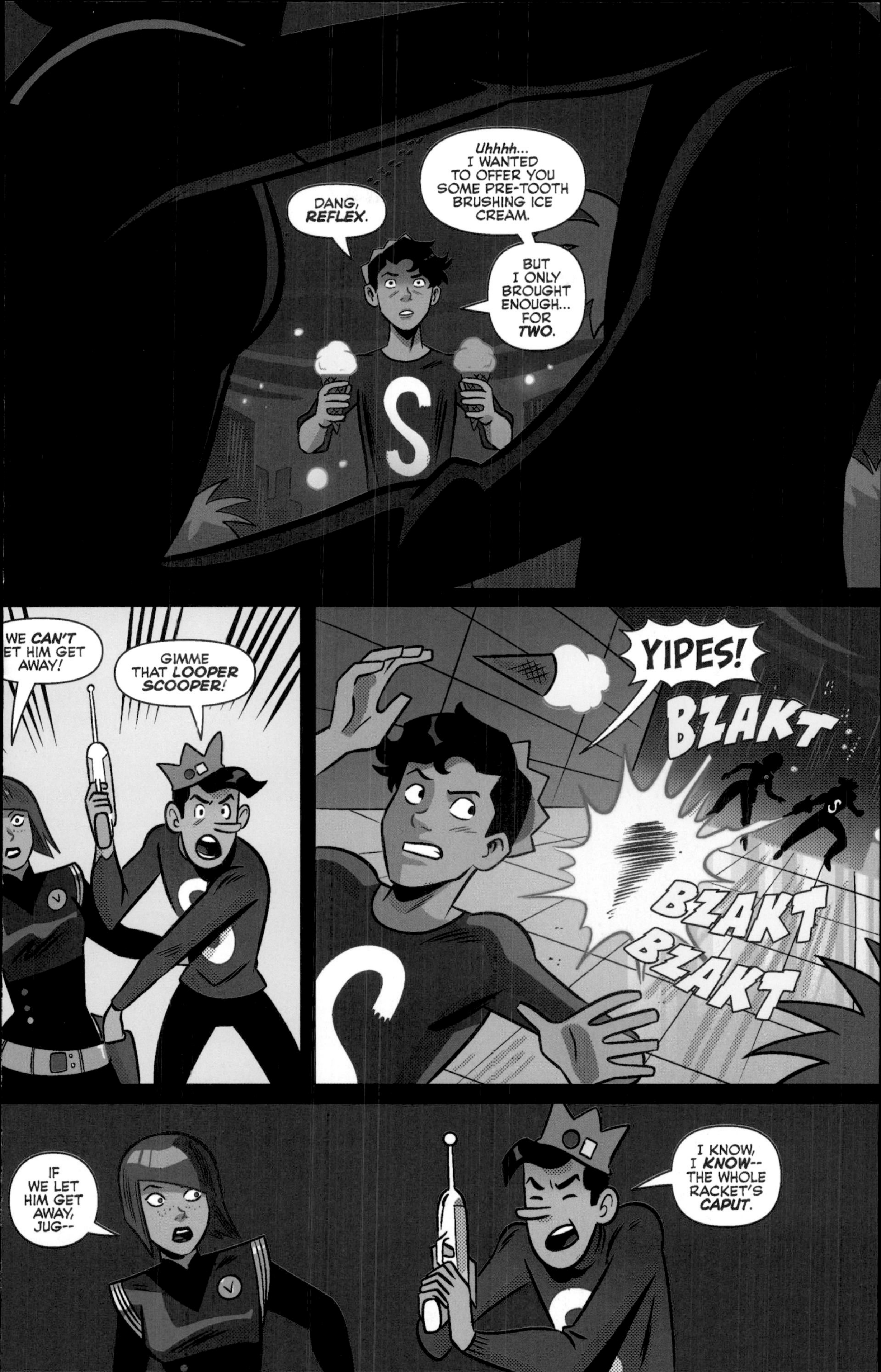

DANG, REFLEX.
Uhhhh... I WANTED TO OFFER YOU SOME PRE-TOOTH BRUSHING ICE CREAM.
BUT I ONLY BROUGHT ENOUGH... FOR TWO.
WE CAN'T LET HIM GET AWAY!
GIMME THAT LOOPER SCOOPER!
YIPES!
BZAKT
BZAKT
BZAKT
IF WE LET HIM GET AWAY, JUG--
I KNOW, I KNOW-- THE WHOLE RACKET'S CAPUT.

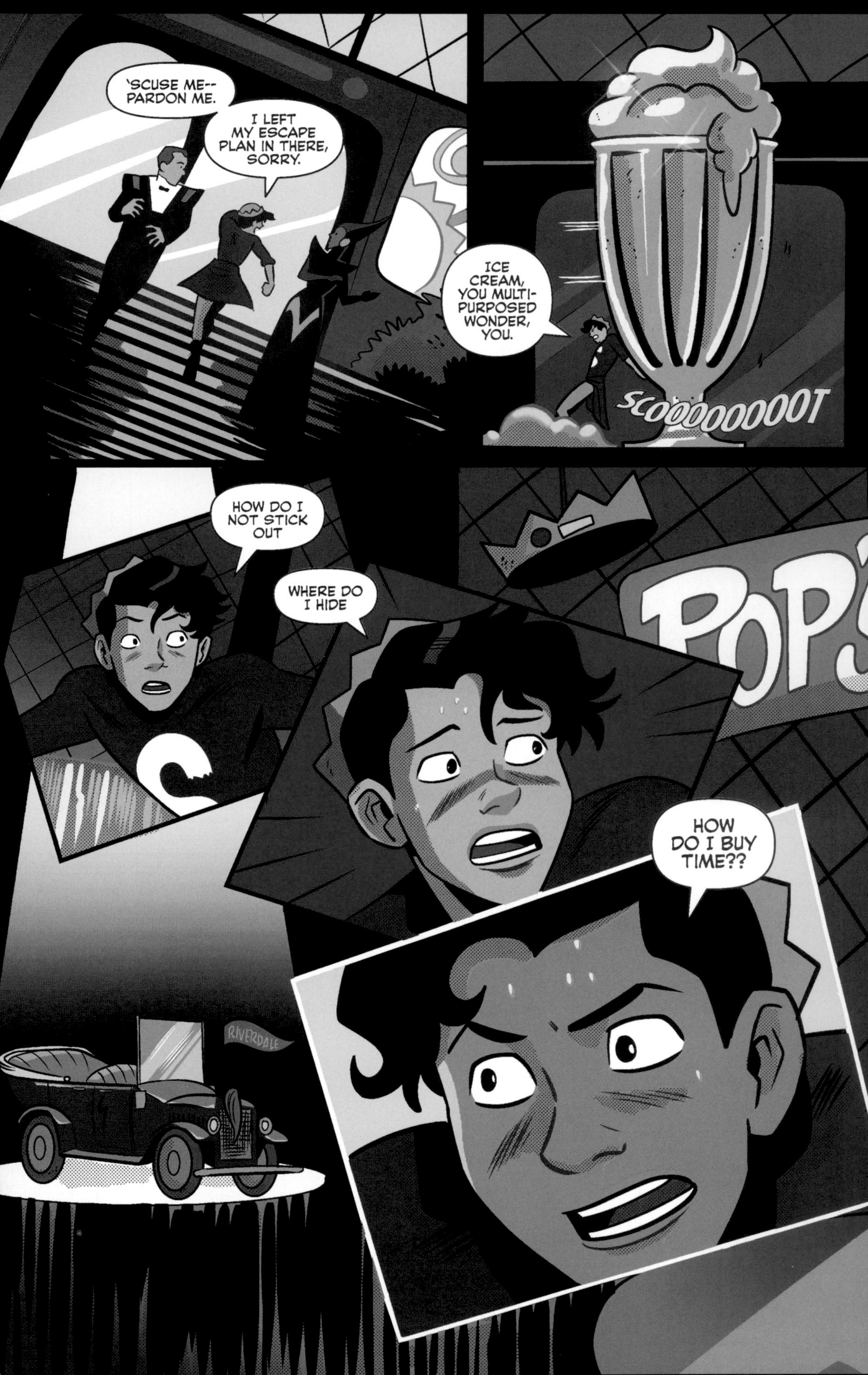
'SCUSE ME--
PARDON ME.
I LEFT MY ESCAPE PLAN IN THERE, SORRY.
ICE CREAM, YOU MULTI-PURPOSED WONDER, YOU.
SCOOOOOOOOOT
HOW DO I NOT STICK OUT
WHERE DO I HIDE
POP'S
HOW DO I BUY TIME??
RIVERDALE

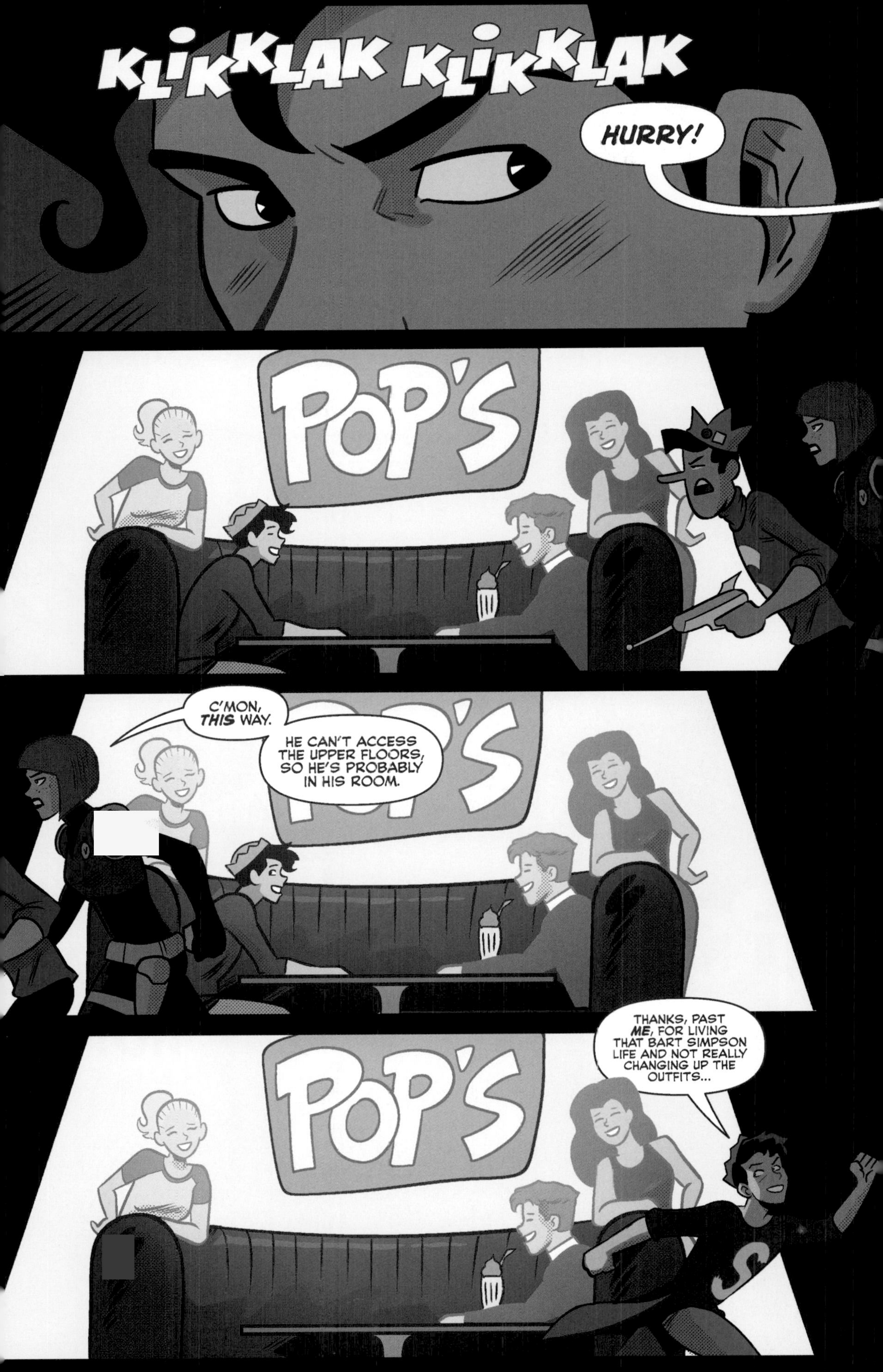
KLIKKLAK KLIKKLAK
HURRY!
POP'S
C'MON, THIS WAY.
HE CAN'T ACCESS THE UPPER FLOORS, SO HE'S PROBABLY IN HIS ROOM.
POP'S
POP'S
THANKS, PAST ME, FOR LIVING THAT BART SIMPSON LIFE AND NOT REALLY CHANGING UP THE OUTFITS...

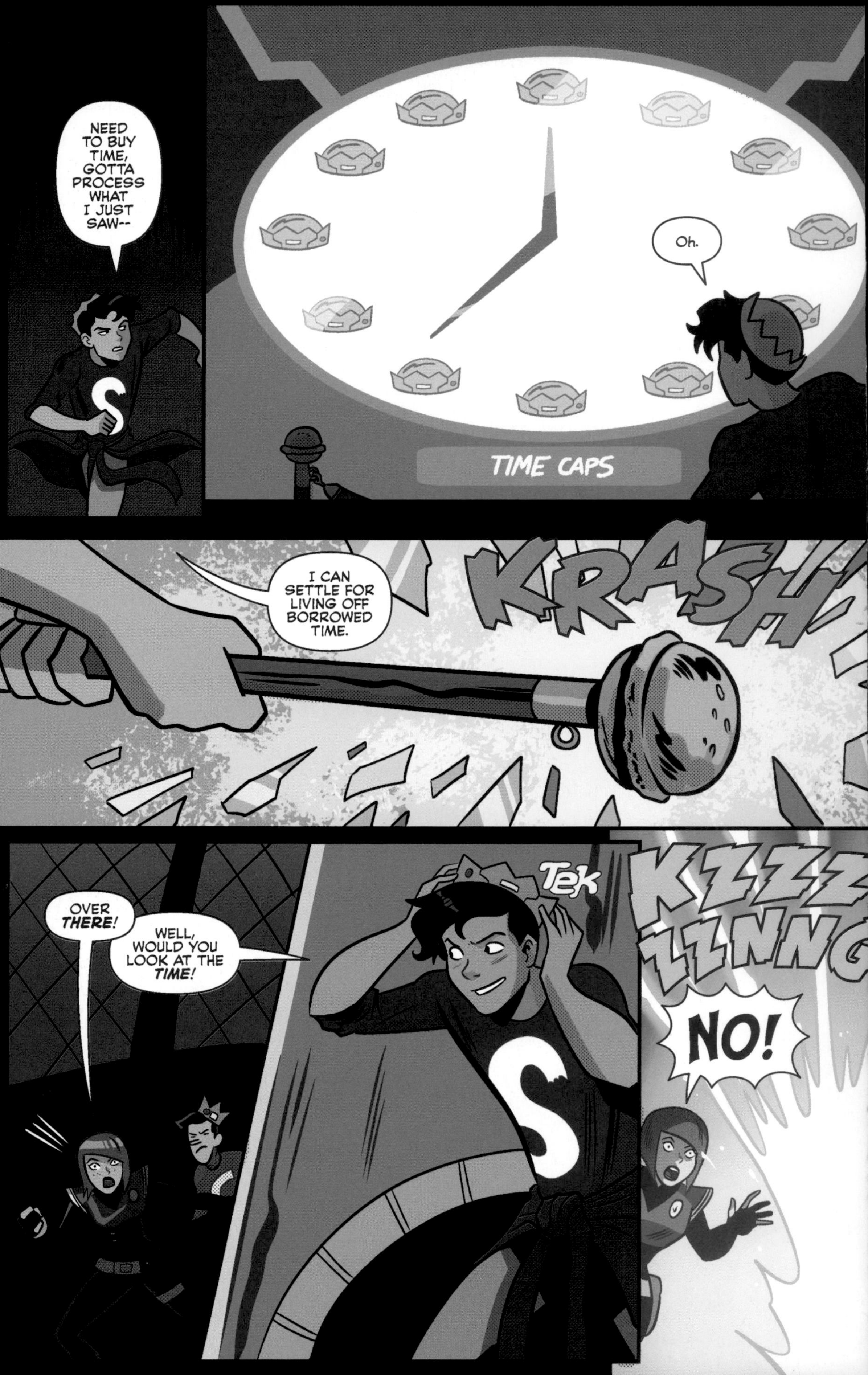
NEED TO BUY TIME, GOTTA PROCESS WHAT I JUST SAW--
Oh.
TIME CAPS
I CAN SETTLE FOR LIVING OFF BORROWED TIME.
KRASH
OVER THERE!
WELL, WOULD YOU LOOK AT THE TIME!
TEK
KZZZZ ZZNNG
NO!

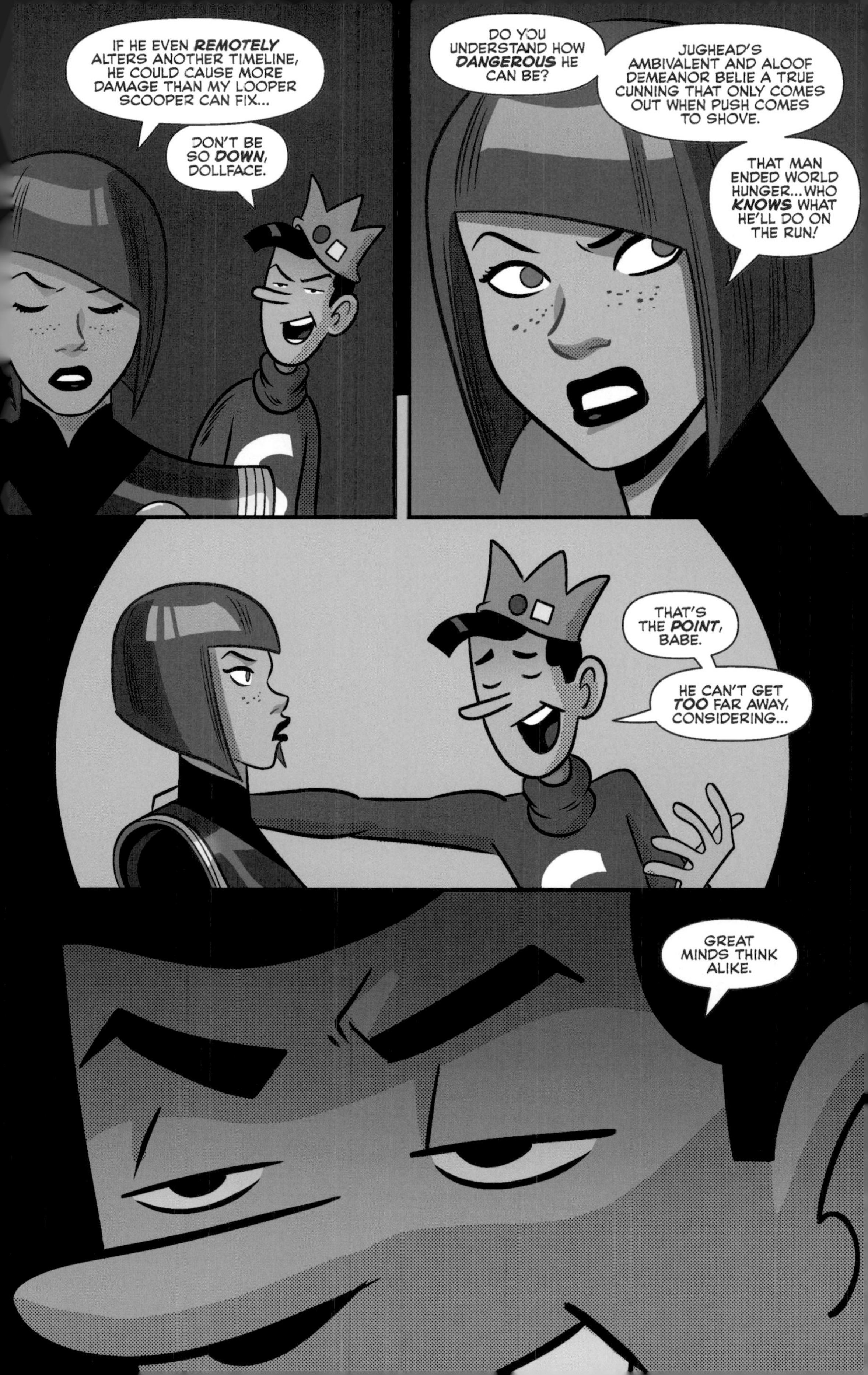
IF HE EVEN REMOTELY ALTERS ANOTHER TIMELINE, HE COULD CAUSE MORE DAMAGE THAN MY LOOPER SCOOPER CAN FIX...
DON'T BE SO DOWN, DOLLFACE.
DO YOU UNDERSTAND HOW DANGEROUS HE CAN BE?
JUGHEAD'S AMBIVALENT AND ALOOF DEMEANOR BELIE A TRUE CUNNING THAT ONLY COMES OUT WHEN PUSH COMES TO SHOVE.
THAT MAN ENDED WORLD HUNGER...WHO KNOWS WHAT HE'LL DO ON THE RUN!
THAT'S THE POINT, BABE.
HE CAN'T GET TOO FAR AWAY, CONSIDERING...
GREAT MINDS THINK ALIKE.

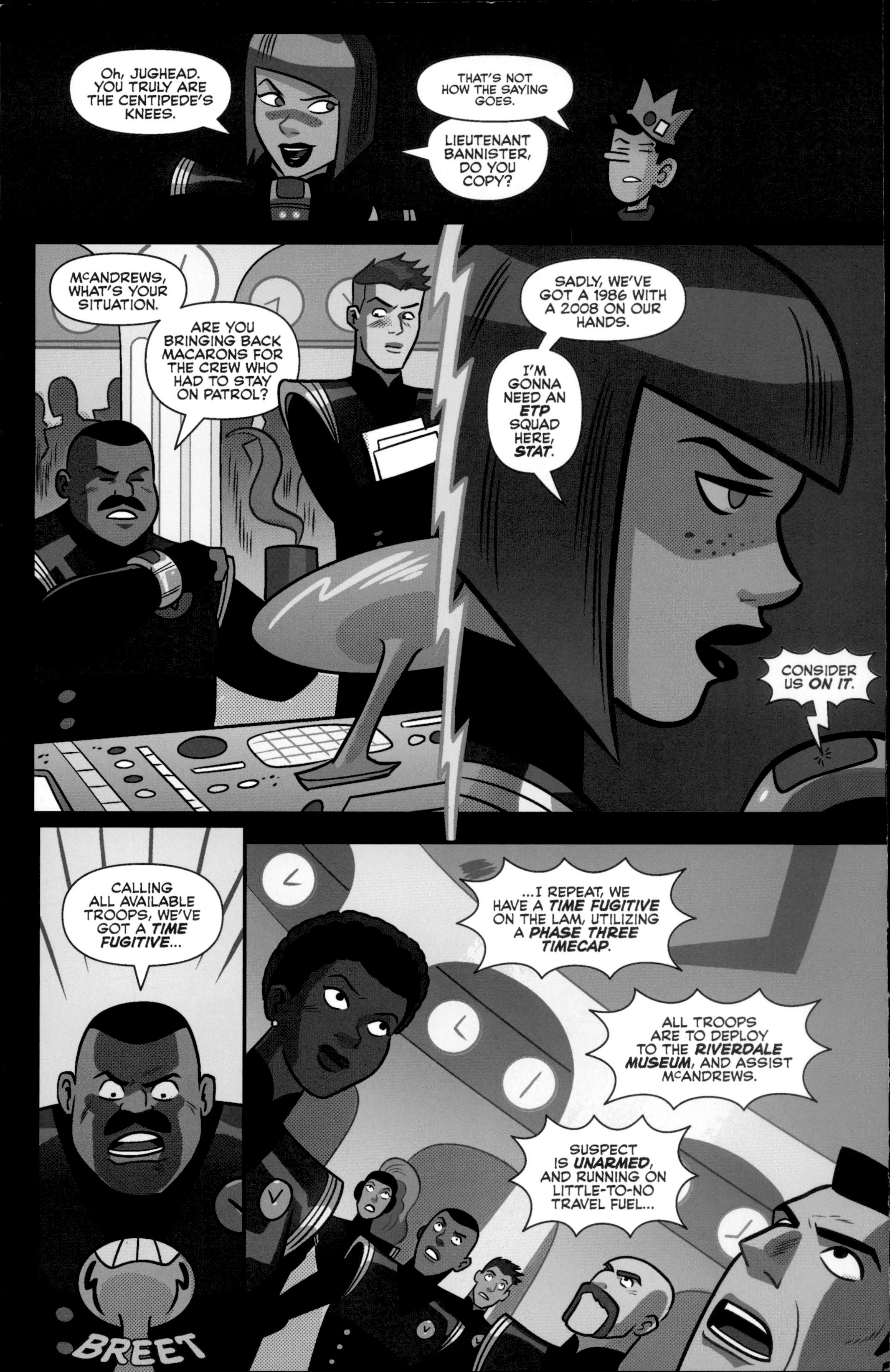
Oh, JUGHEAD. YOU TRULY ARE THE CENTIPEDE'S KNEES.
THAT'S NOT HOW THE SAYING GOES.
LIEUTENANT BANNISTER, DO YOU COPY?
McANDREWS, WHAT'S YOUR SITUATION.
ARE YOU BRINGING BACK MACARONS FOR THE CREW WHO HAD TO STAY ON PATROL?
SADLY, WE'VE GOT A 1986 WITH A 2008 ON OUR HANDS.
I'M GONNA NEED AN ETP SQUAD HERE, STAT.
CONSIDER US ON IT.
CALLING ALL AVAILABLE TROOPS, WE'VE GOT A TIME FUGITIVE...
...I REPEAT, WE HAVE A TIME FUGITIVE ON THE LAM, UTILIZING A PHASE THREE TIMECAP.
ALL TROOPS ARE TO DEPLOY TO THE RIVERDALE MUSEUM, AND ASSIST McANDREWS.
SUSPECT IS UNARMED, AND RUNNING ON LITTLE-TO-NO TRAVEL FUEL...
BREET

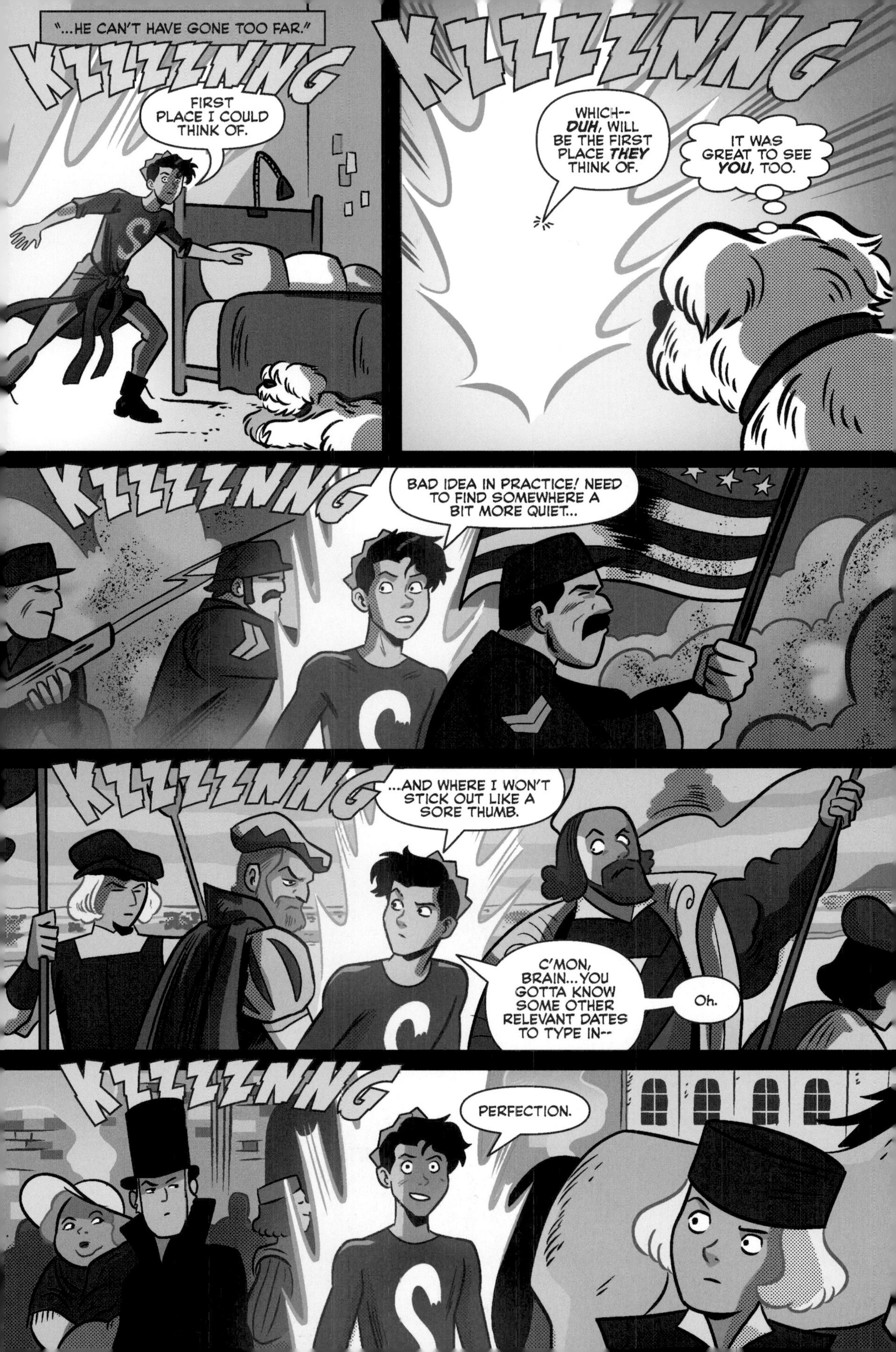
"...HE CAN'T HAVE GONE TOO FAR."
KZZZZZNNG
FIRST PLACE I COULD THINK OF.
KZZZZZNNG
WHICH-- DUH, WILL BE THE FIRST PLACE THEY THINK OF.
IT WAS GREAT TO SEE YOU, TOO.
KZZZZZNNG
BAD IDEA IN PRACTICE! NEED TO FIND SOMEWHERE A BIT MORE QUIET...
KZZZZZNNG
...AND WHERE I WON'T STICK OUT LIKE A SORE THUMB.
C'MON, BRAIN...YOU GOTTA KNOW SOME OTHER RELEVANT DATES TO TYPE IN--
Oh.
KZZZZZNNG
PERFECTION.

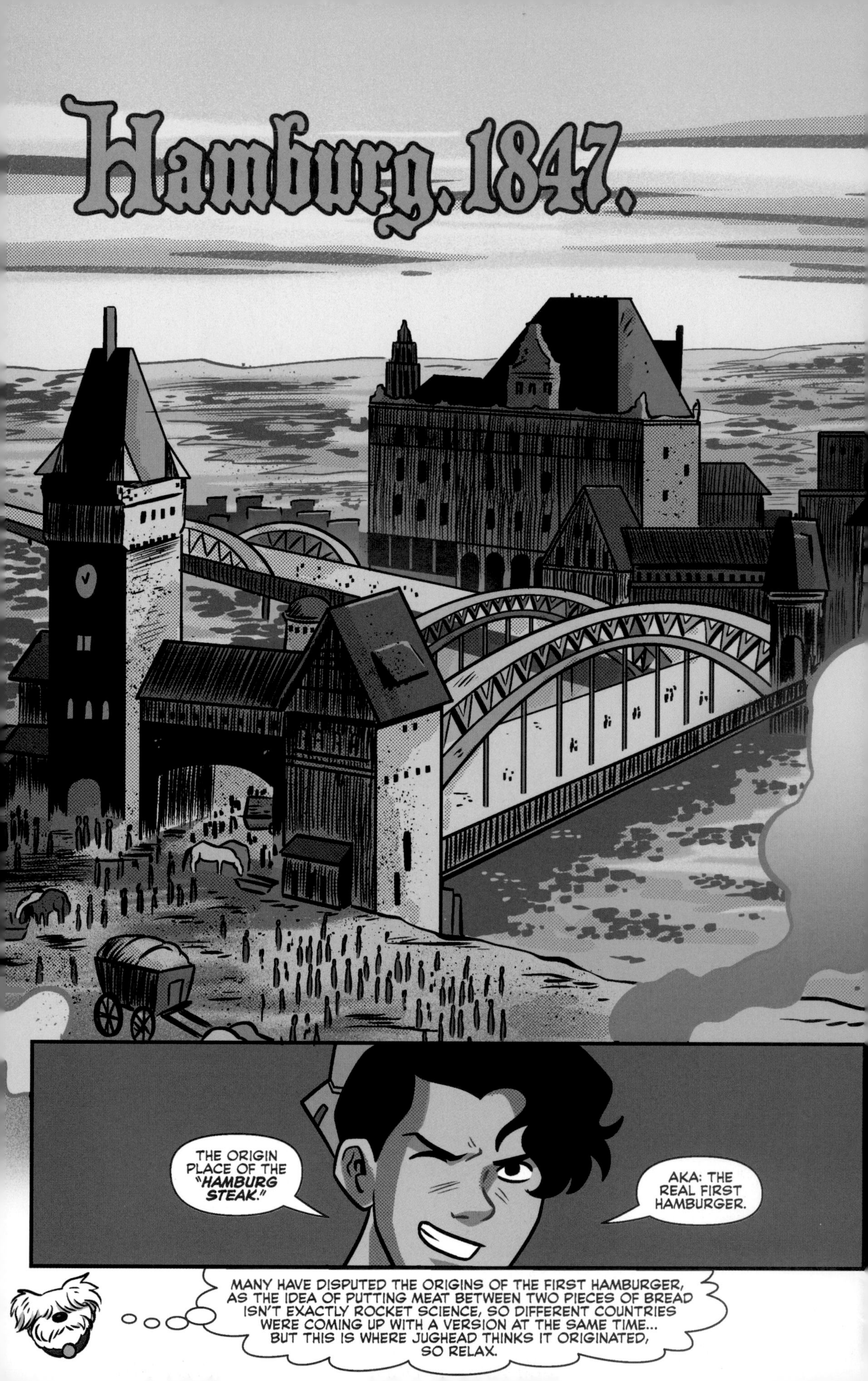
Hamburg, 1847.
THE ORIGIN PLACE OF THE "HAMBURG STEAK."
AKA: THE REAL FIRST HAMBURGER.
MANY HAVE DISPUTED THE ORIGINS OF THE FIRST HAMBURGER, AS THE IDEA OF PUTTING MEAT BETWEEN TWO PIECES OF BREAD ISN'T EXACTLY ROCKET SCIENCE, SO DIFFERENT COUNTRIES WERE COMING UP WITH A VERSION AT THE SAME TIME... BUT THIS IS WHERE JUGHEAD THINKS IT ORIGINATED, SO RELAX.

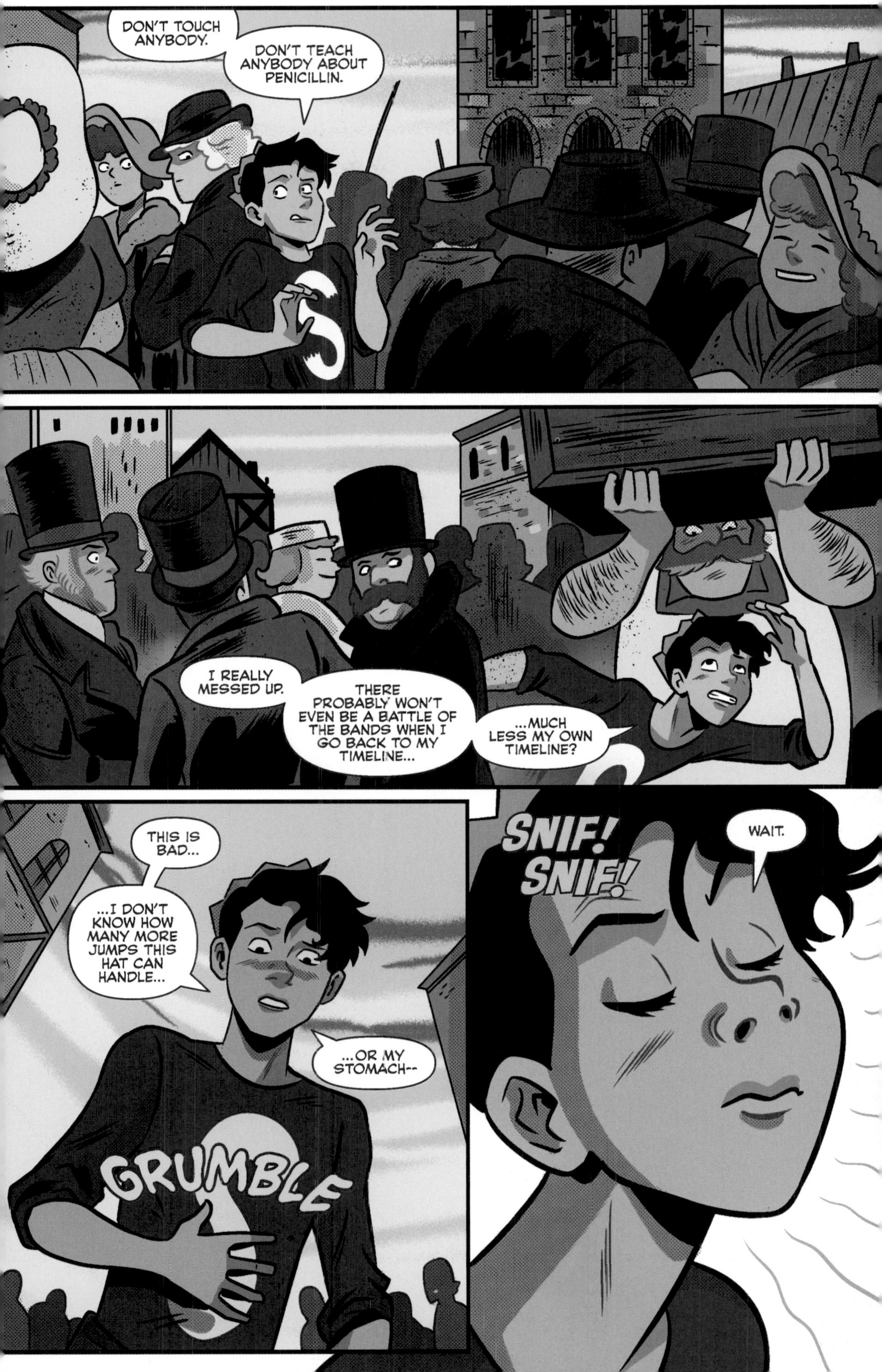
DON'T TOUCH ANYBODY.
DON'T TEACH ANYBODY ABOUT PENICILLIN.
I REALLY MESSED UP.
THERE PROBABLY WON'T EVEN BE A BATTLE OF THE BANDS WHEN I GO BACK TO MY TIMELINE...
...MUCH LESS MY OWN TIMELINE?
THIS IS BAD...
...I DON'T KNOW HOW MANY MORE JUMPS THIS HAT CAN HANDLE...
...OR MY STOMACH--
GRUMBLE
SNIF! SNIF!
WAIT.

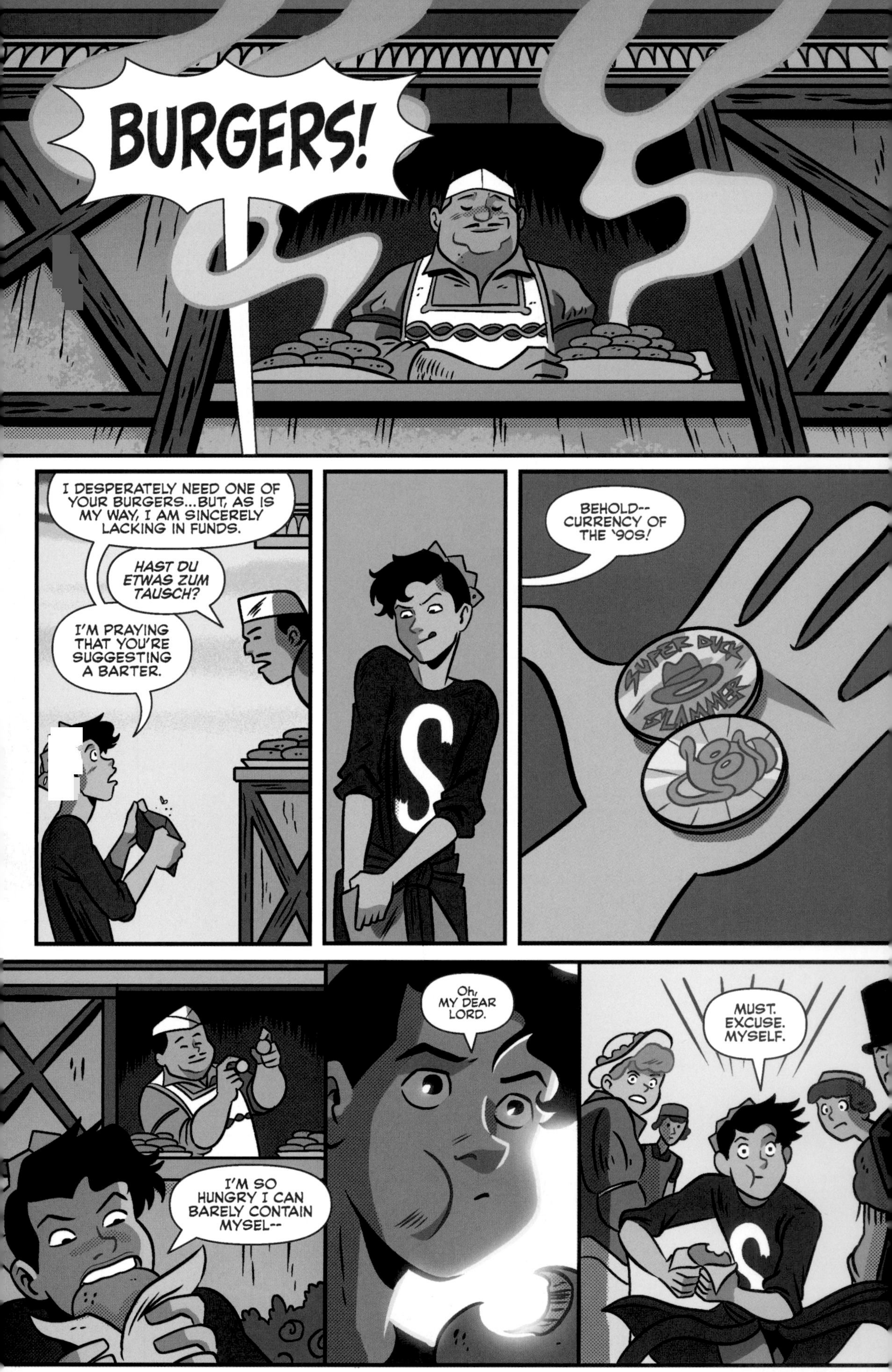
BURGERS!
I DESPERATELY NEED ONE OF YOUR BURGERS...BUT, AS IS MY WAY, I AM SINCERELY LACKING IN FUNDS.
HAST DU ETWAS ZUM TAUSCH?
I'M PRAYING THAT YOU'RE SUGGESTING A BARTER.
BEHOLD-- CURRENCY OF THE '90S!
SUPER DUCK SLAMMER
I'M SO HUNGRY I CAN BARELY CONTAIN MYSEL--
Oh, MY DEAR LORD.
MUST. EXCUSE. MYSELF.

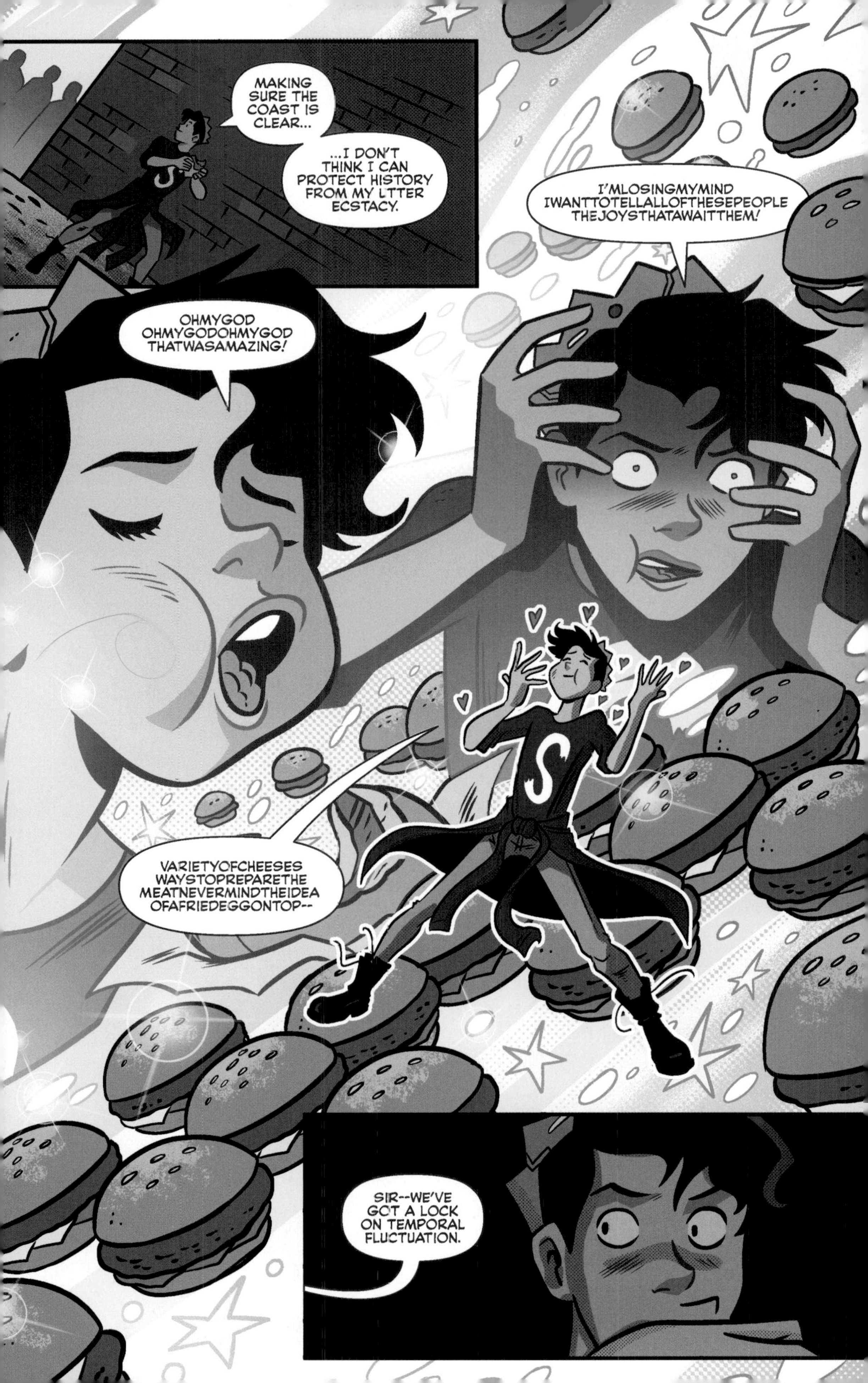
MAKING SURE THE COAST IS CLEAR...
...I DON'T THINK I CAN PROTECT HISTORY FROM MY UTTER ECSTACY.
I'MLOSINGMYMIND IWANTTOTELLALLOFTHESEPEOPLE THEJOYSTHATAWAITTHEM!
OHMYGOD OHMYGODOHMYGOD THATWASAMAZING!
VARIETYOFCHEESES WAYSTOPREPARETHE MEATNEVERMINDTHEIDEA OFAFRIEDEGGONTOP--
SIR--WE'VE GOT A LOCK ON TEMPORAL FLUCTUATION.

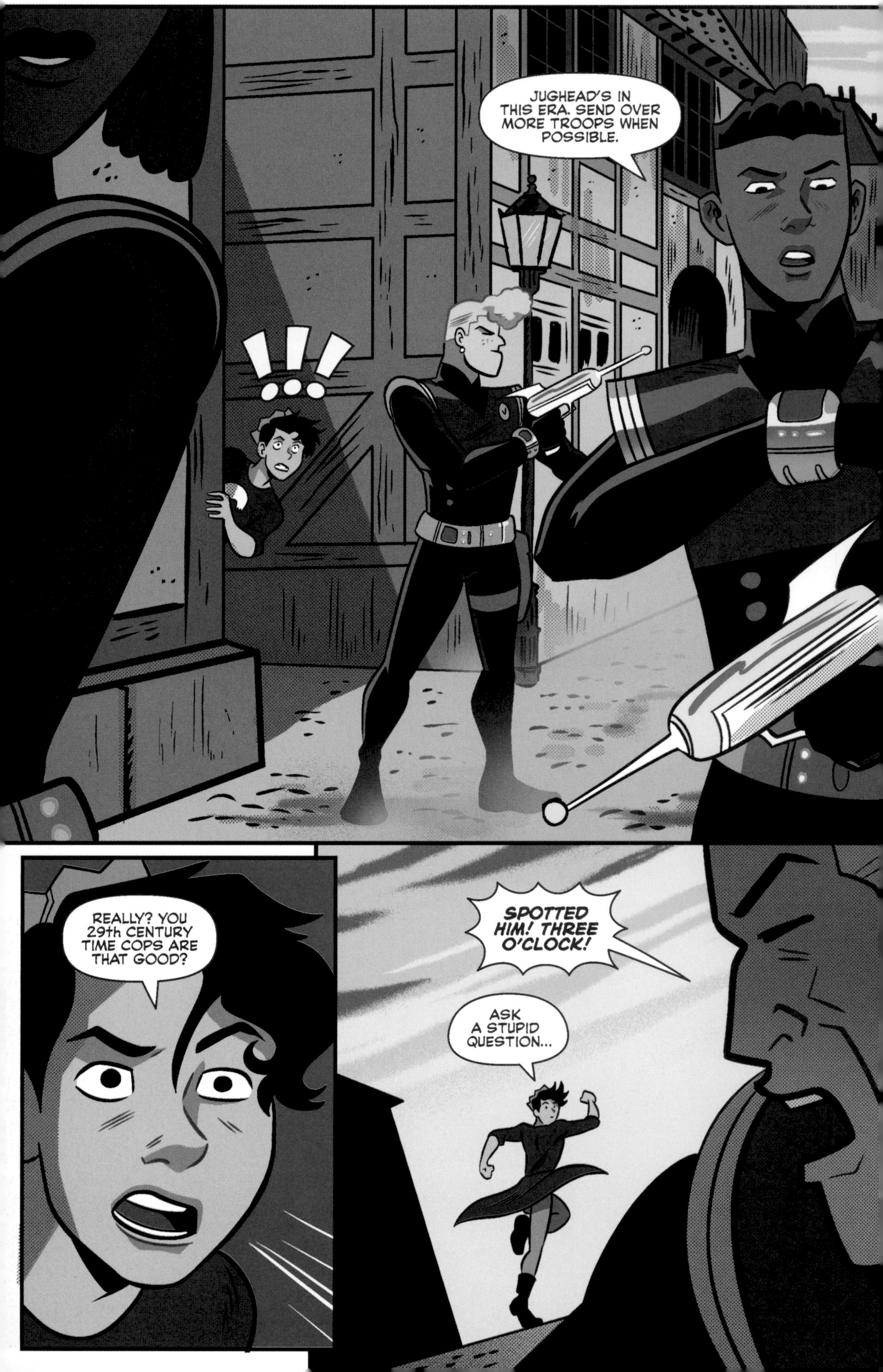
JUGHEAD'S IN THIS ERA. SEND OVER MORE TROOPS WHEN POSSIBLE.
!!!...
REALLY? YOU 29th CENTURY TIME COPS ARE THAT GOOD?
SPOTTED HIM! THREE O'CLOCK!
ASK A STUPID QUESTION...

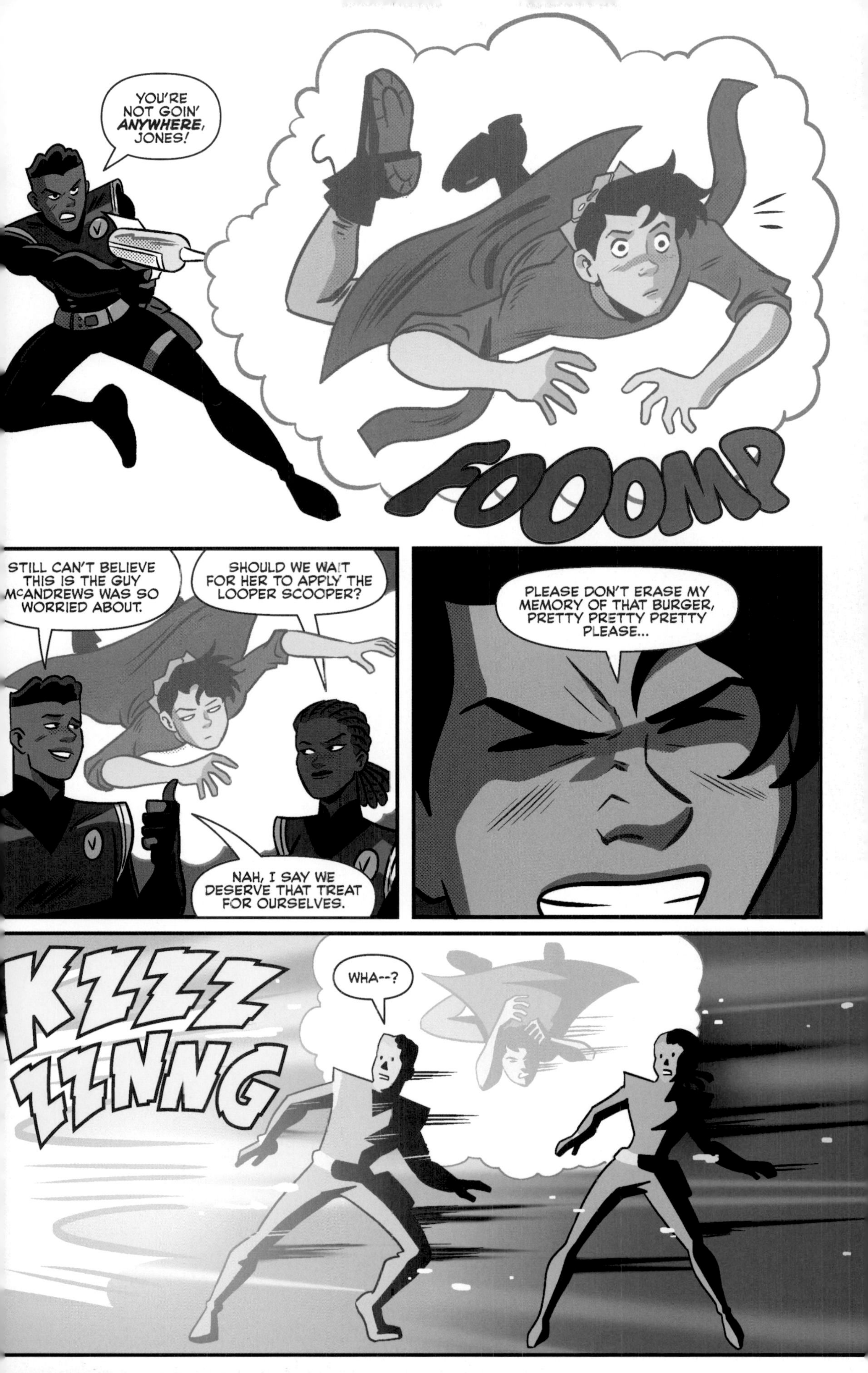
YOU'RE NOT GOIN' ANYWHERE, JONES!
FOOOMP
STILL CAN'T BELIEVE THIS IS THE GUY McANDREWS WAS SO WORRIED ABOUT.
SHOULD WE WAIT FOR HER TO APPLY THE LOOPER SCOOPER?
NAH, I SAY WE DESERVE THAT TREAT FOR OURSELVES.
PLEASE DON'T ERASE MY MEMORY OF THAT BURGER, PRETTY PRETTY PRETTY PLEASE...
KZZZZ ZZNNG
WHA--?

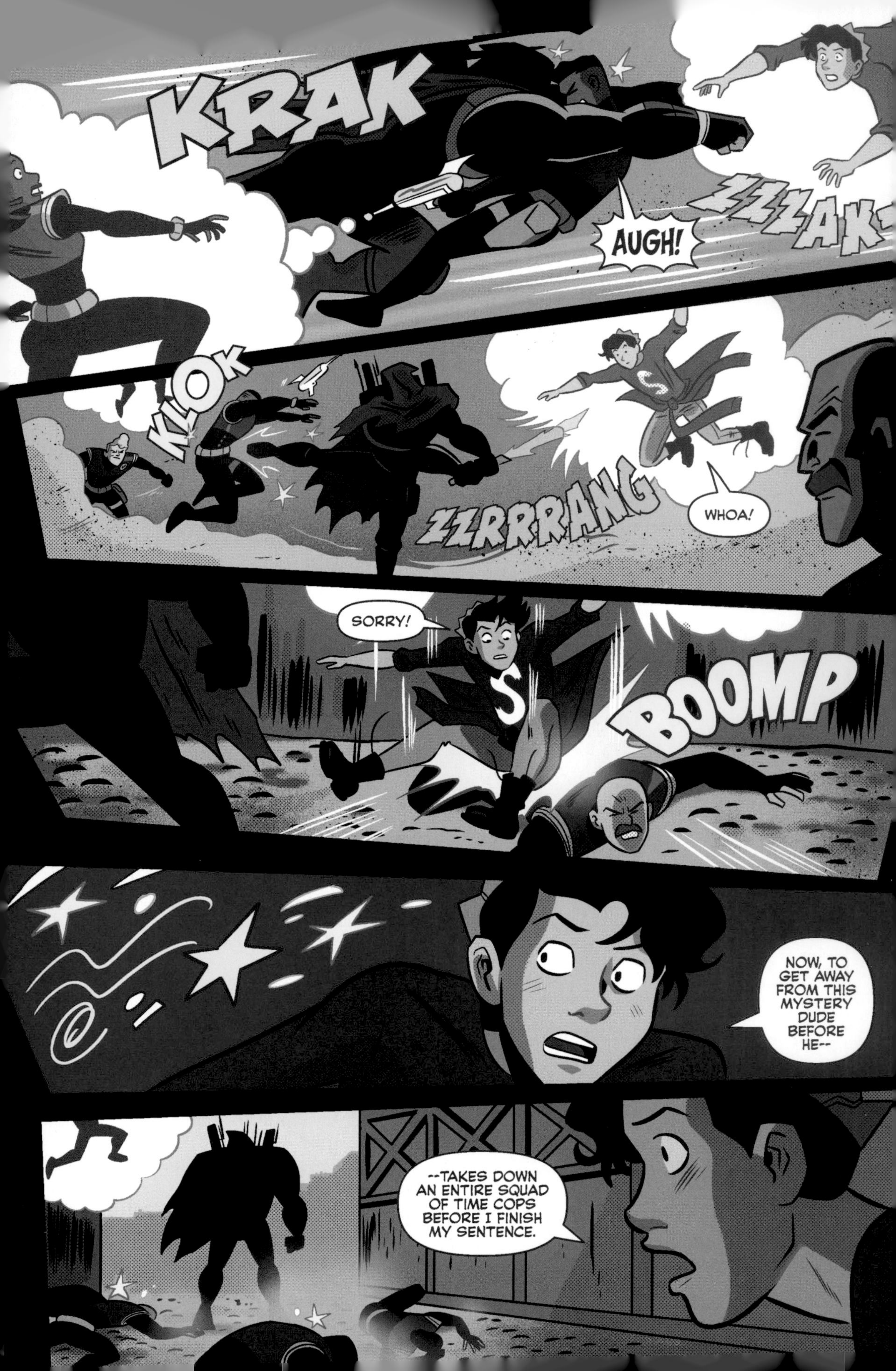
KRAK
AUGH!
ZZZZAK
KLOK
ZZRRRRANG
WHOA!
SORRY!
BOOMP
NOW, TO GET AWAY FROM THIS MYSTERY DUDE BEFORE HE--
--TAKES DOWN AN ENTIRE SQUAD OF TIME COPS BEFORE I FINISH MY SENTENCE.

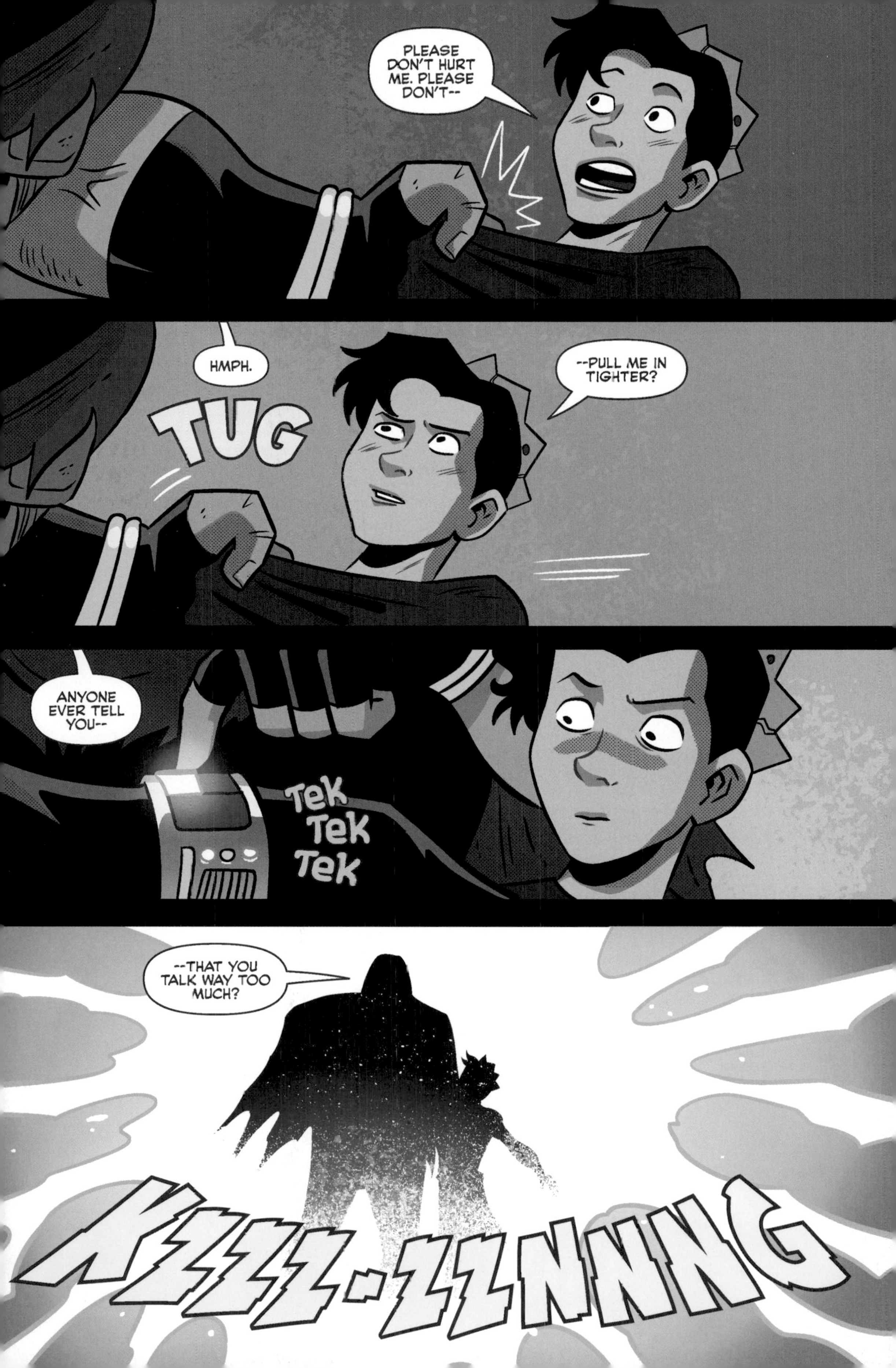
PLEASE DON'T HURT ME. PLEASE DON'T--
HMPH.
--PULL ME IN TIGHTER?
TUG
ANYONE EVER TELL YOU--
TEK TEK TEK
--THAT YOU TALK WAY TOO MUCH?
KZZZ-ZZNNNG

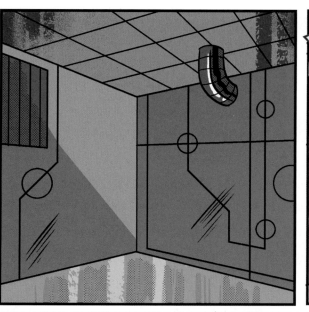

KZZZNNG

WAAAAAAH!!

GOTTA ESCAPE FOR MY DEAR LIFE--

--NEED TO FIND ANOTHER--

OOF!

KLONK

Oh, MAN! OUT OF THE TIME COPS' CLUTCHES AND INTO A TIME THIEF'S!

PLEASE, PLEASE, PLEASE FEED ME SOMETHING BEFORE YOU THROW ME IN AN AUCTION LED BY A DEN OF BLACK MARKET TIME CRIMINALS...

...MY CONSTITUTION CAN'T TAKE ANY MORE.

RELAX, KID. I'M NOT A TIME THIEF.

THEY WON'T KNOW WHERE TO FIND YOU.

THEY'LL NEVER BE ABLE TO FIGURE OUT WHERE YOU ARE, SO LONG AS...

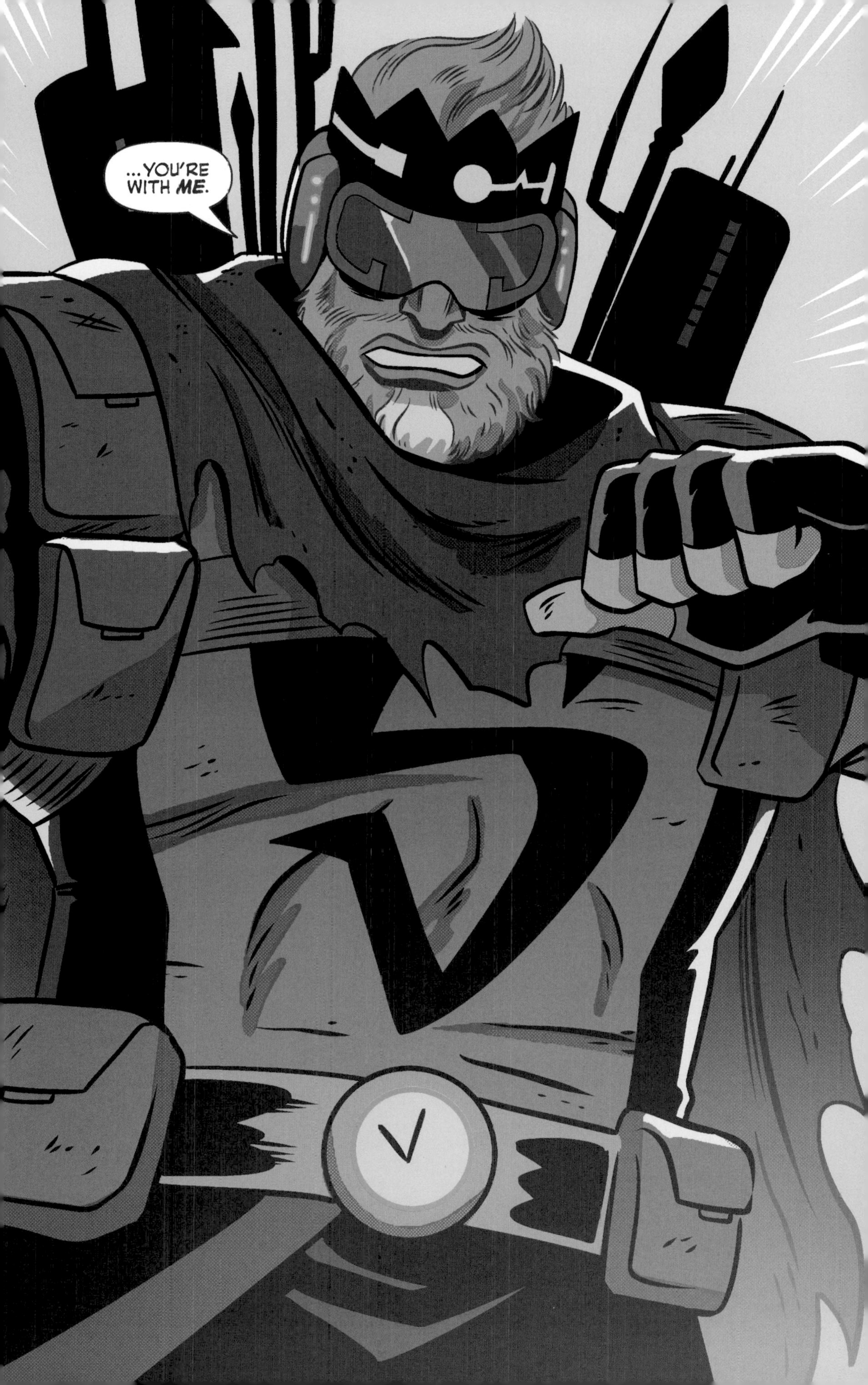
...YOU'RE WITH ME.

CHAPTER 4

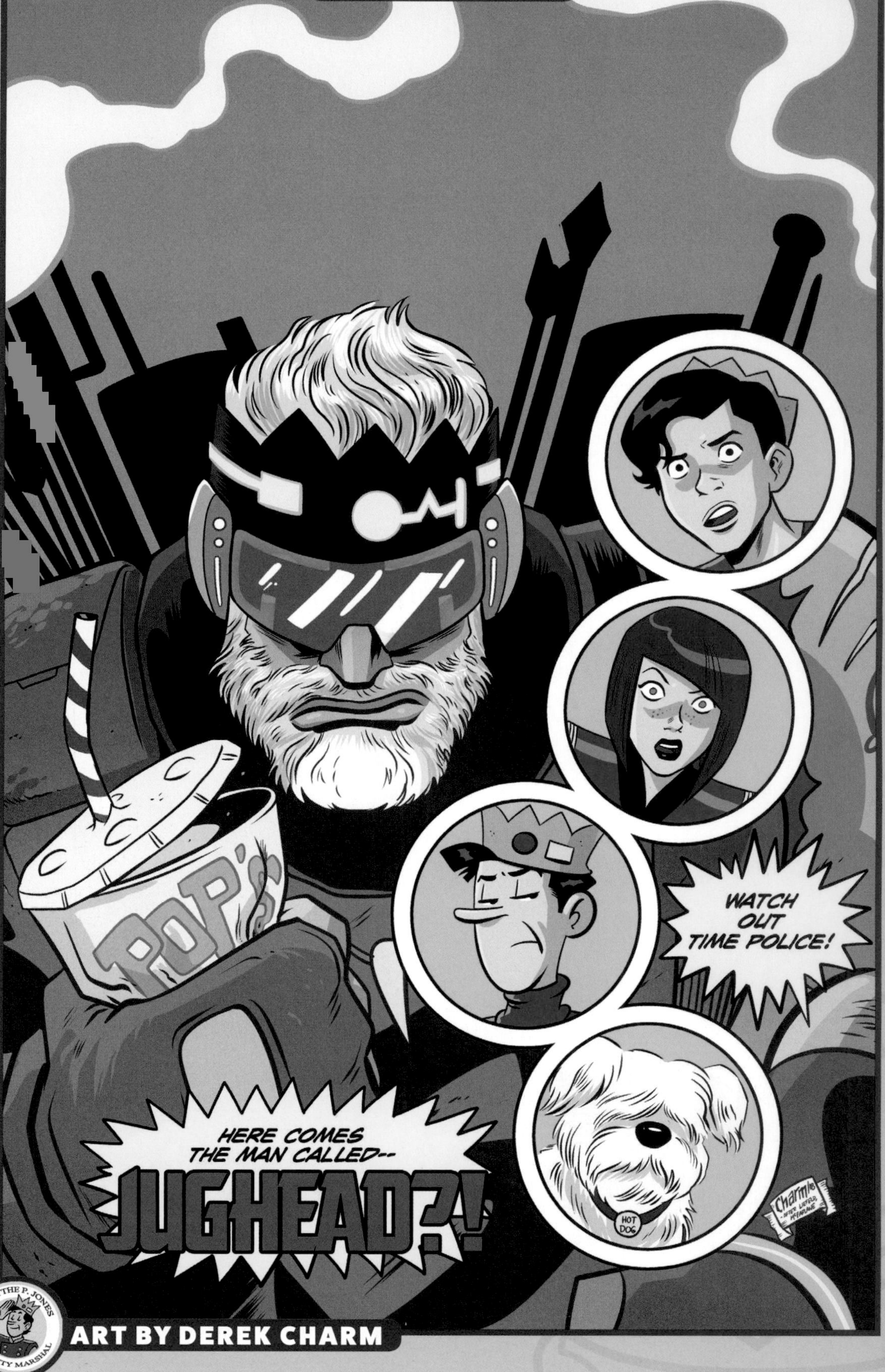
WATCH OUT TIME POLICE!
POP'S
HOT DOG
HERE COMES THE MAN CALLED--
JUGHEAD?!

FORSYTHE P. JONES
DEPUTY MARSHAL

ART BY DEREK CHARM

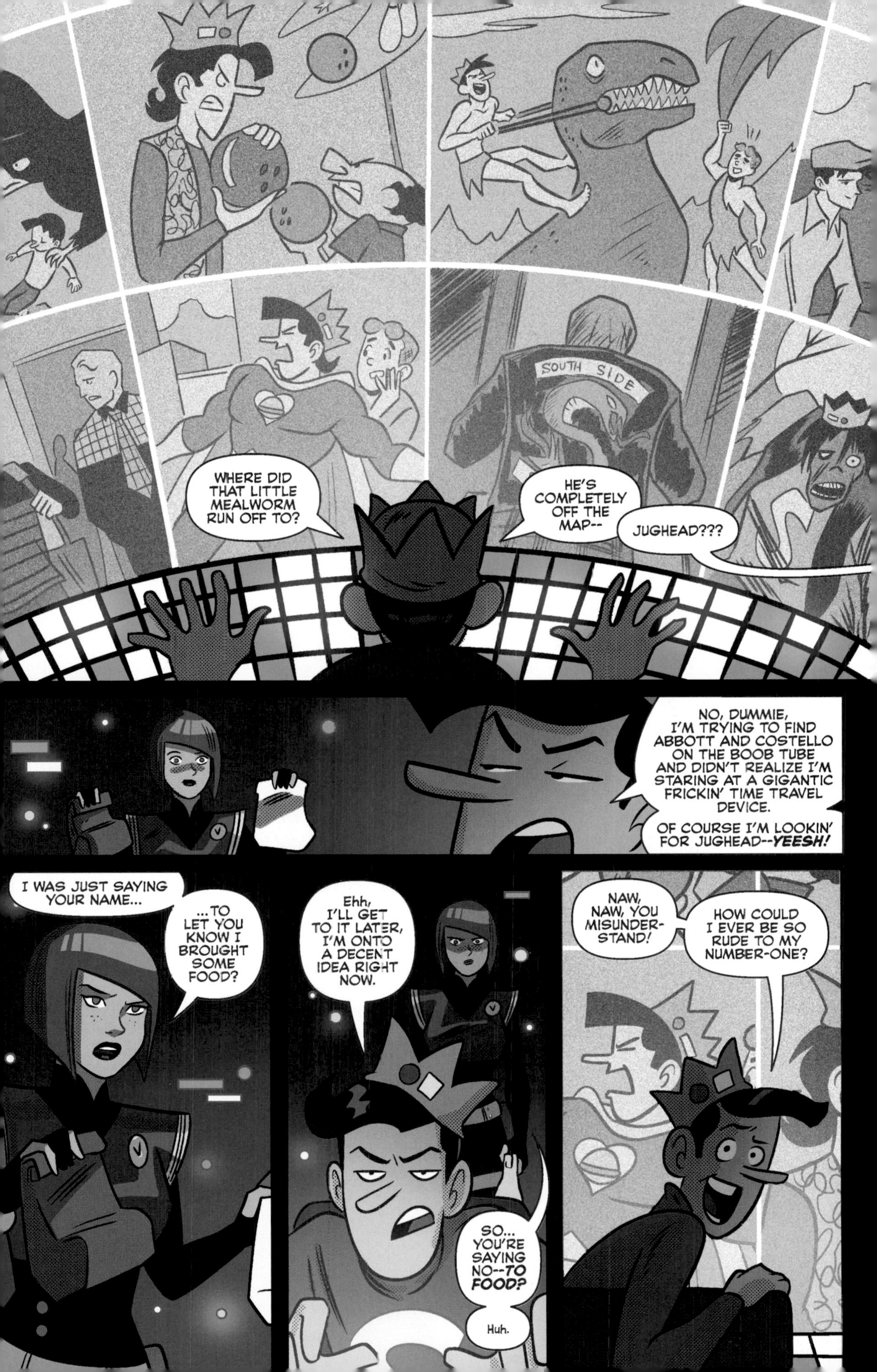

SOUTH SIDE
WHERE DID THAT LITTLE MEALWORM RUN OFF TO?
HE'S COMPLETELY OFF THE MAP--
JUGHEAD???
NO, DUMMIE, I'M TRYING TO FIND ABBOTT AND COSTELLO ON THE BOOB TUBE AND DIDN'T REALIZE I'M STARING AT A GIGANTIC FRICKIN' TIME TRAVEL DEVICE.
OF COURSE I'M LOOKIN' FOR JUGHEAD--*YEESH!*
I WAS JUST SAYING YOUR NAME...
...TO LET YOU KNOW I BROUGHT SOME FOOD?
Ehh, I'LL GET TO IT LATER, I'M ONTO A DECENT IDEA RIGHT NOW.
SO... YOU'RE SAYING NO--*TO FOOD?*
Huh.
NAW, NAW, YOU MISUNDER-STAND!
HOW COULD I EVER BE SO RUDE TO MY NUMBER-ONE?

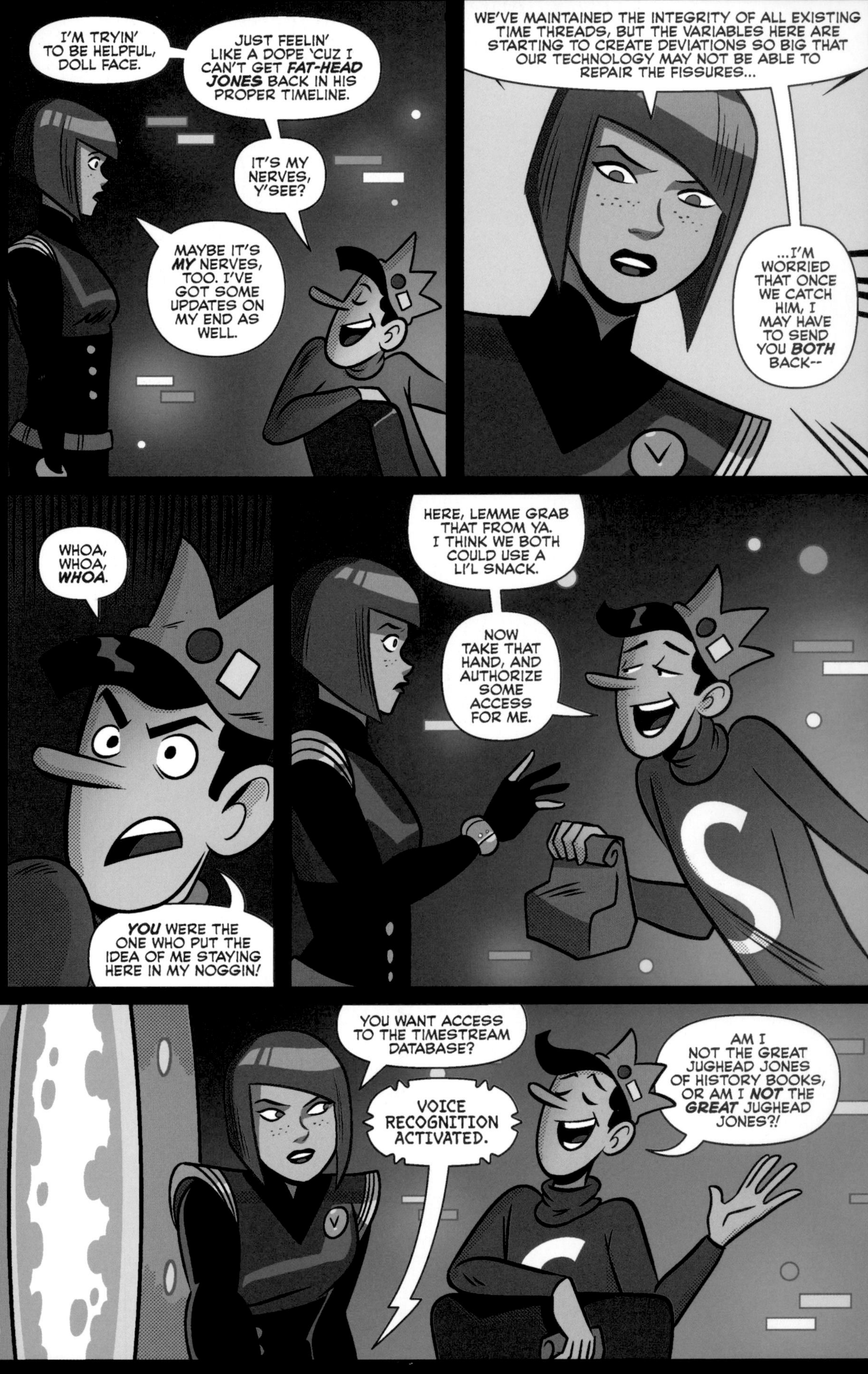
I'M TRYIN' TO BE HELPFUL, DOLL FACE.
JUST FEELIN' LIKE A DOPE 'CUZ I CAN'T GET **FAT-HEAD JONES** BACK IN HIS PROPER TIMELINE.
IT'S MY NERVES, Y'SEE?
MAYBE IT'S **MY** NERVES, TOO. I'VE GOT SOME UPDATES ON MY END AS WELL.
WE'VE MAINTAINED THE INTEGRITY OF ALL EXISTING TIME THREADS, BUT THE VARIABLES HERE ARE STARTING TO CREATE DEVIATIONS SO BIG THAT OUR TECHNOLOGY MAY NOT BE ABLE TO REPAIR THE FISSURES...
...I'M WORRIED THAT ONCE WE CATCH HIM, I MAY HAVE TO SEND YOU **BOTH** BACK--
WHOA, WHOA, **WHOA**.
YOU WERE THE ONE WHO PUT THE IDEA OF ME STAYING HERE IN MY NOGGIN!
HERE, LEMME GRAB THAT FROM YA. I THINK WE BOTH COULD USE A LI'L SNACK.
NOW TAKE THAT HAND, AND AUTHORIZE SOME ACCESS FOR ME.
YOU WANT ACCESS TO THE TIMESTREAM DATABASE?
VOICE RECOGNITION ACTIVATED.
AM I NOT THE GREAT JUGHEAD JONES OF HISTORY BOOKS, OR AM I **NOT** THE **GREAT** JUGHEAD JONES?!

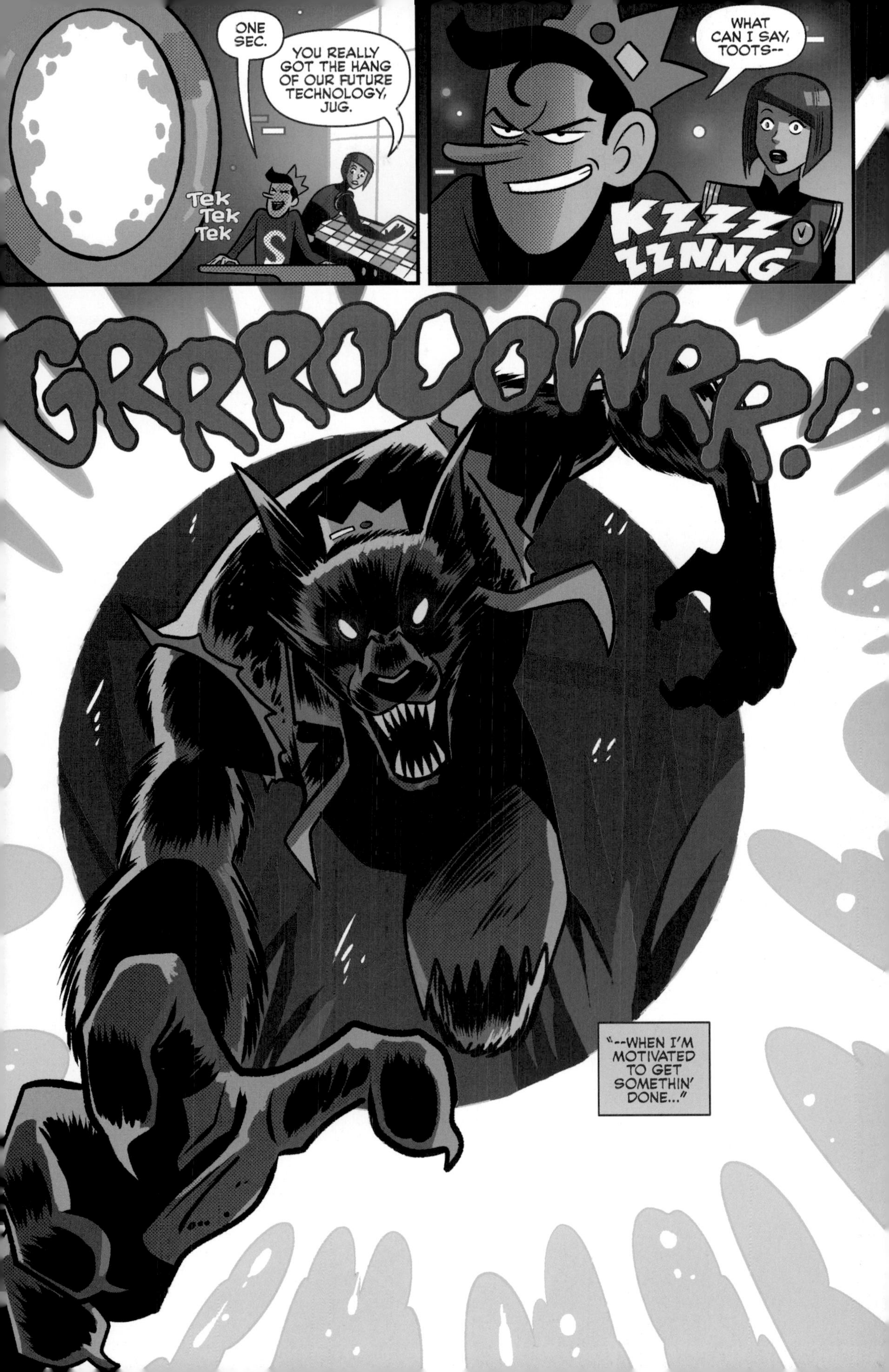
ONE SEC.
YOU REALLY GOT THE HANG OF OUR FUTURE TECHNOLOGY, JUG.
Tek Tek Tek
WHAT CAN I SAY, TOOTS--
KZZZ ZZNNG
GRRROOOWRR!!
"--WHEN I'M MOTIVATED TO GET SOMETHIN' DONE..."

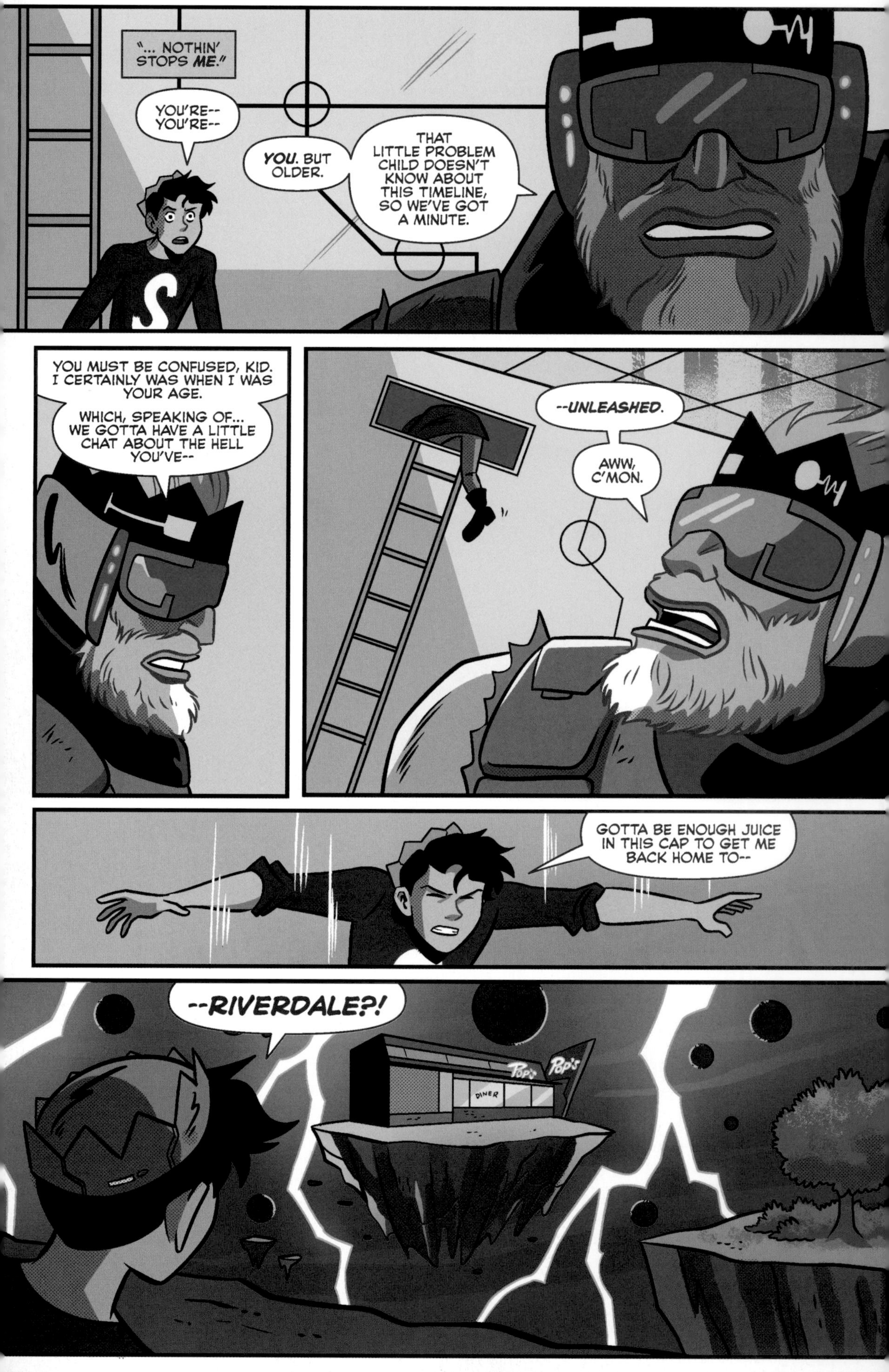
"... NOTHIN' STOPS ME."
YOU'RE-- YOU'RE--
YOU. BUT OLDER.
THAT LITTLE PROBLEM CHILD DOESN'T KNOW ABOUT THIS TIMELINE, SO WE'VE GOT A MINUTE.
YOU MUST BE CONFUSED, KID. I CERTAINLY WAS WHEN I WAS YOUR AGE.
WHICH, SPEAKING OF... WE GOTTA HAVE A LITTLE CHAT ABOUT THE HELL YOU'VE--
--UNLEASHED.
AWW, C'MON.
GOTTA BE ENOUGH JUICE IN THIS CAP TO GET ME BACK HOME TO--
--RIVERDALE?!
POP'S
POP'S
DINER

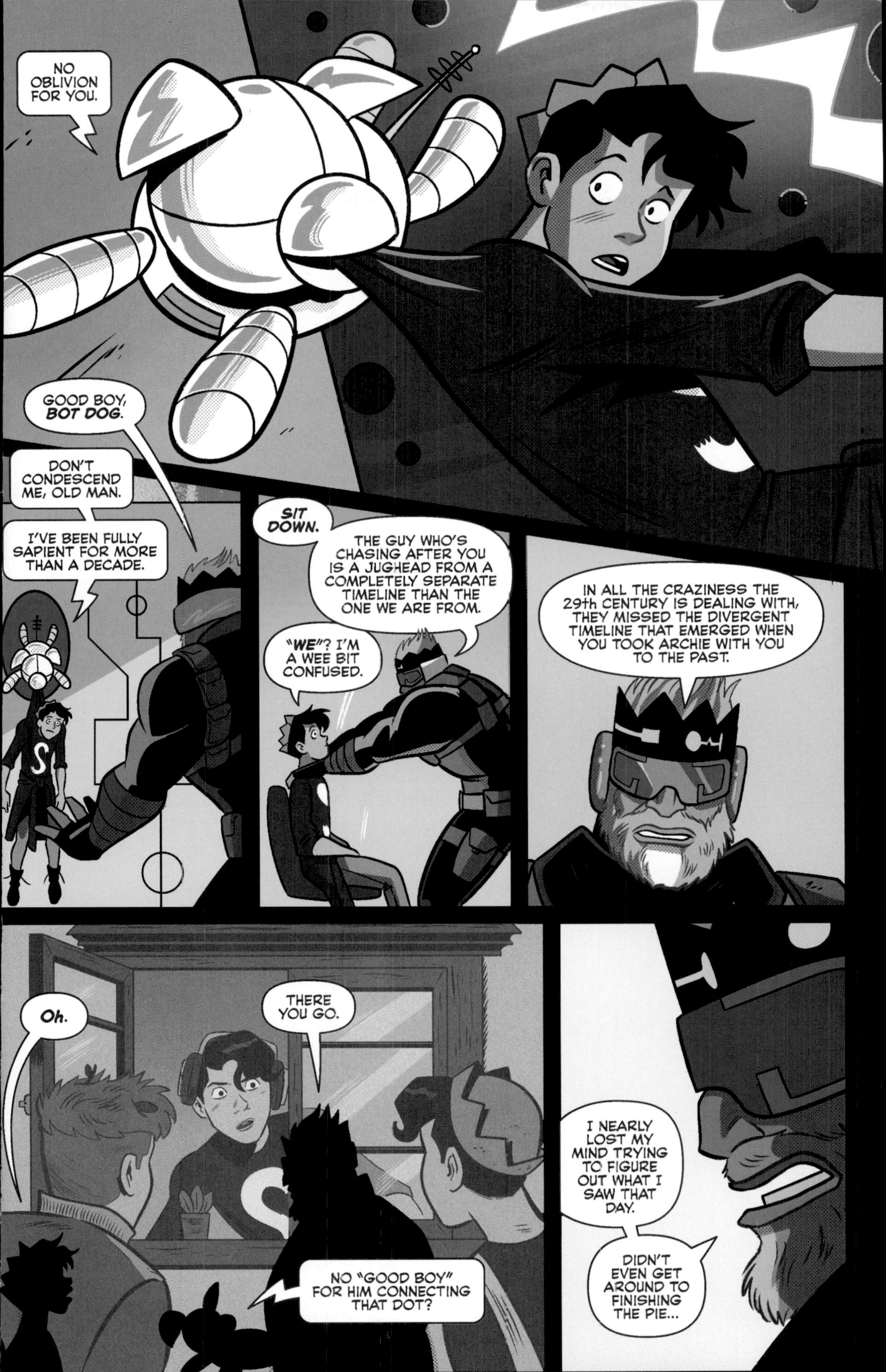
NO OBLIVION FOR YOU.
GOOD BOY, *BOT DOG*.
DON'T CONDESCEND ME, OLD MAN.
I'VE BEEN FULLY SAPIENT FOR MORE THAN A DECADE.
SIT DOWN.
THE GUY WHO'S CHASING AFTER YOU IS A JUGHEAD FROM A COMPLETELY SEPARATE TIMELINE THAN THE ONE WE ARE FROM.
"*WE*"? I'M A WEE BIT CONFUSED.
IN ALL THE CRAZINESS THE 29th CENTURY IS DEALING WITH, THEY MISSED THE DIVERGENT TIMELINE THAT EMERGED WHEN YOU TOOK ARCHIE WITH YOU TO THE PAST.
Oh.
THERE YOU GO.
NO "GOOD BOY" FOR HIM CONNECTING THAT DOT?
I NEARLY LOST MY MIND TRYING TO FIGURE OUT WHAT I SAW THAT DAY.
DIDN'T EVEN GET AROUND TO FINISHING THE PIE...

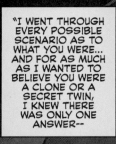 "I WENT THROUGH EVERY POSSIBLE SCENARIO AS TO WHAT YOU WERE... AND FOR AS MUCH AS I WANTED TO BELIEVE YOU WERE A CLONE OR A SECRET TWIN, I KNEW THERE WAS ONLY ONE ANSWER--

 "--TIME TRAVEL.

"BY THE TIME I FIGURED THE TECHNOLOGY OUT AND WENT LOOKIN' TO THE FUTURE... I WAS TOO LATE.

"THE JUGHEAD WHO'S BEEN COMIN' AFTER YOU HAD ALREADY DONE THE DAMAGE.

 "IT MESSED WITH THAT KID'S HEAD TOO MUCH TO SEE HE WASN'T SO *ORIGINAL*--

--THE RIVERDALE HE CAME UP IN WAS A BIT TOO HUMDRUM FOR HIS TASTES."

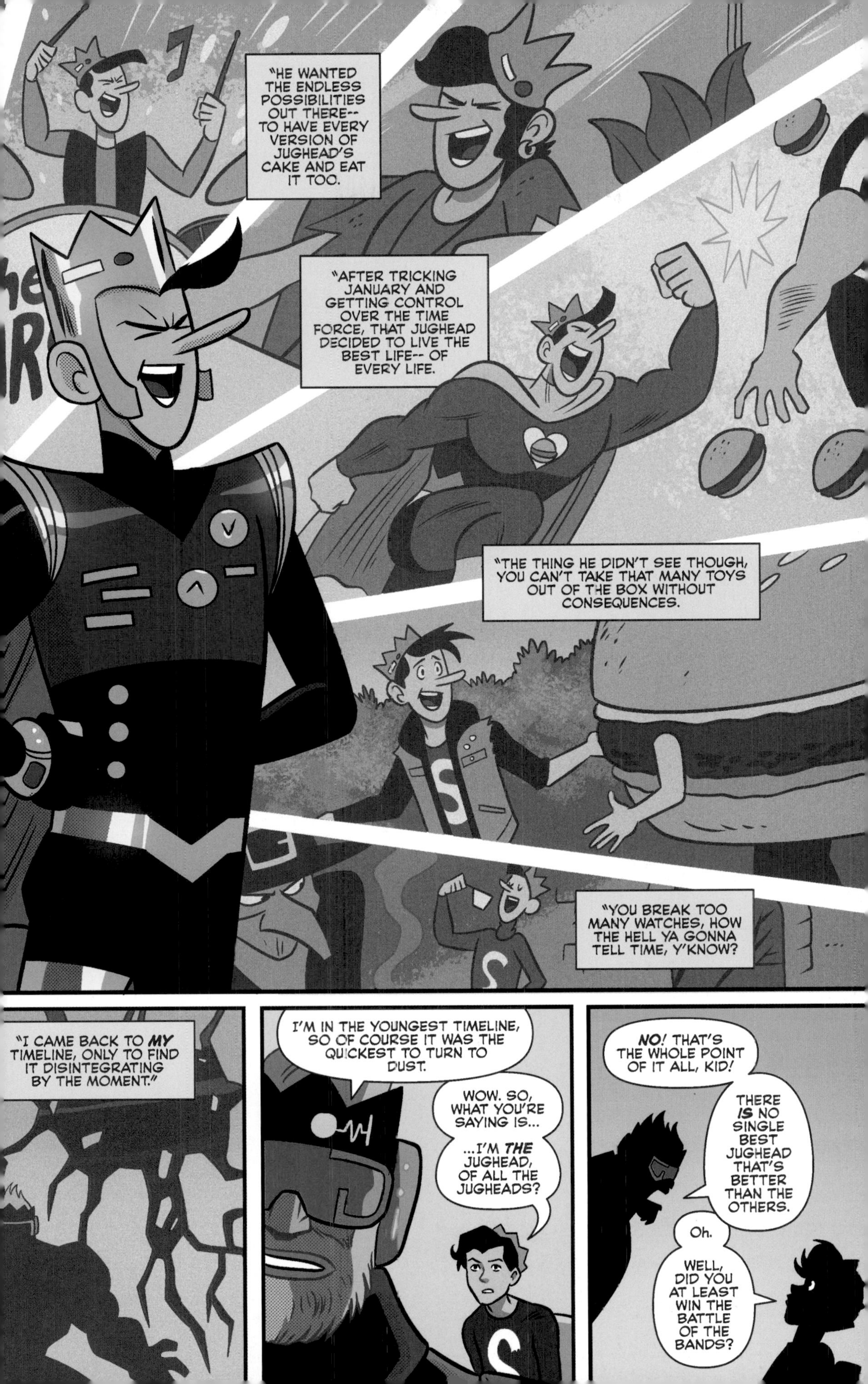
"HE WANTED THE ENDLESS POSSIBILITIES OUT THERE-- TO HAVE EVERY VERSION OF JUGHEAD'S CAKE AND EAT IT TOO.
"AFTER TRICKING JANUARY AND GETTING CONTROL OVER THE TIME FORCE, THAT JUGHEAD DECIDED TO LIVE THE BEST LIFE-- OF EVERY LIFE.
"THE THING HE DIDN'T SEE THOUGH, YOU CAN'T TAKE THAT MANY TOYS OUT OF THE BOX WITHOUT CONSEQUENCES.
"YOU BREAK TOO MANY WATCHES, HOW THE HELL YA GONNA TELL TIME, Y'KNOW?
"I CAME BACK TO MY TIMELINE, ONLY TO FIND IT DISINTEGRATING BY THE MOMENT."
I'M IN THE YOUNGEST TIMELINE, SO OF COURSE IT WAS THE QUICKEST TO TURN TO DUST.
WOW. SO, WHAT YOU'RE SAYING IS...
...I'M THE JUGHEAD, OF ALL THE JUGHEADS?
NO! THAT'S THE WHOLE POINT OF IT ALL, KID!
THERE IS NO SINGLE BEST JUGHEAD THAT'S BETTER THAN THE OTHERS.
Oh.
WELL, DID YOU AT LEAST WIN THE BATTLE OF THE BANDS?

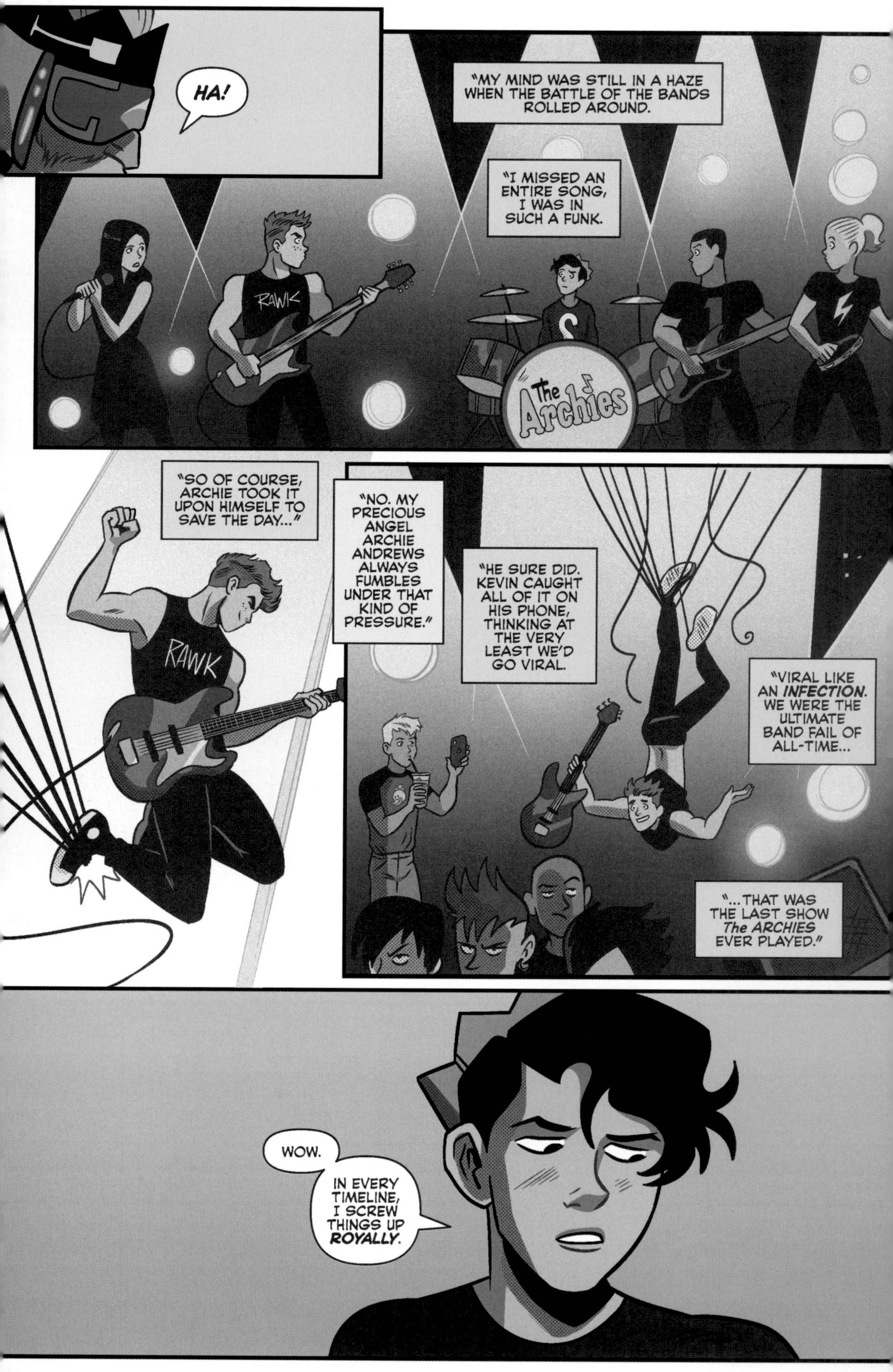
HA!
"MY MIND WAS STILL IN A HAZE WHEN THE BATTLE OF THE BANDS ROLLED AROUND.
"I MISSED AN ENTIRE SONG, I WAS IN SUCH A FUNK.
RAWK
The Archies
"SO OF COURSE, ARCHIE TOOK IT UPON HIMSELF TO SAVE THE DAY..."
"NO. MY PRECIOUS ANGEL ARCHIE ANDREWS ALWAYS FUMBLES UNDER THAT KIND OF PRESSURE."
RAWK
"HE SURE DID. KEVIN CAUGHT ALL OF IT ON HIS PHONE, THINKING AT THE VERY LEAST WE'D GO VIRAL.
"VIRAL LIKE AN INFECTION. WE WERE THE ULTIMATE BAND FAIL OF ALL-TIME...
"...THAT WAS THE LAST SHOW The ARCHIES EVER PLAYED."
WOW.
IN EVERY TIMELINE, I SCREW THINGS UP ROYALLY.

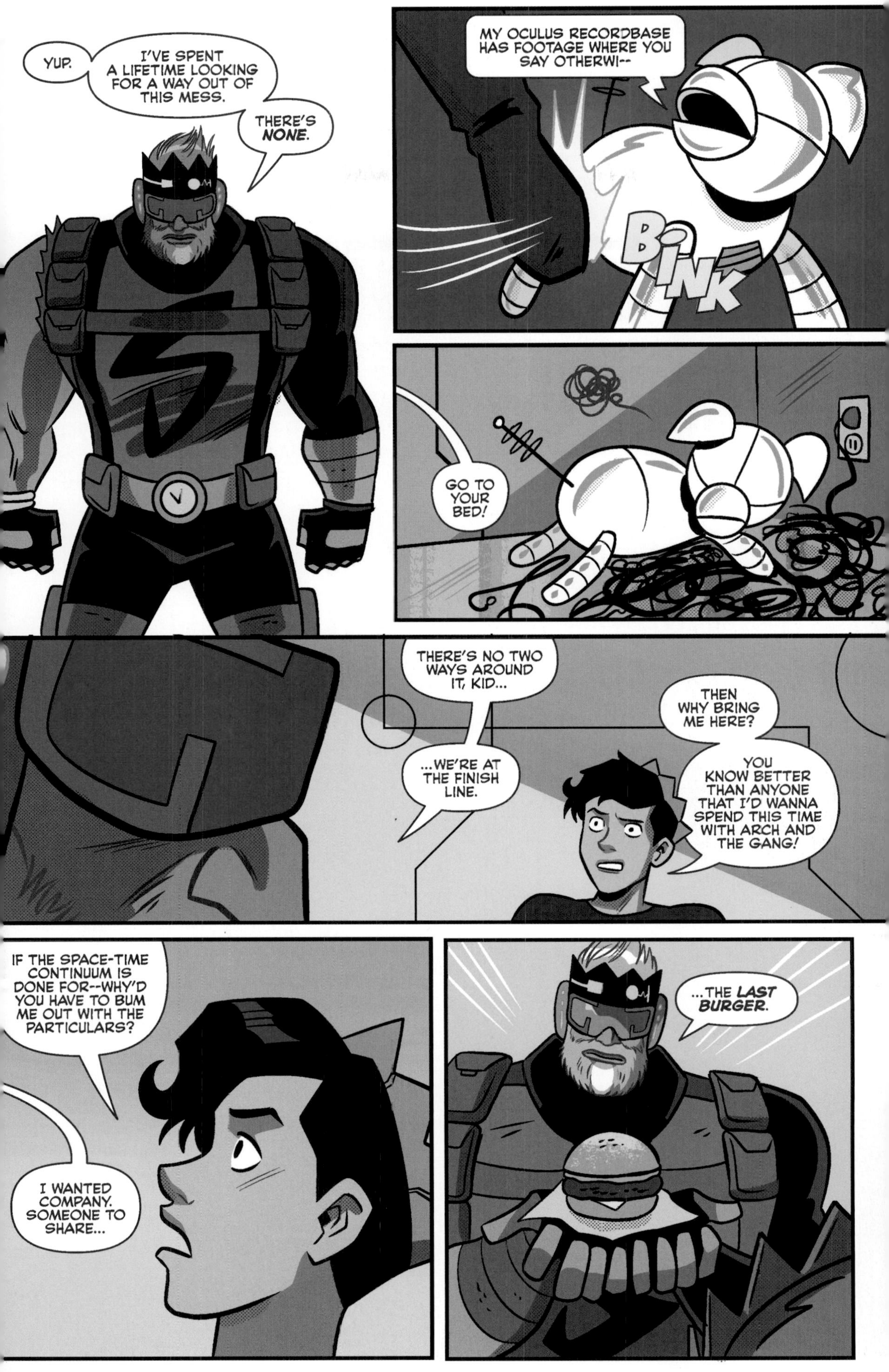
YUP.
I'VE SPENT A LIFETIME LOOKING FOR A WAY OUT OF THIS MESS.
THERE'S NONE.
MY OCULUS RECORDBASE HAS FOOTAGE WHERE YOU SAY OTHERWI--
BINK
GO TO YOUR BED!
THERE'S NO TWO WAYS AROUND IT, KID...
...WE'RE AT THE FINISH LINE.
THEN WHY BRING ME HERE?
YOU KNOW BETTER THAN ANYONE THAT I'D WANNA SPEND THIS TIME WITH ARCH AND THE GANG!
IF THE SPACE-TIME CONTINUUM IS DONE FOR--WHY'D YOU HAVE TO BUM ME OUT WITH THE PARTICULARS?
I WANTED COMPANY. SOMEONE TO SHARE...
...THE LAST BURGER.

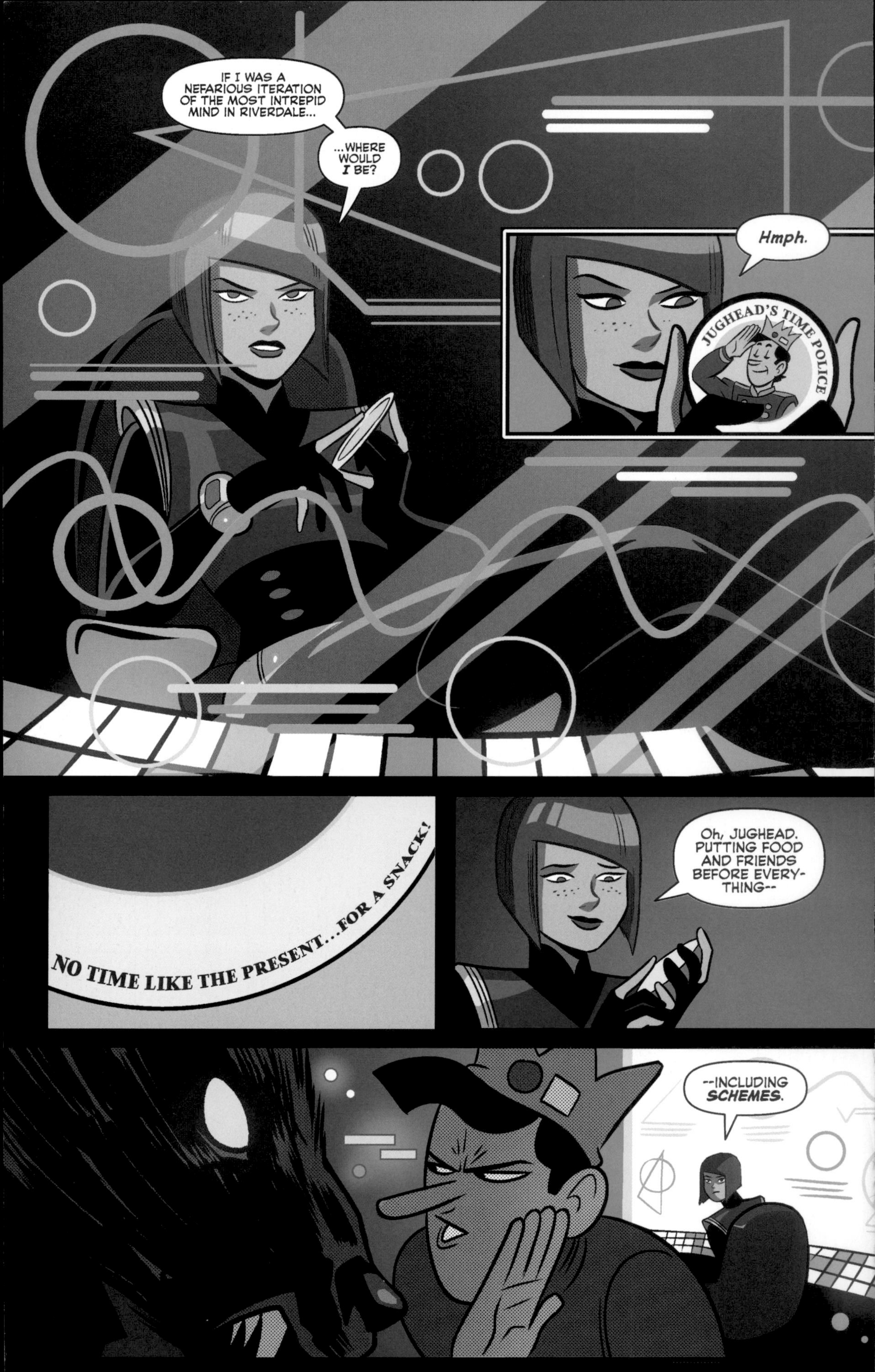
IF I WAS A NEFARIOUS ITERATION OF THE MOST INTREPID MIND IN RIVERDALE...
...WHERE WOULD I BE?
Hmph.
JUGHEAD'S TIME POLICE
NO TIME LIKE THE PRESENT...FOR A SNACK!
Oh, JUGHEAD. PUTTING FOOD AND FRIENDS BEFORE EVERY-THING--
--INCLUDING SCHEMES.

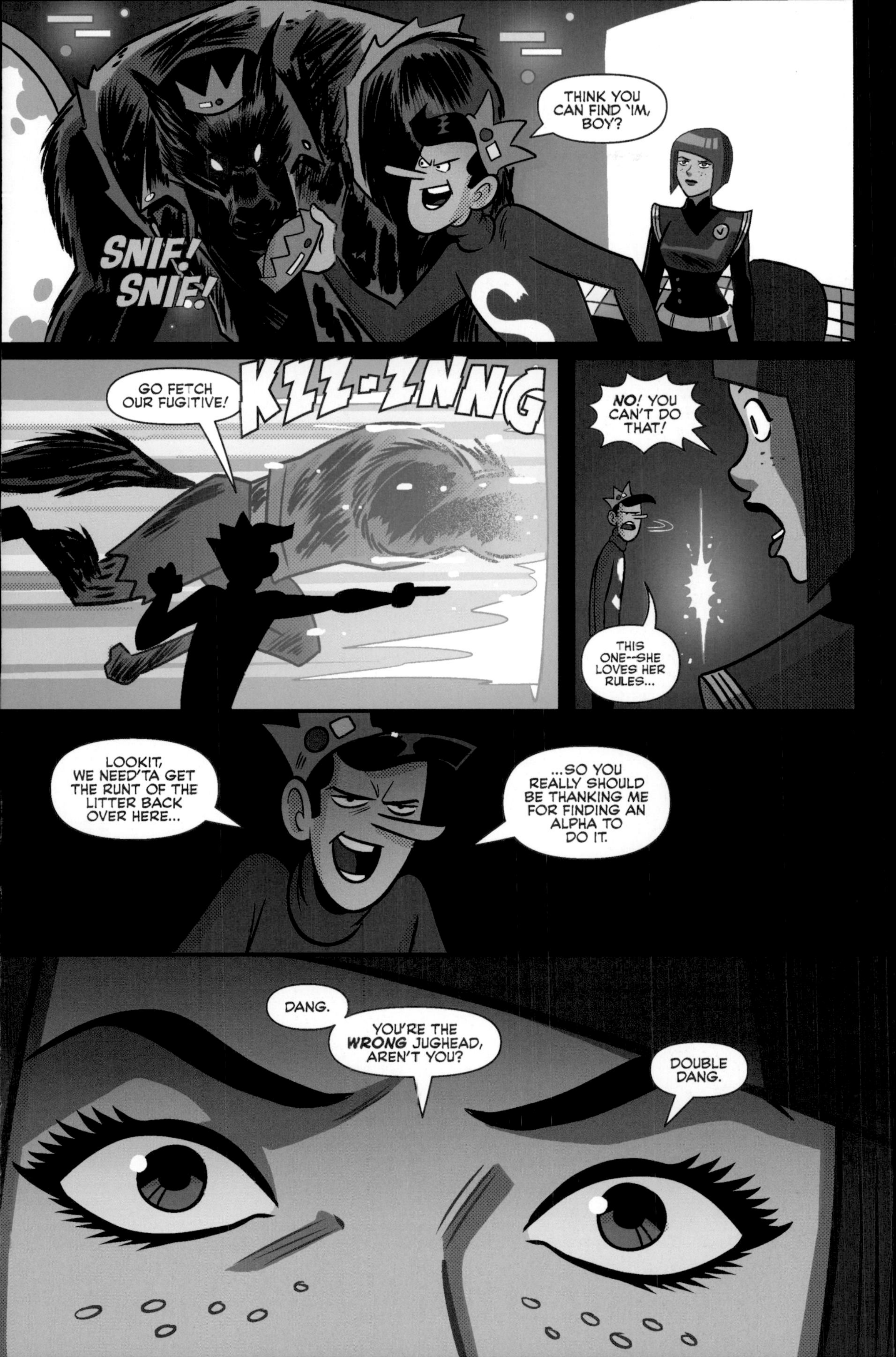

THINK YOU CAN FIND 'IM, BOY?
SNIF! SNIF!
GO FETCH OUR FUGITIVE!
KZZ-ZNNG
NO! YOU CAN'T DO THAT!
THIS ONE--SHE LOVES HER RULES...
LOOKIT, WE NEED'TA GET THE RUNT OF THE LITTER BACK OVER HERE...
...SO YOU REALLY SHOULD BE THANKING ME FOR FINDING AN ALPHA TO DO IT.
DANG.
YOU'RE THE WRONG JUGHEAD, AREN'T YOU?
DOUBLE DANG.

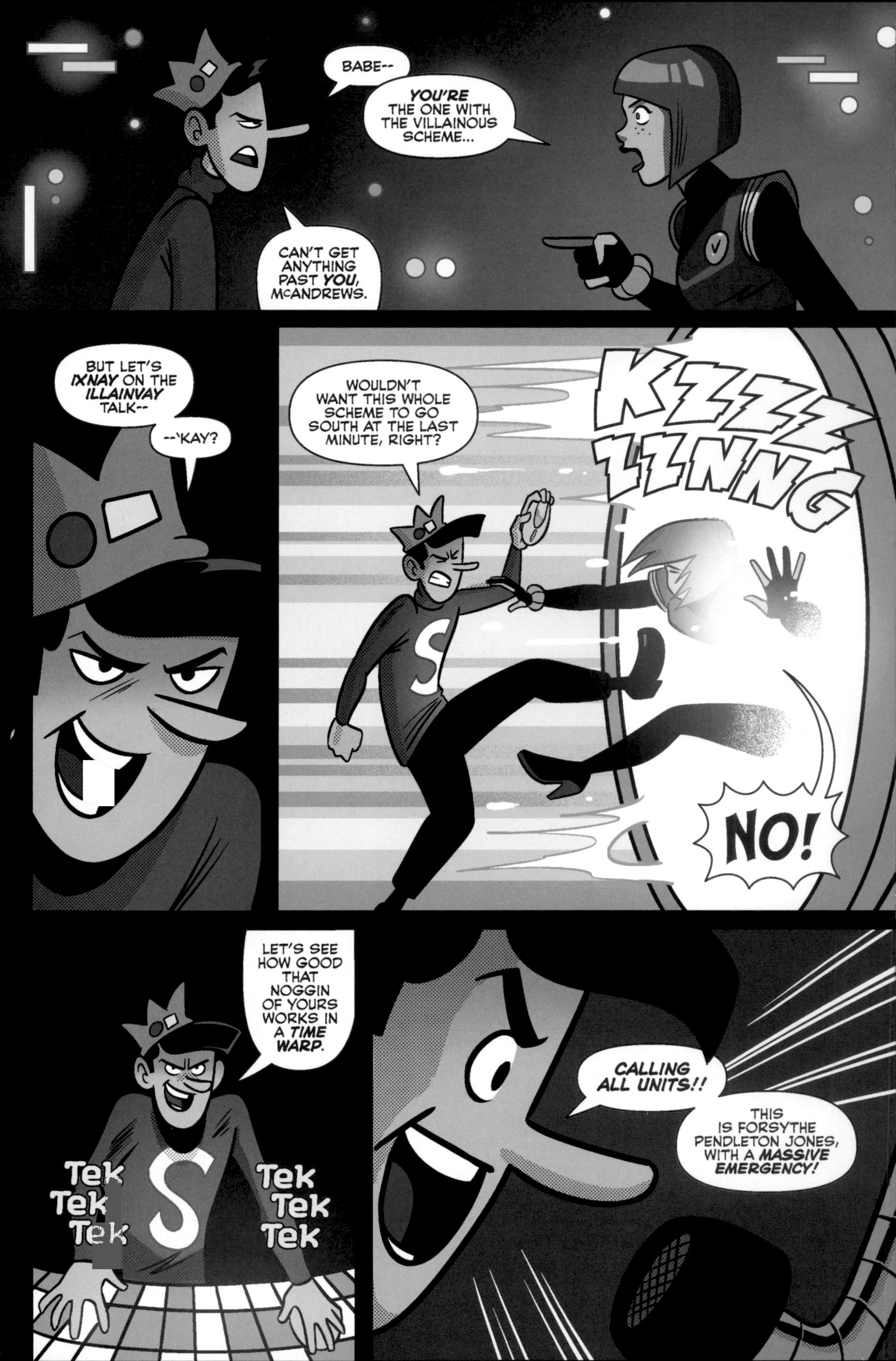
BABE--
YOU'RE THE ONE WITH THE VILLAINOUS SCHEME...
CAN'T GET ANYTHING PAST *YOU*, McANDREWS.
BUT LET'S *IXNAY* ON THE *ILLAINVAY* TALK--
--'KAY?
WOULDN'T WANT THIS WHOLE SCHEME TO GO SOUTH AT THE LAST MINUTE, RIGHT?
KZZZ ZZNNG
NO!
LET'S SEE HOW GOOD THAT NOGGIN OF YOURS WORKS IN A *TIME WARP*.
Tek Tek Tek
Tek Tek Tek
CALLING ALL UNITS!!
THIS IS FORSYTHE PENDLETON JONES, WITH A *MASSIVE EMERGENCY!*

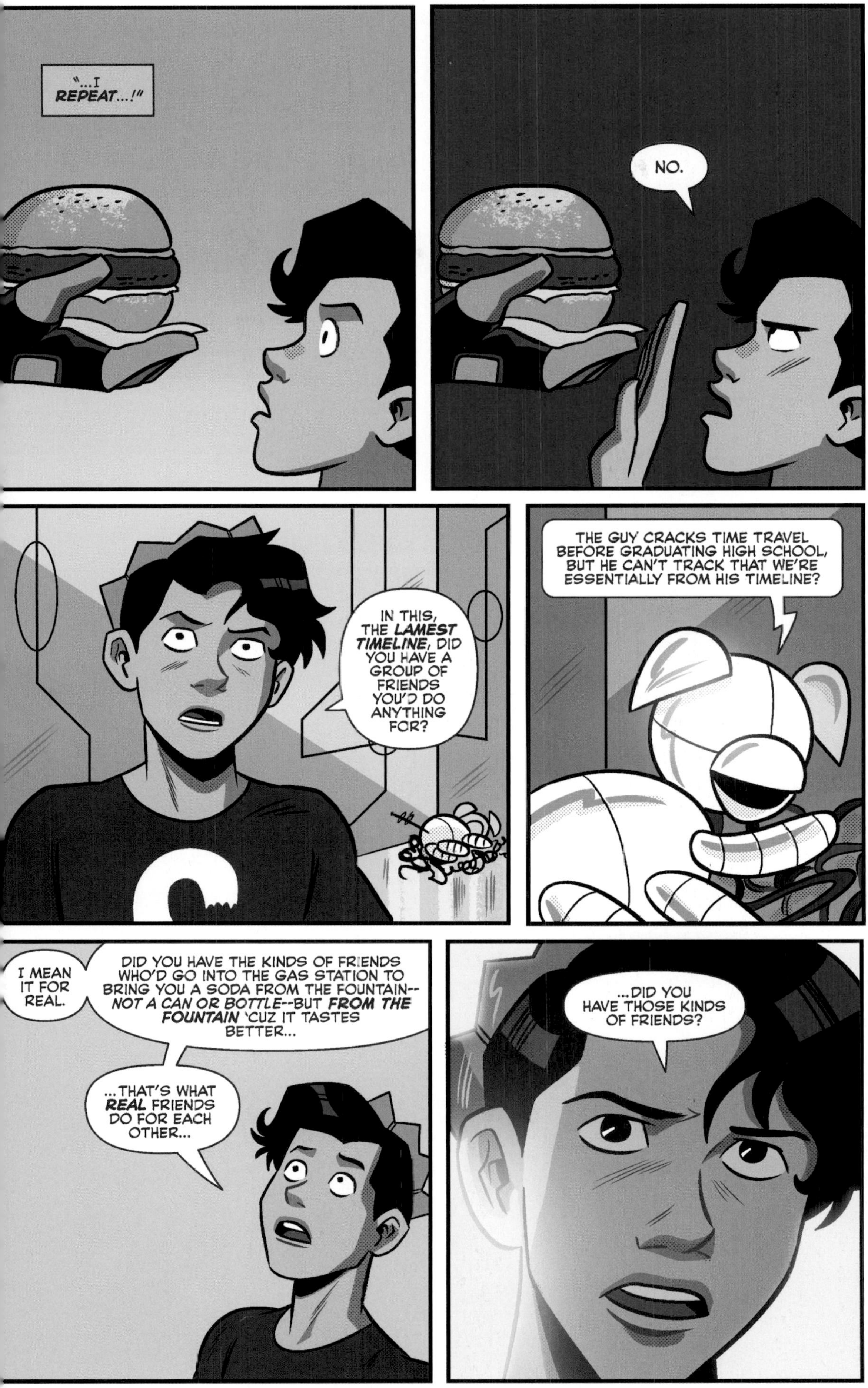
"...I REPEAT...!"
NO.
IN THIS, THE LAMEST TIMELINE, DID YOU HAVE A GROUP OF FRIENDS YOU'D DO ANYTHING FOR?
THE GUY CRACKS TIME TRAVEL BEFORE GRADUATING HIGH SCHOOL, BUT HE CAN'T TRACK THAT WE'RE ESSENTIALLY FROM HIS TIMELINE?
I MEAN IT FOR REAL.
DID YOU HAVE THE KINDS OF FRIENDS WHO'D GO INTO THE GAS STATION TO BRING YOU A SODA FROM THE FOUNTAIN--NOT A CAN OR BOTTLE--BUT FROM THE FOUNTAIN 'CUZ IT TASTES BETTER...
...THAT'S WHAT REAL FRIENDS DO FOR EACH OTHER...
...DID YOU HAVE THOSE KINDS OF FRIENDS?

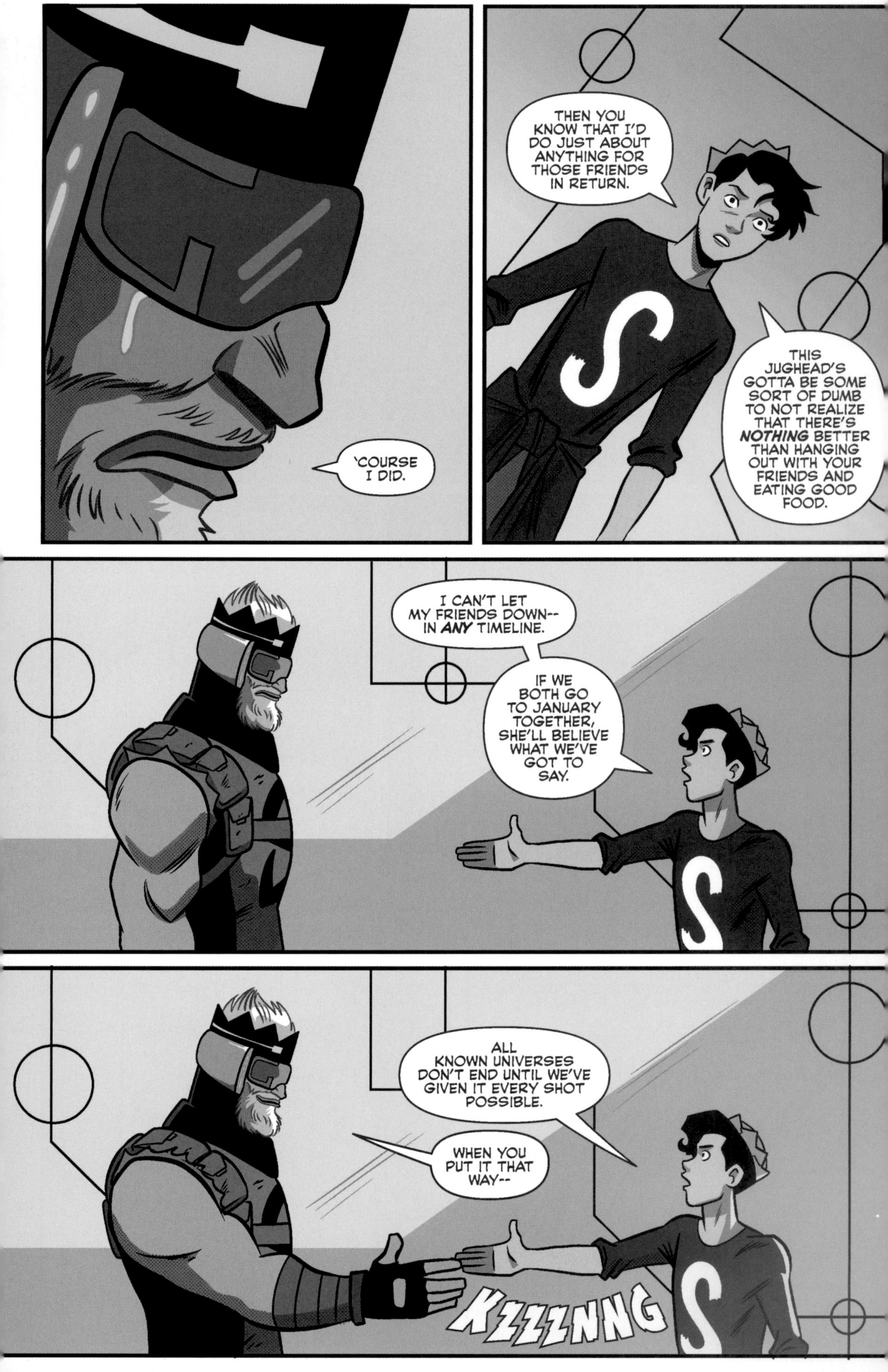
'COURSE I DID.
THEN YOU KNOW THAT I'D DO JUST ABOUT ANYTHING FOR THOSE FRIENDS IN RETURN.
THIS JUGHEAD'S GOTTA BE SOME SORT OF DUMB TO NOT REALIZE THAT THERE'S **NOTHING** BETTER THAN HANGING OUT WITH YOUR FRIENDS AND EATING GOOD FOOD.
I CAN'T LET MY FRIENDS DOWN-- IN ***ANY*** TIMELINE.
IF WE BOTH GO TO JANUARY TOGETHER, SHE'LL BELIEVE WHAT WE'VE GOT TO SAY.
ALL KNOWN UNIVERSES DON'T END UNTIL WE'VE GIVEN IT EVERY SHOT POSSIBLE.
WHEN YOU PUT IT THAT WAY--
KZZZNNG

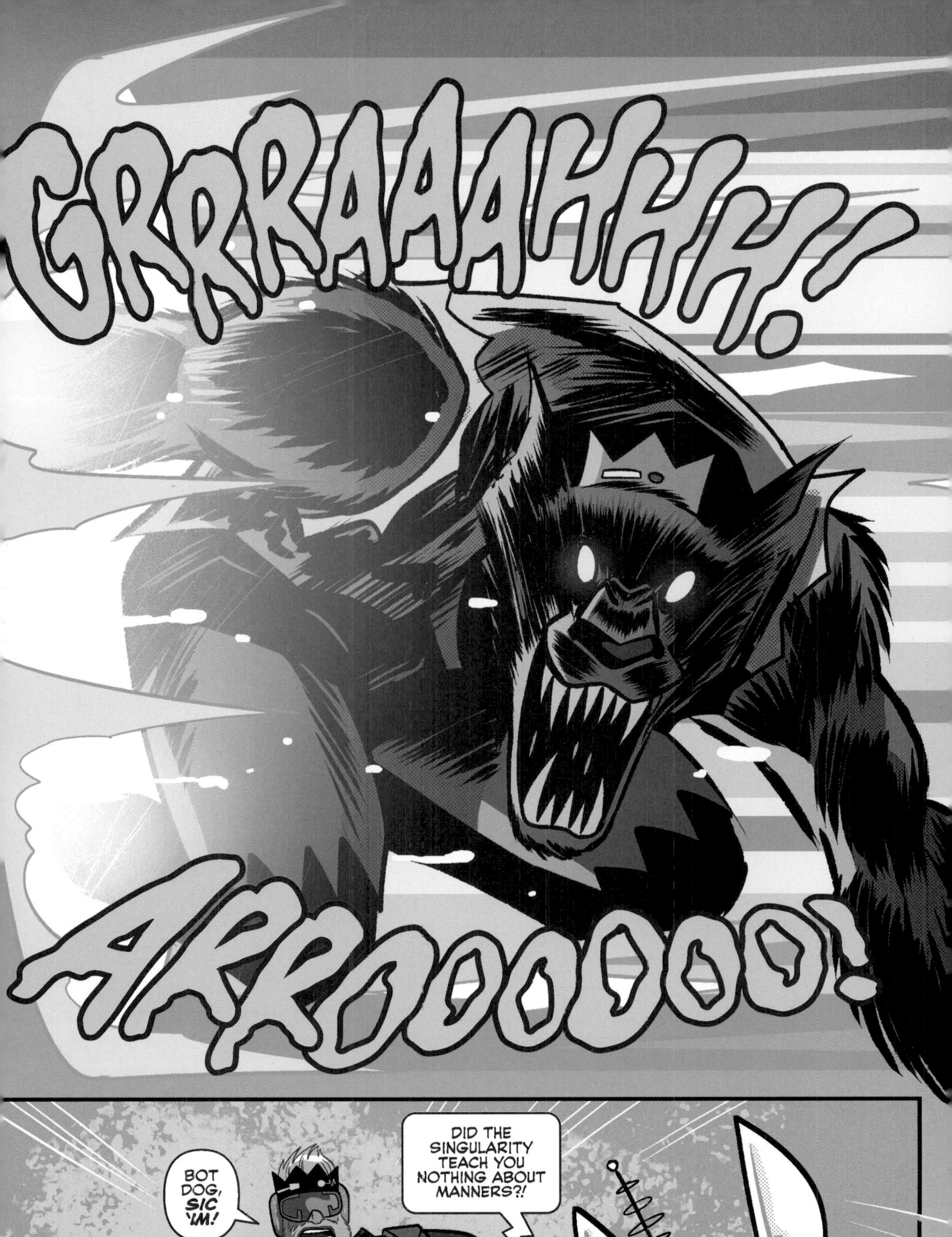
GRRRAAAHHHH!!
ARROOOOOO!

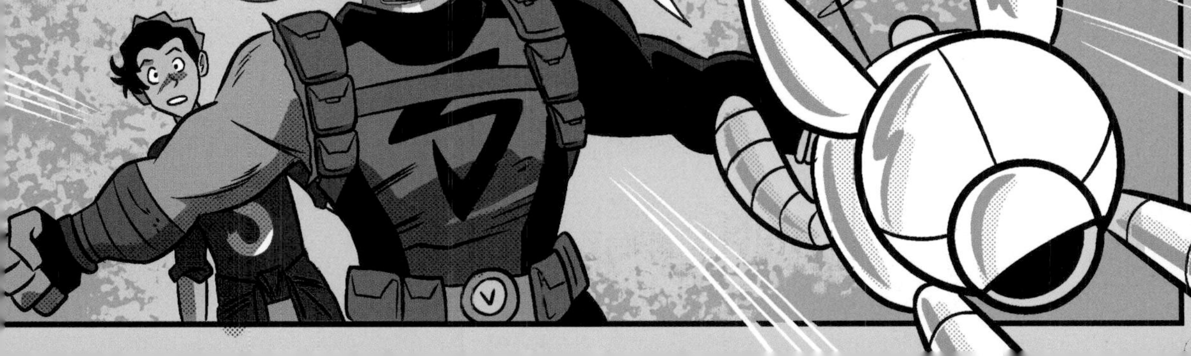
BOT DOG, SIC 'IM!
DID THE SINGULARITY TEACH YOU NOTHING ABOUT MANNERS?!

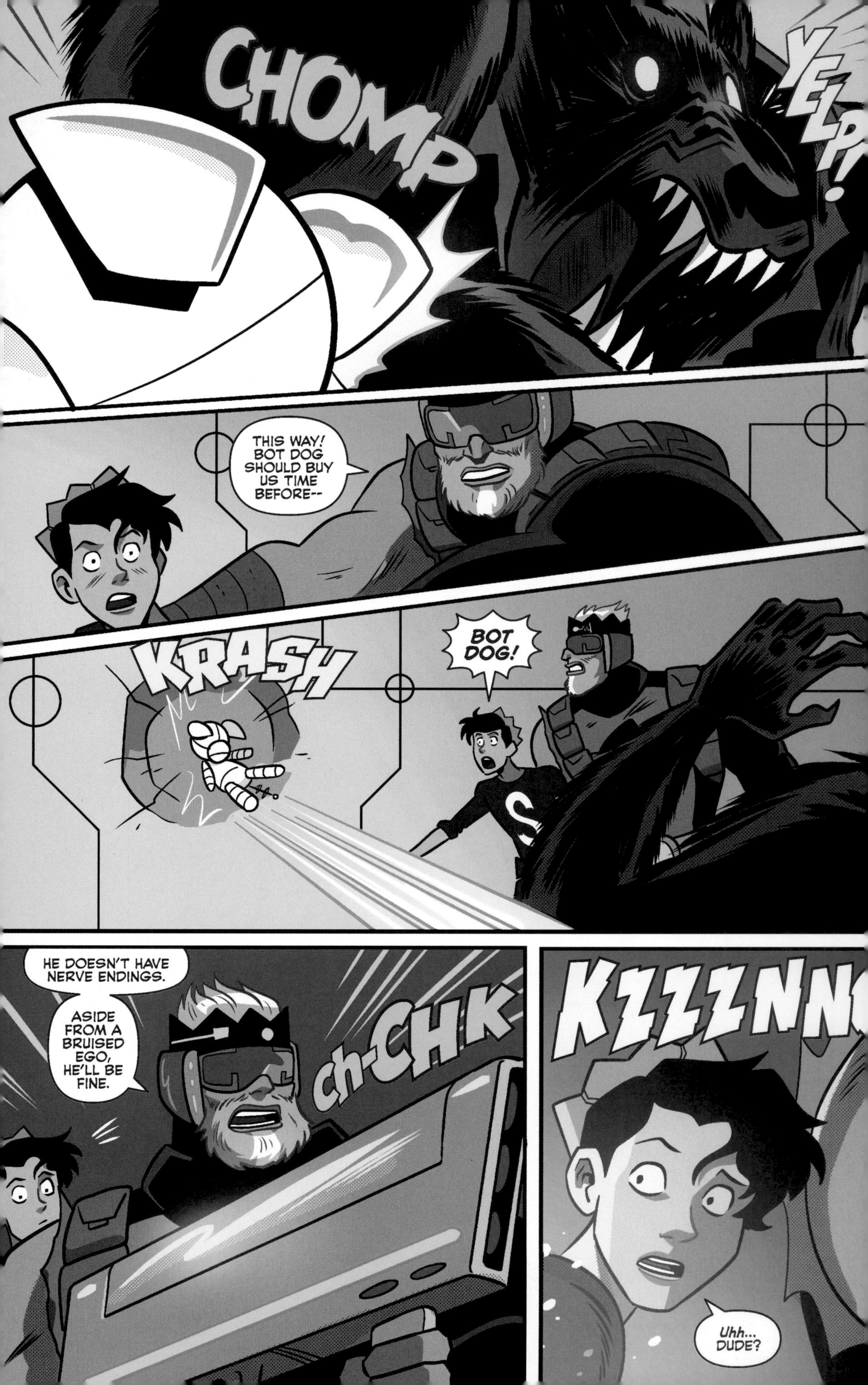
CHOMP
YELP!
THIS WAY! BOT DOG SHOULD BUY US TIME BEFORE--
KRASH
BOT DOG!
HE DOESN'T HAVE NERVE ENDINGS.
ASIDE FROM A BRUISED EGO, HE'LL BE FINE.
ch-CHK
KZZZNN
Uhh... DUDE?

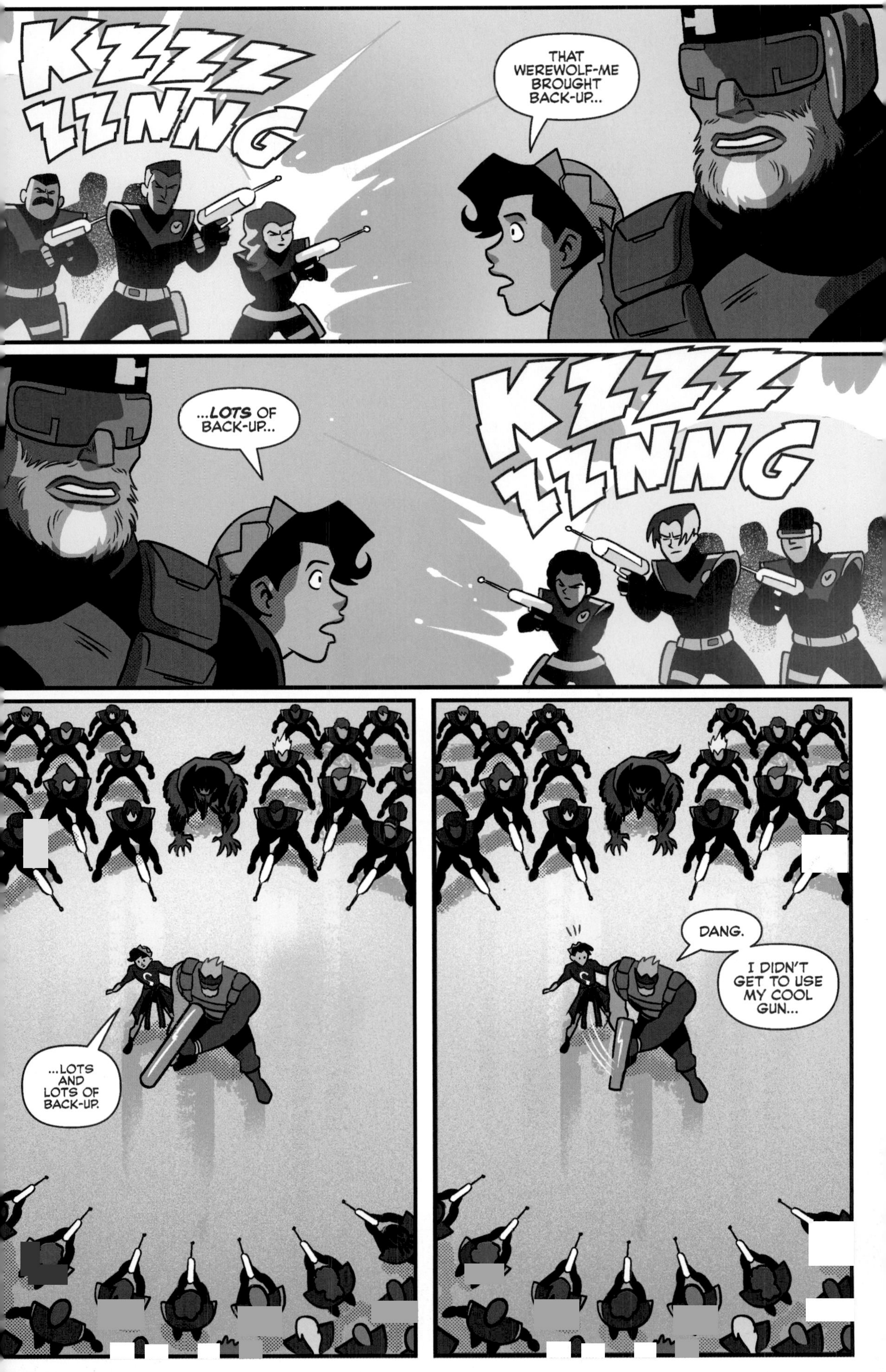
KZZZZ ZZNNG
THAT WEREWOLF-ME BROUGHT BACK-UP...
...LOTS OF BACK-UP...
KZZZZ ZZNNG
...LOTS AND LOTS OF BACK-UP.
DANG.
I DIDN'T GET TO USE MY COOL GUN...

"...DOUBLE DANG."

THERE THEY ARE!

THOSE ARE THE CROOKS WHO HAD THE MOXIE TO THROW MY DAME INTO A TIME WARP!

GIVE US SOME ROOM... THIS SLIPPERY CAT CAN GRAB ONE OF YER GUNS QUICKER THAN YOU CAN SAY, "WHEATCAKES."

DO I SOUND THIS CORNY?

WE ALL DO, BUT IT'S WHY PEOPLE LIKE US.

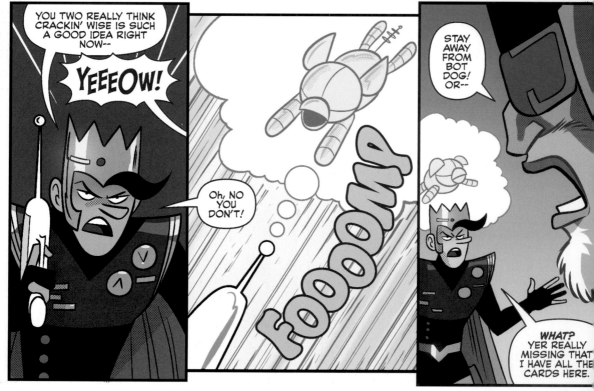

YOU TWO REALLY THINK CRACKIN' WISE IS SUCH A GOOD IDEA RIGHT NOW--

YEEEOW!

OH, NO YOU DON'T!

FOOOOMP

STAY AWAY FROM BOT DOG! OR--

WHAT? YER REALLY MISSING THAT I HAVE ALL THE CARDS HERE.

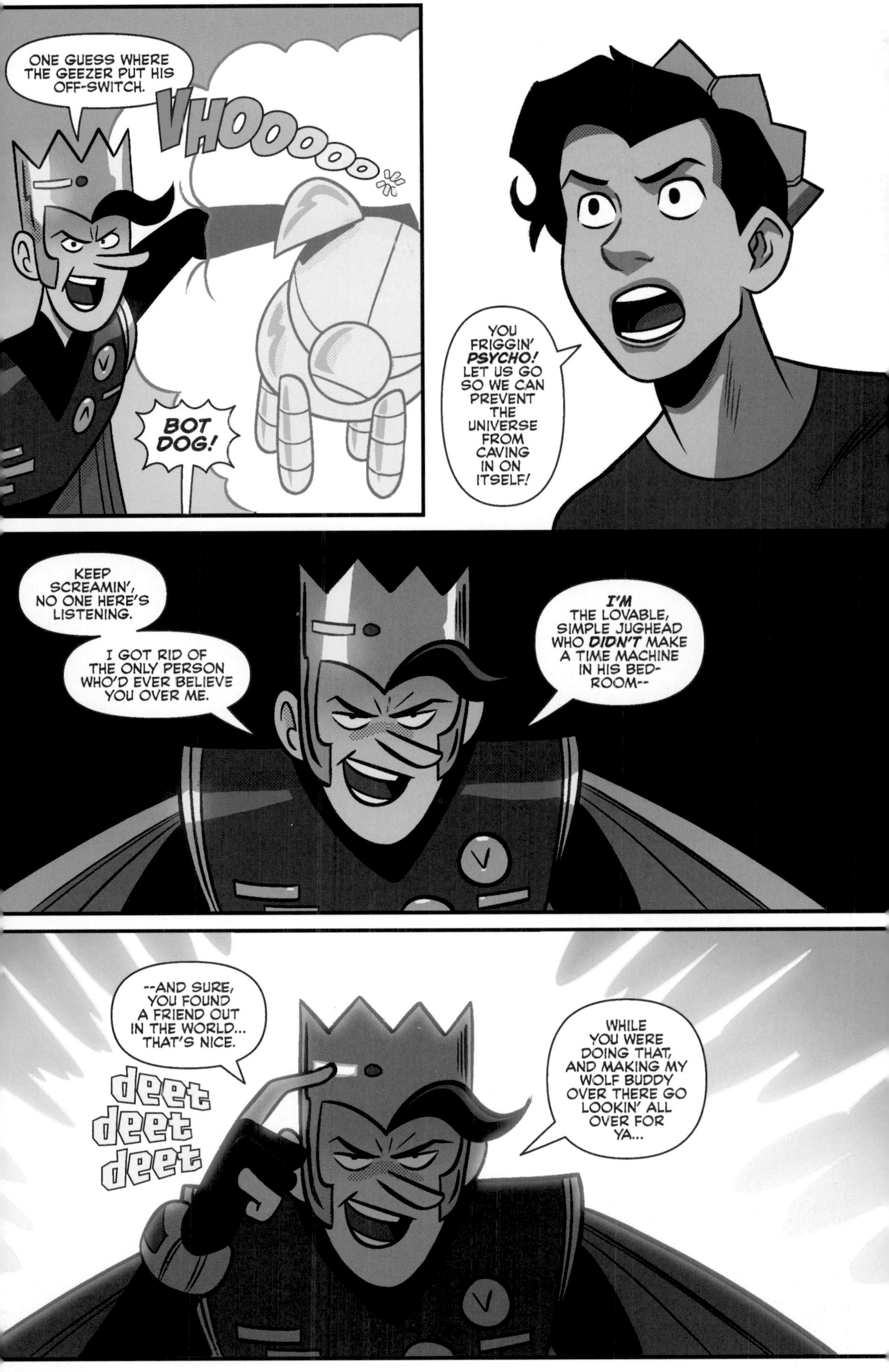
ONE GUESS WHERE THE GEEZER PUT HIS OFF-SWITCH.
VHOOOOOO
BOT DOG!
YOU FRIGGIN' PSYCHO! LET US GO SO WE CAN PREVENT THE UNIVERSE FROM CAVING IN ON ITSELF!
KEEP SCREAMIN', NO ONE HERE'S LISTENING.
I GOT RID OF THE ONLY PERSON WHO'D EVER BELIEVE YOU OVER ME.
I'M THE LOVABLE, SIMPLE JUGHEAD WHO DIDN'T MAKE A TIME MACHINE IN HIS BED-ROOM--
--AND SURE, YOU FOUND A FRIEND OUT IN THE WORLD... THAT'S NICE.
deet deet deet
WHILE YOU WERE DOING THAT, AND MAKING MY WOLF BUDDY OVER THERE GO LOOKIN' ALL OVER FOR YA...

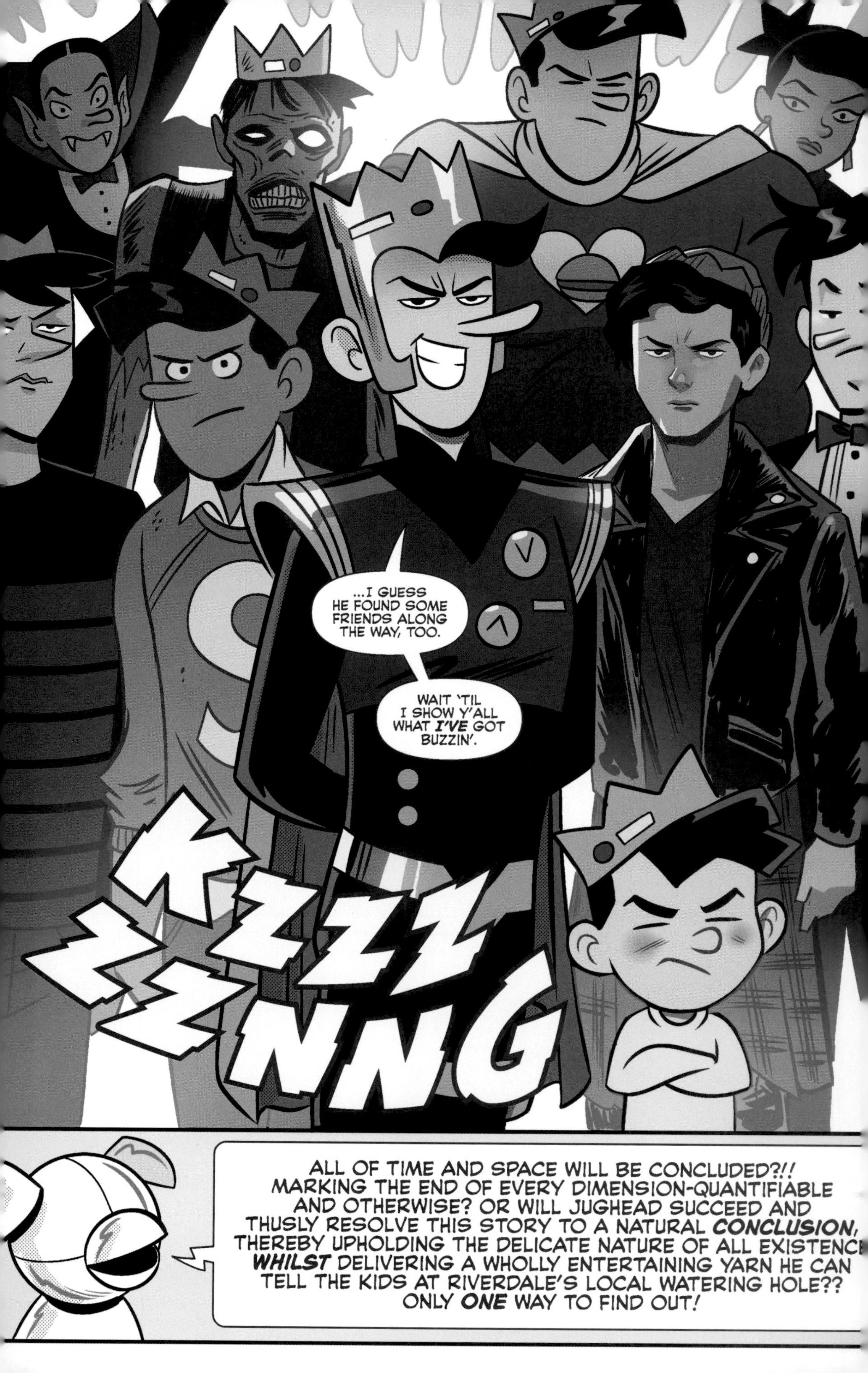
...I GUESS HE FOUND SOME FRIENDS ALONG THE WAY, TOO.
WAIT 'TIL I SHOW Y'ALL WHAT *I'VE* GOT BUZZIN'.
KZZZ ZZNNG
ALL OF TIME AND SPACE WILL BE CONCLUDED?!! MARKING THE END OF EVERY DIMENSION-QUANTIFIABLE AND OTHERWISE? OR WILL JUGHEAD SUCCEED AND THUSLY RESOLVE THIS STORY TO A NATURAL *CONCLUSION*, THEREBY UPHOLDING THE DELICATE NATURE OF ALL EXISTENCE *WHILST* DELIVERING A WHOLLY ENTERTAINING YARN HE CAN TELL THE KIDS AT RIVERDALE'S LOCAL WATERING HOLE?? ONLY *ONE* WAY TO FIND OUT!

Jughead's® Time Police™

SPECIAL FEATURE

CHARACTER CONCEPTS

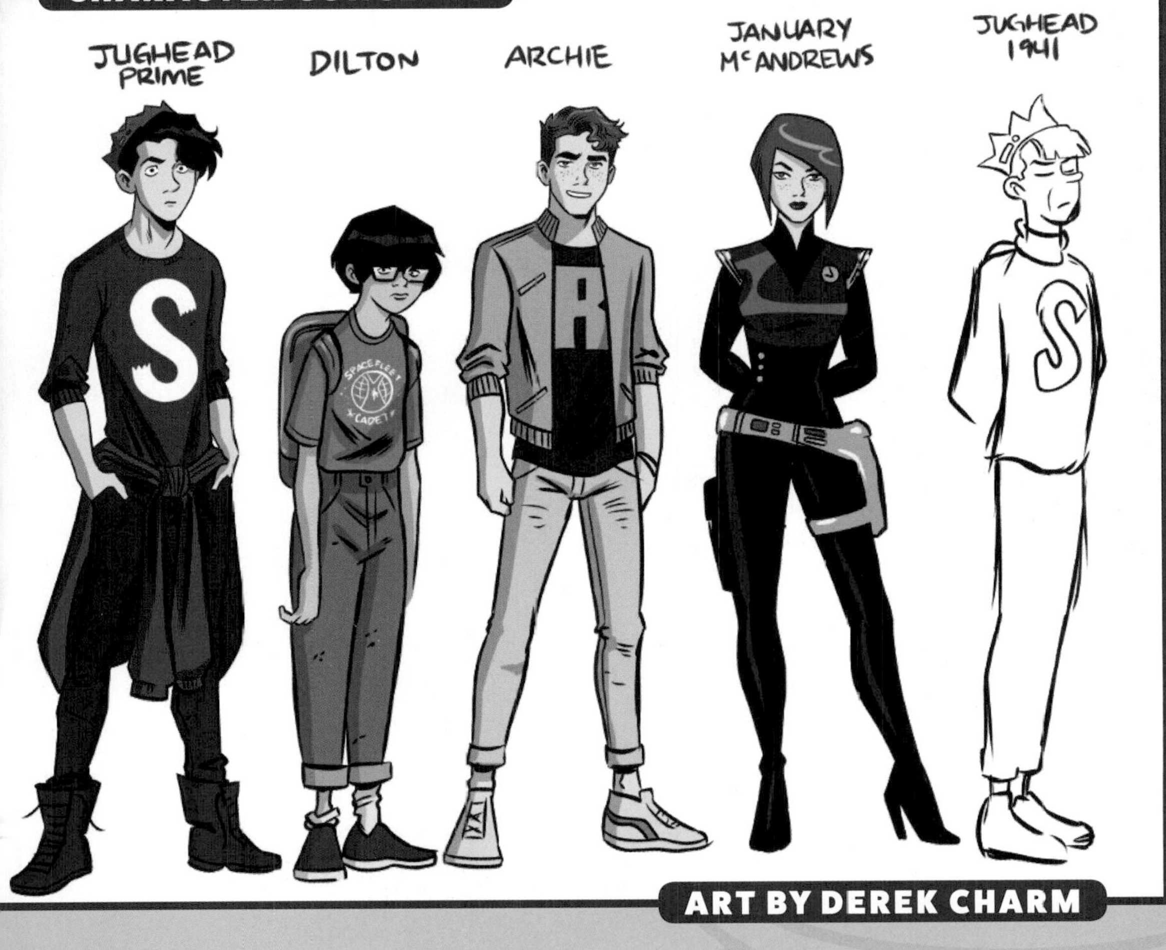

JUGHEAD PRIME
DILTON
ARCHIE
JANUARY McANDREWS
JUGHEAD 1941
SPACE FLEET CADET

ART BY DEREK CHARM

CHAPTER 5

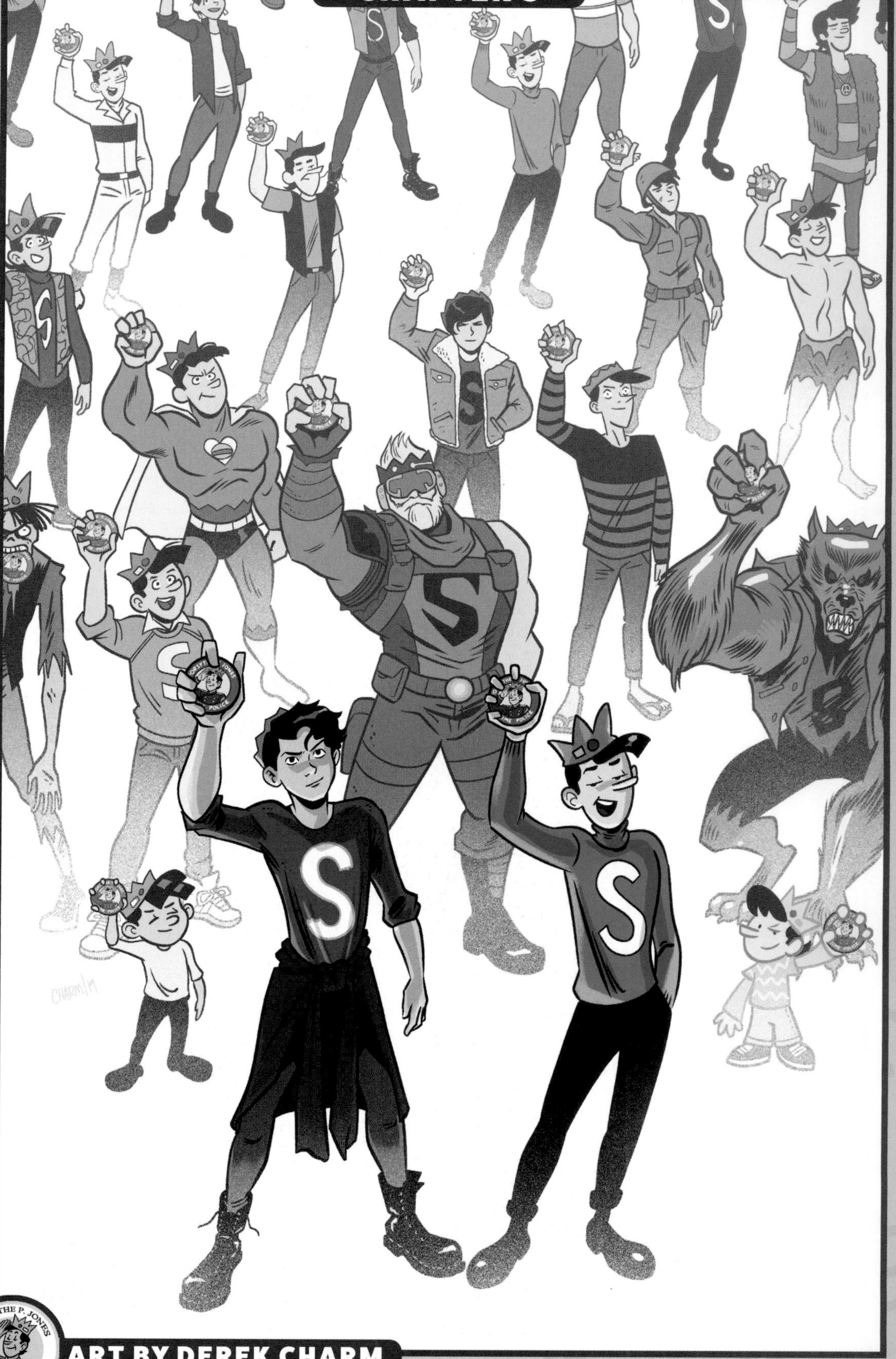
CHARM/19

ART BY DEREK CHARM

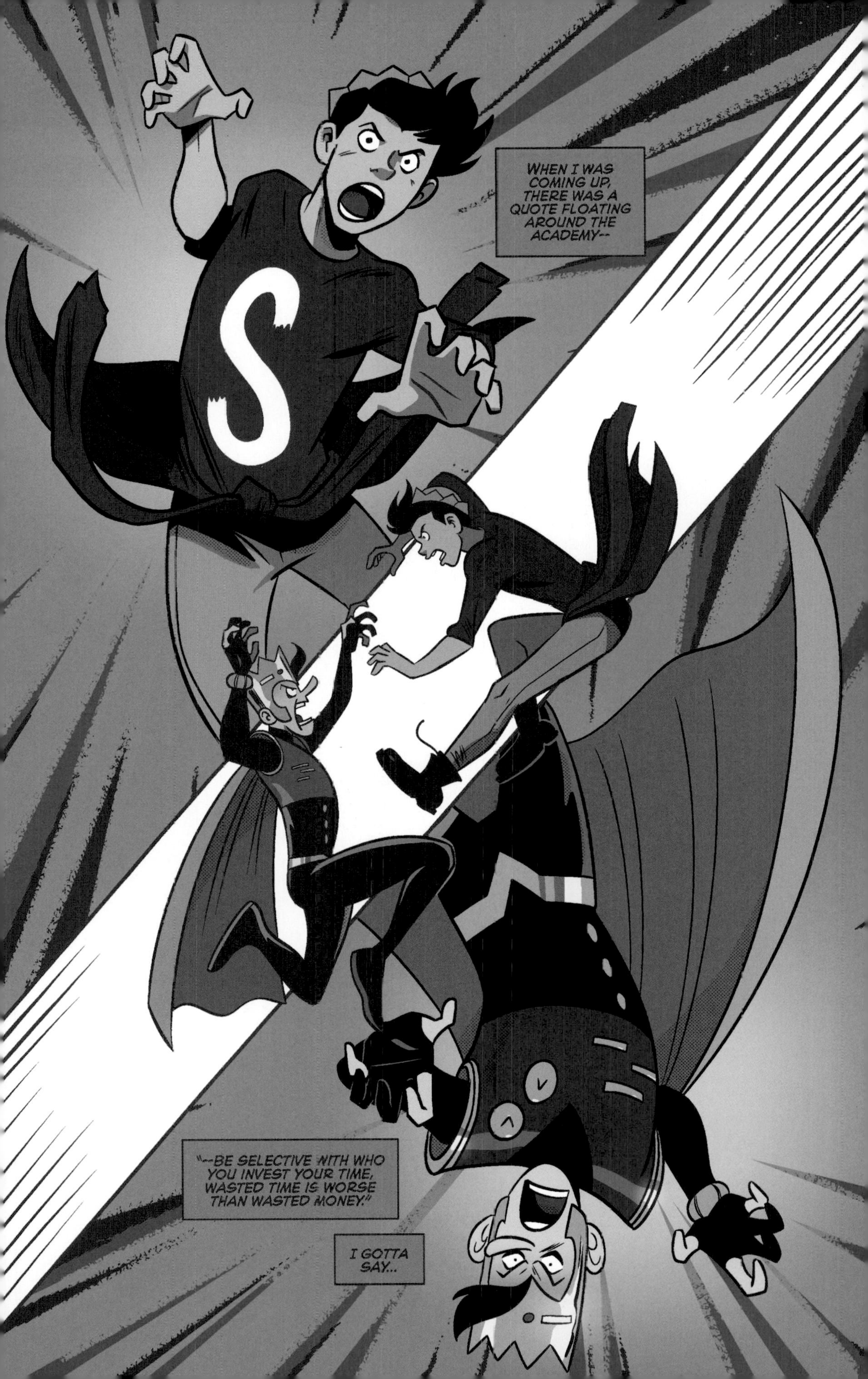
WHEN I WAS COMING UP, THERE WAS A QUOTE FLOATING AROUND THE ACADEMY--
"--BE SELECTIVE WITH WHO YOU INVEST YOUR TIME, WASTED TIME IS WORSE THAN WASTED MONEY."
I GOTTA SAY...

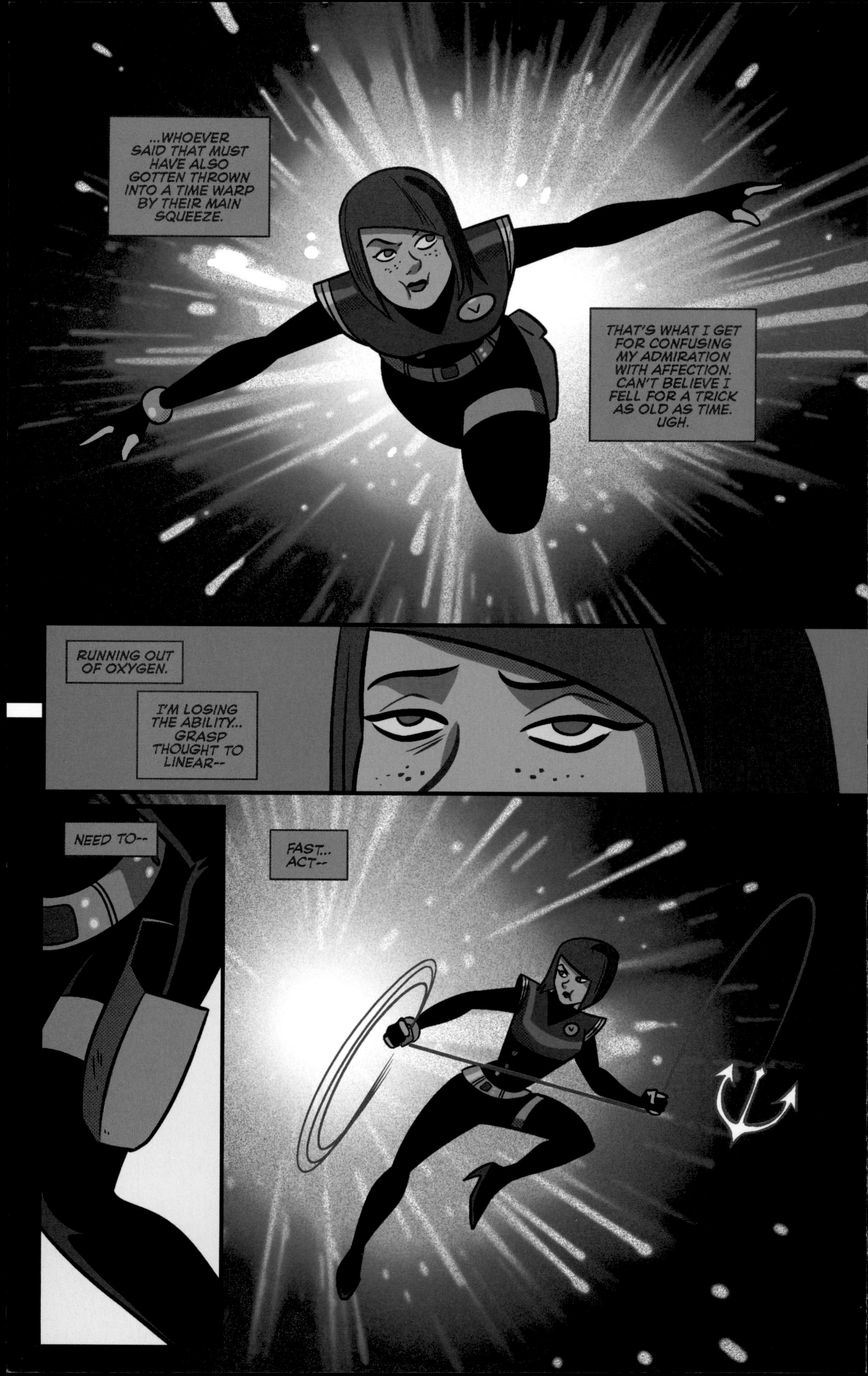
...WHOEVER SAID THAT MUST HAVE ALSO GOTTEN THROWN INTO A TIME WARP BY THEIR MAIN SQUEEZE.
THAT'S WHAT I GET FOR CONFUSING MY ADMIRATION WITH AFFECTION. CAN'T BELIEVE I FELL FOR A TRICK AS OLD AS TIME. UGH.
RUNNING OUT OF OXYGEN.
I'M LOSING THE ABILITY... GRASP THOUGHT TO LINEAR--
NEED TO--
FAST... ACT--

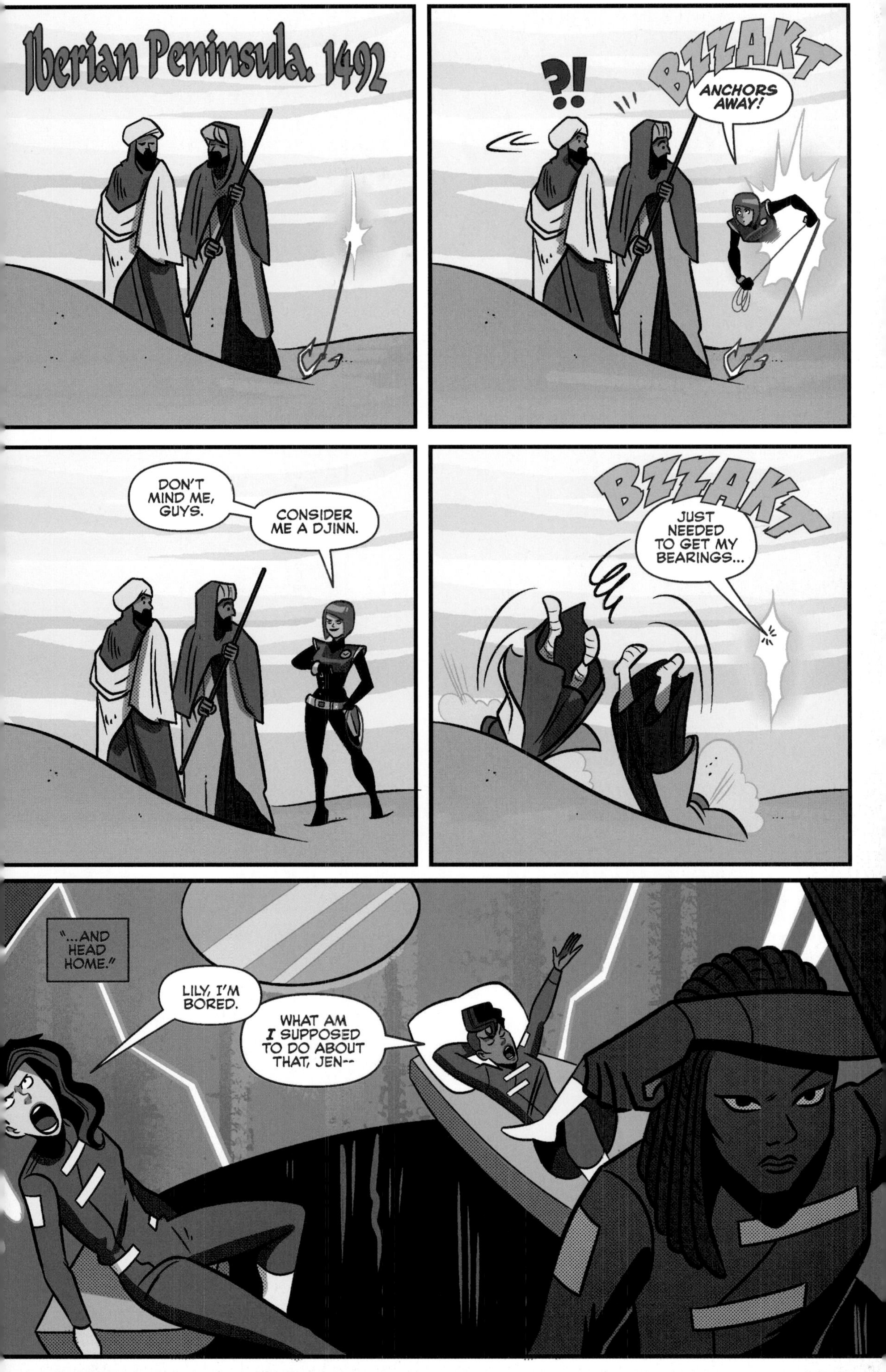
Iberian Peninsula. 1492
?!
BZZAKT
ANCHORS AWAY!
DON'T MIND ME, GUYS.
CONSIDER ME A DJINN.
BZZAKT
JUST NEEDED TO GET MY BEARINGS...
"...AND HEAD HOME."
LILY, I'M BORED.
WHAT AM I SUPPOSED TO DO ABOUT THAT, JEN--

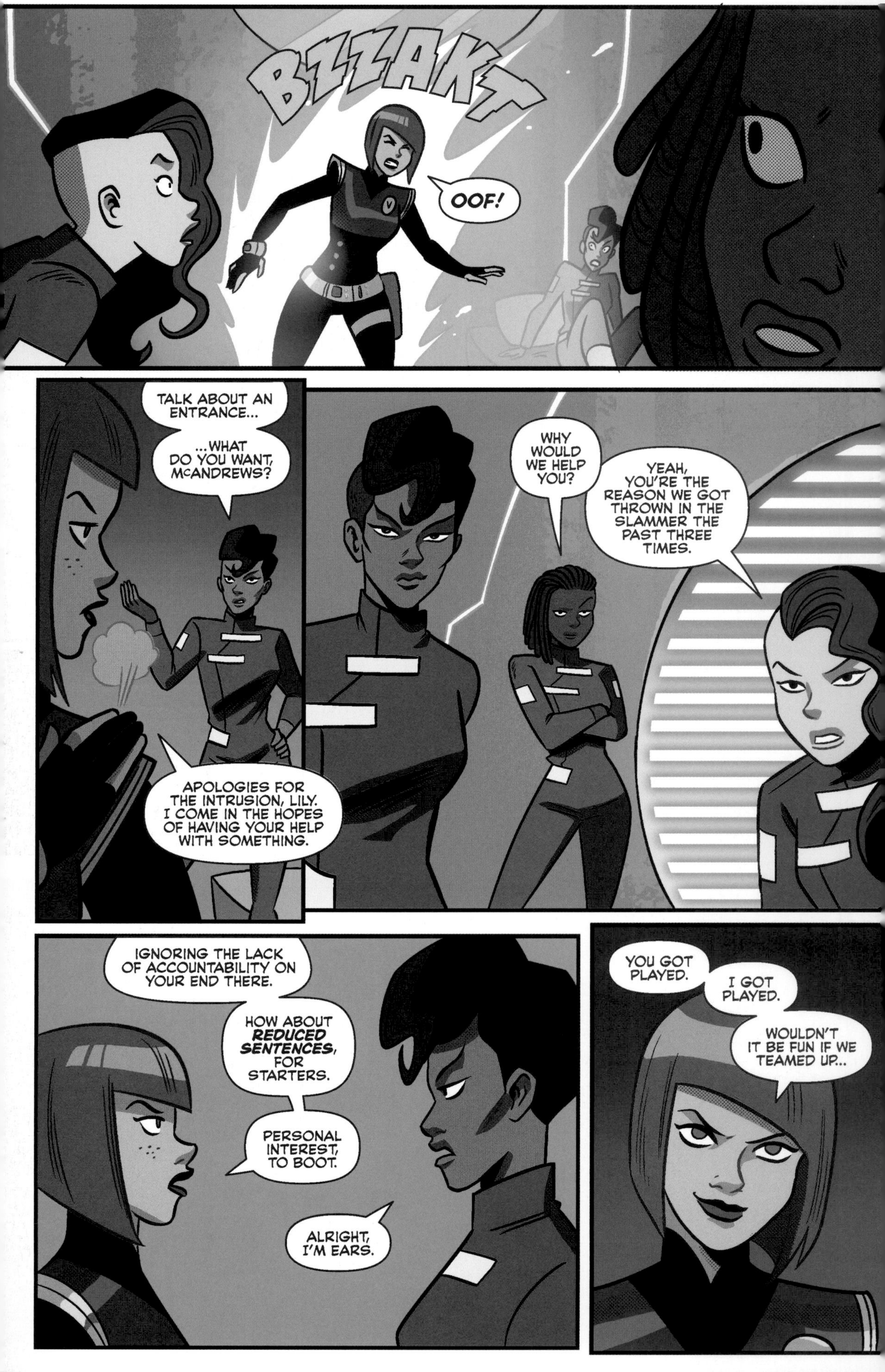
BZZAKT
OOF!
TALK ABOUT AN ENTRANCE...
...WHAT DO YOU WANT, McANDREWS?
APOLOGIES FOR THE INTRUSION, LILY. I COME IN THE HOPES OF HAVING YOUR HELP WITH SOMETHING.
WHY WOULD WE HELP YOU?
YEAH, YOU'RE THE REASON WE GOT THROWN IN THE SLAMMER THE PAST THREE TIMES.
IGNORING THE LACK OF ACCOUNTABILITY ON YOUR END THERE.
HOW ABOUT ***REDUCED SENTENCES***, FOR STARTERS.
PERSONAL INTEREST, TO BOOT.
ALRIGHT, I'M EARS.
YOU GOT PLAYED.
I GOT PLAYED.
WOULDN'T IT BE FUN IF WE TEAMED UP...

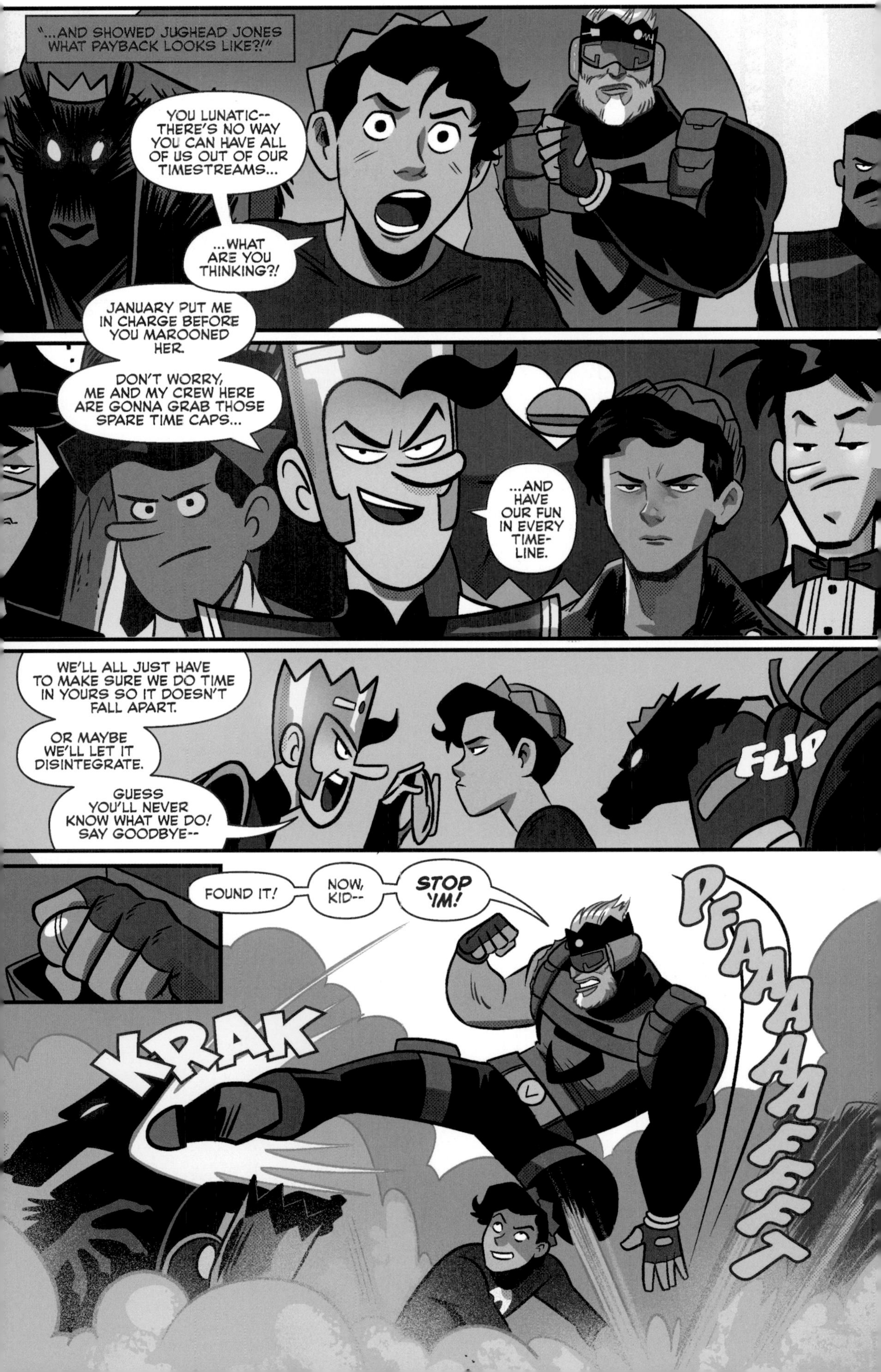
"...AND SHOWED JUGHEAD JONES WHAT PAYBACK LOOKS LIKE?!"
YOU LUNATIC-- THERE'S NO WAY YOU CAN HAVE ALL OF US OUT OF OUR TIMESTREAMS...
...WHAT ARE YOU THINKING?!
JANUARY PUT ME IN CHARGE BEFORE YOU MAROONED HER.
DON'T WORRY, ME AND MY CREW HERE ARE GONNA GRAB THOSE SPARE TIME CAPS...
...AND HAVE OUR FUN IN EVERY TIME-LINE.
WE'LL ALL JUST HAVE TO MAKE SURE WE DO TIME IN YOURS SO IT DOESN'T FALL APART.
OR MAYBE WE'LL LET IT DISINTEGRATE.
GUESS YOU'LL NEVER KNOW WHAT WE DO! SAY GOODBYE--
FLIP
FOUND IT!
NOW, KID--
STOP 'IM!
PFAAAAAAFFFT
KRAK

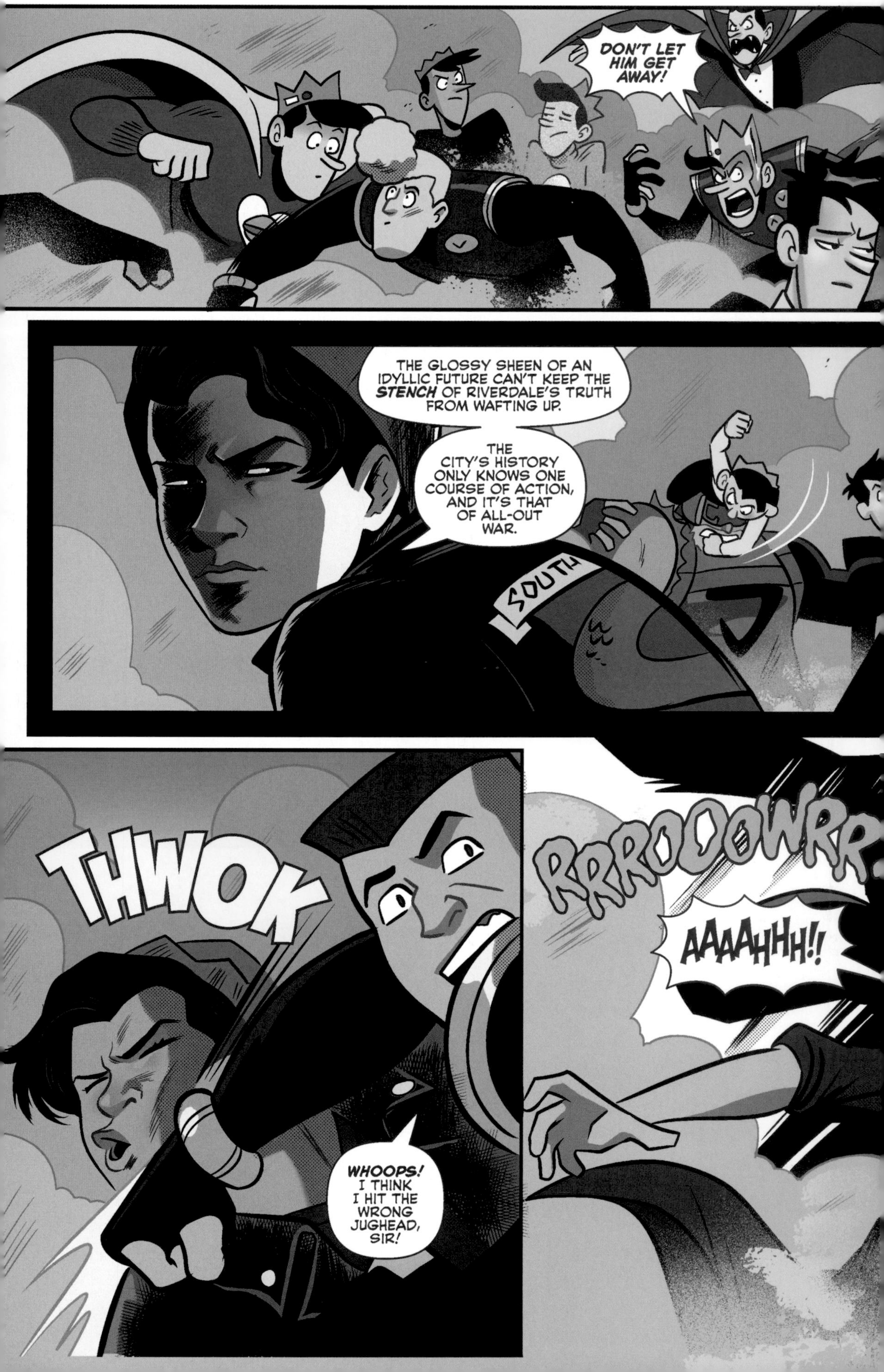
DON'T LET HIM GET AWAY!
THE GLOSSY SHEEN OF AN IDYLLIC FUTURE CAN'T KEEP THE STENCH OF RIVERDALE'S TRUTH FROM WAFTING UP.
THE CITY'S HISTORY ONLY KNOWS ONE COURSE OF ACTION, AND IT'S THAT OF ALL-OUT WAR.
SOUTH
THWOK
WHOOPS! I THINK I HIT THE WRONG JUGHEAD, SIR!
RRROOOWRR
AAAAHHH!!

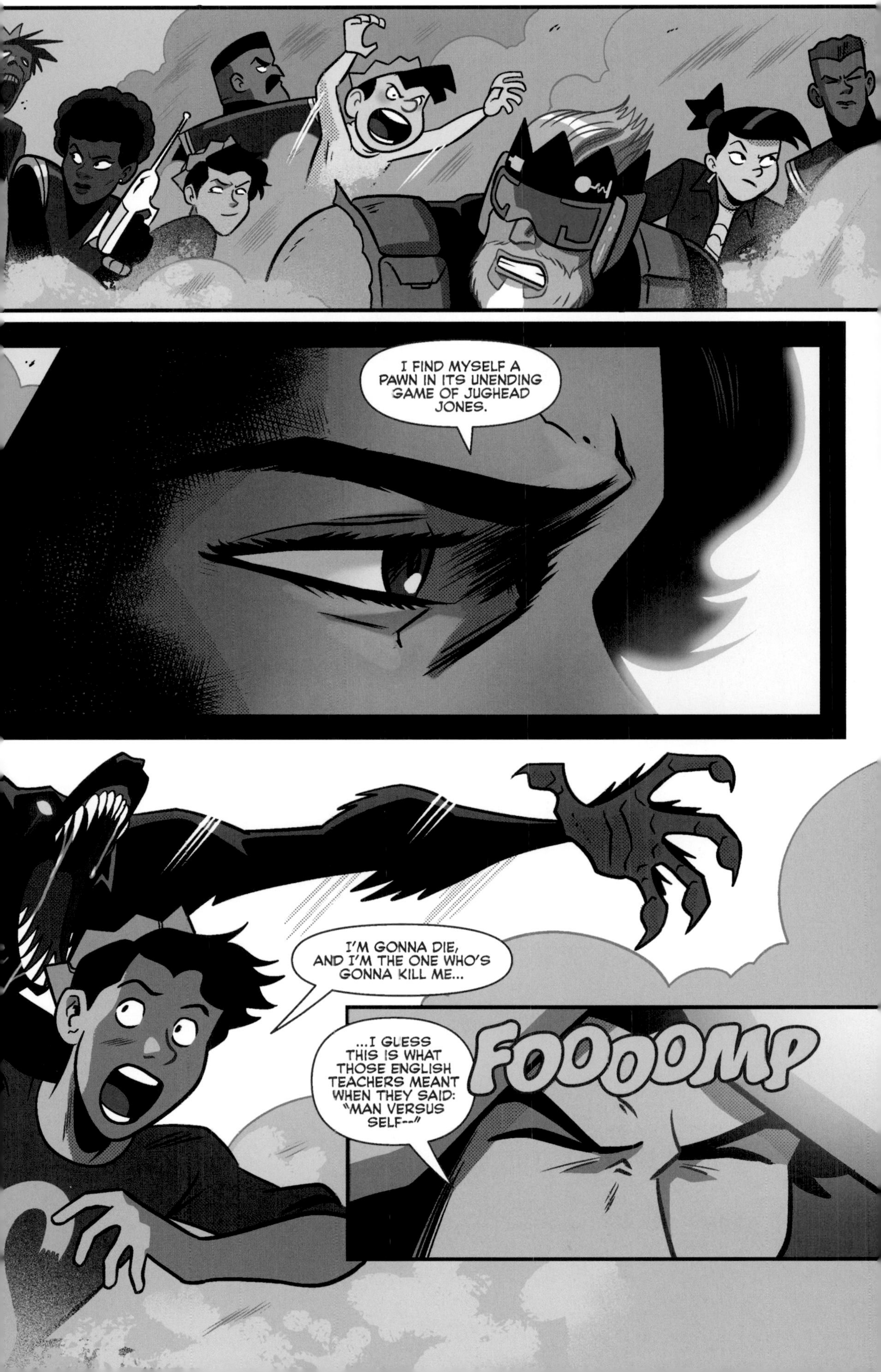
I FIND MYSELF A PAWN IN ITS UNENDING GAME OF JUGHEAD JONES.
I'M GONNA DIE, AND I'M THE ONE WHO'S GONNA KILL ME...
...I GUESS THIS IS WHAT THOSE ENGLISH TEACHERS MEANT WHEN THEY SAID: "MAN VERSUS SELF--"
FOOOOMP

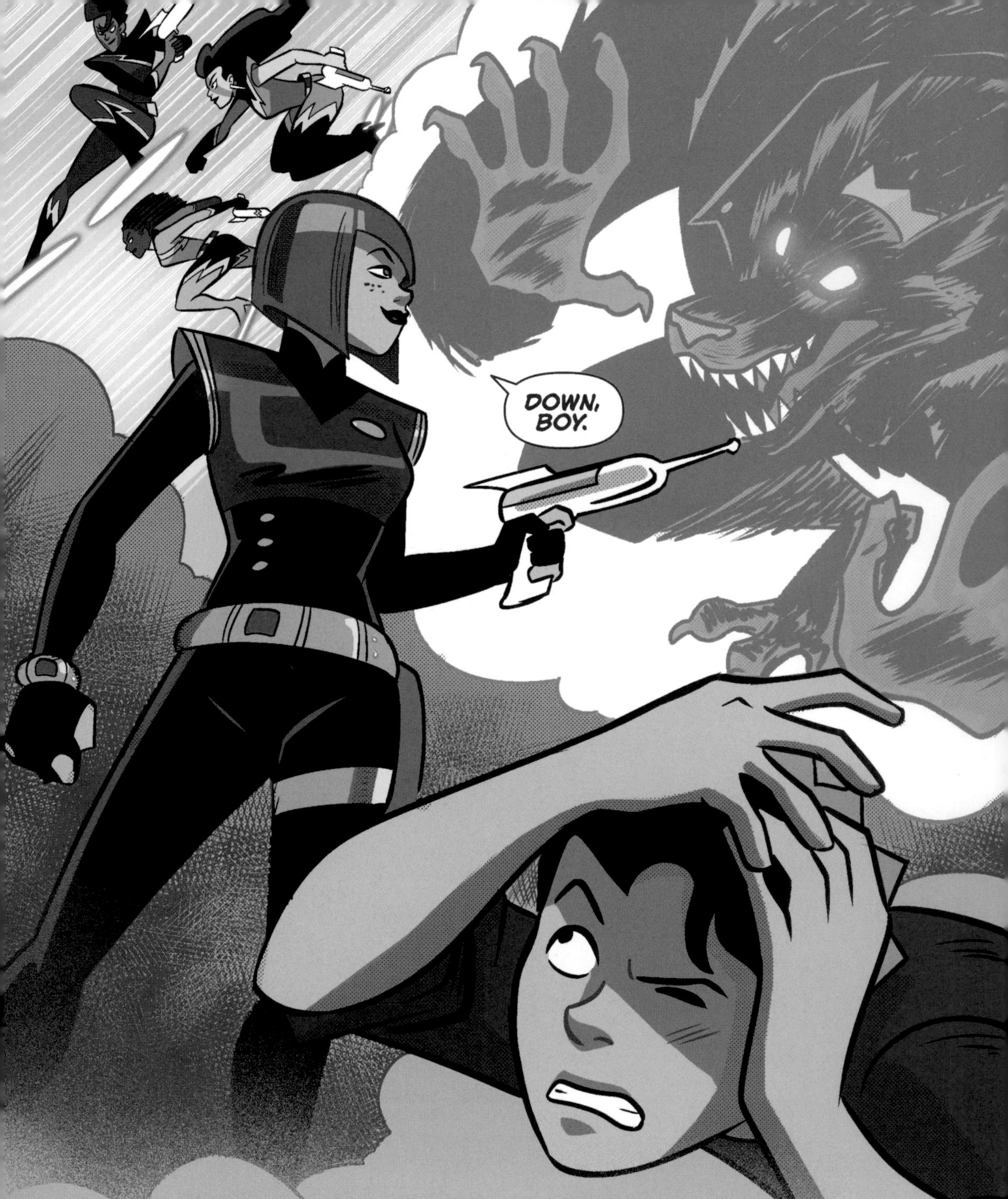
DOWN, BOY.

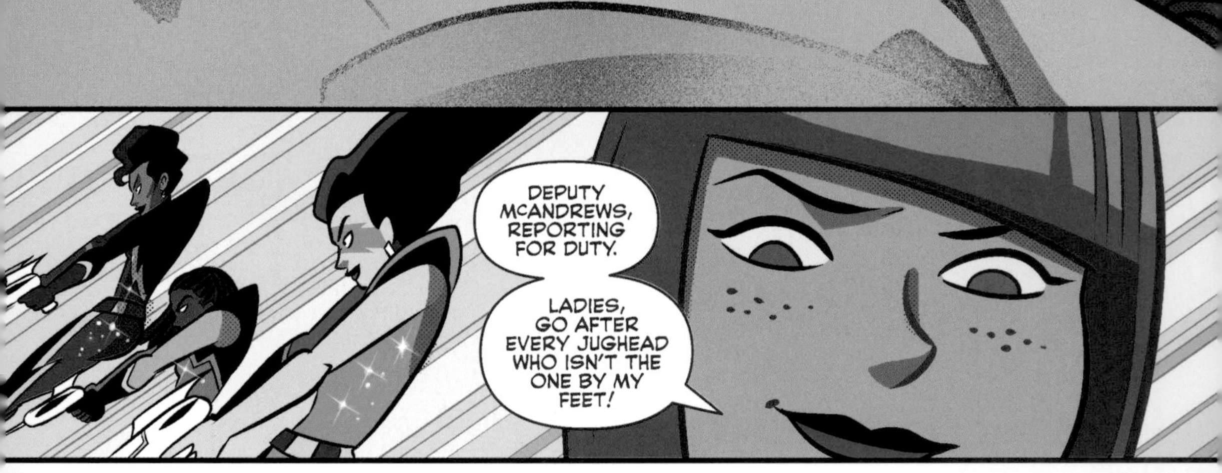
DEPUTY McANDREWS, REPORTING FOR DUTY.
LADIES, GO AFTER EVERY JUGHEAD WHO ISN'T THE ONE BY MY FEET!

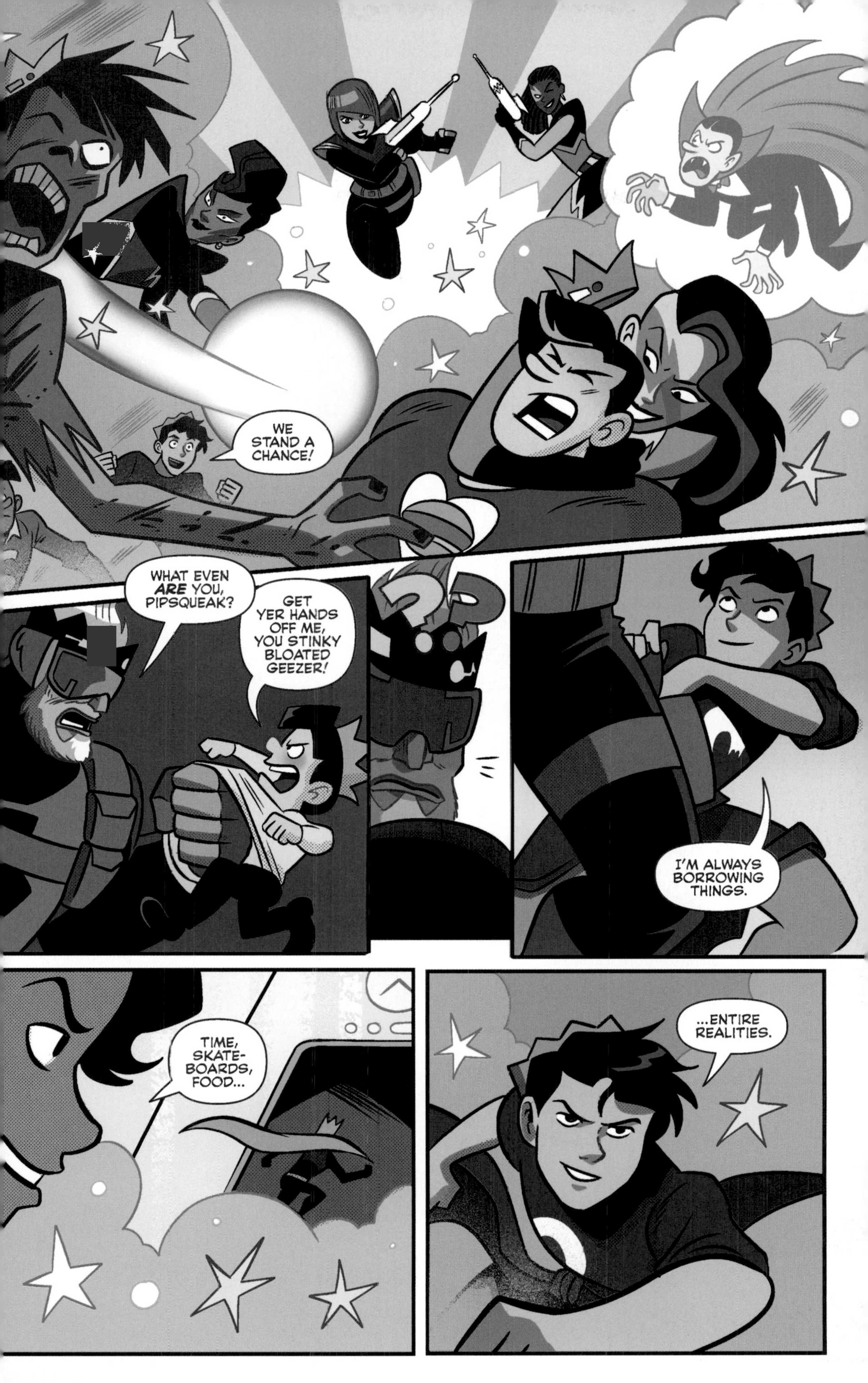
WE STAND A CHANCE!
WHAT EVEN ***ARE*** YOU, PIPSQUEAK?
GET YER HANDS OFF ME, YOU STINKY BLOATED GEEZER!
I'M ALWAYS BORROWING THINGS.
TIME, SKATE-BOARDS, FOOD...
...ENTIRE REALITIES.

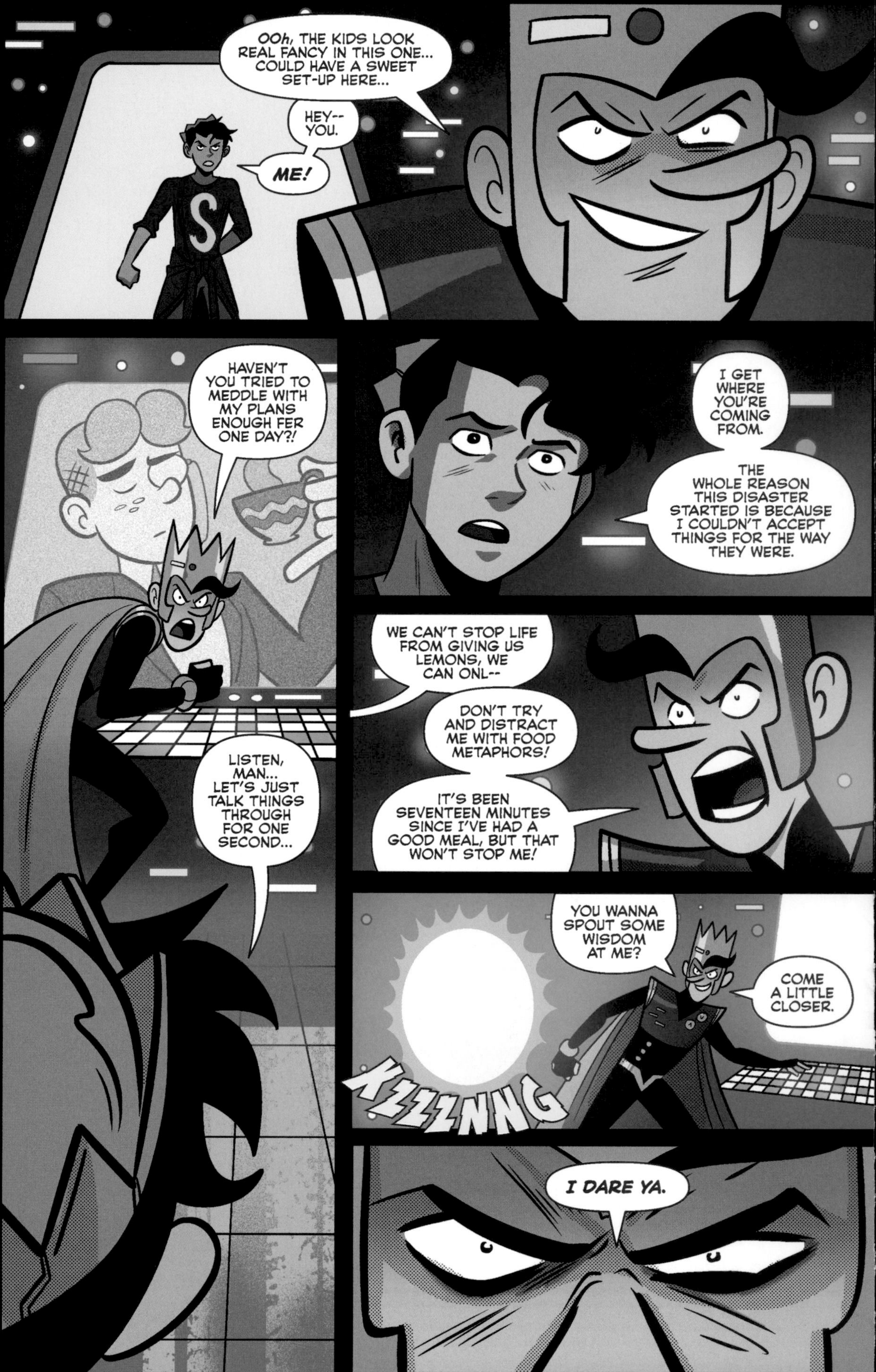
OOh, THE KIDS LOOK REAL FANCY IN THIS ONE... COULD HAVE A SWEET SET-UP HERE...
HEY-- YOU.
ME!
HAVEN'T YOU TRIED TO MEDDLE WITH MY PLANS ENOUGH FER ONE DAY?!
I GET WHERE YOU'RE COMING FROM.
THE WHOLE REASON THIS DISASTER STARTED IS BECAUSE I COULDN'T ACCEPT THINGS FOR THE WAY THEY WERE.
WE CAN'T STOP LIFE FROM GIVING US LEMONS, WE CAN ONL--
DON'T TRY AND DISTRACT ME WITH FOOD METAPHORS!
IT'S BEEN SEVENTEEN MINUTES SINCE I'VE HAD A GOOD MEAL, BUT THAT WON'T STOP ME!
LISTEN, MAN... LET'S JUST TALK THINGS THROUGH FOR ONE SECOND...
YOU WANNA SPOUT SOME WISDOM AT ME?
COME A LITTLE CLOSER.
KZZZNNG
I DARE YA.

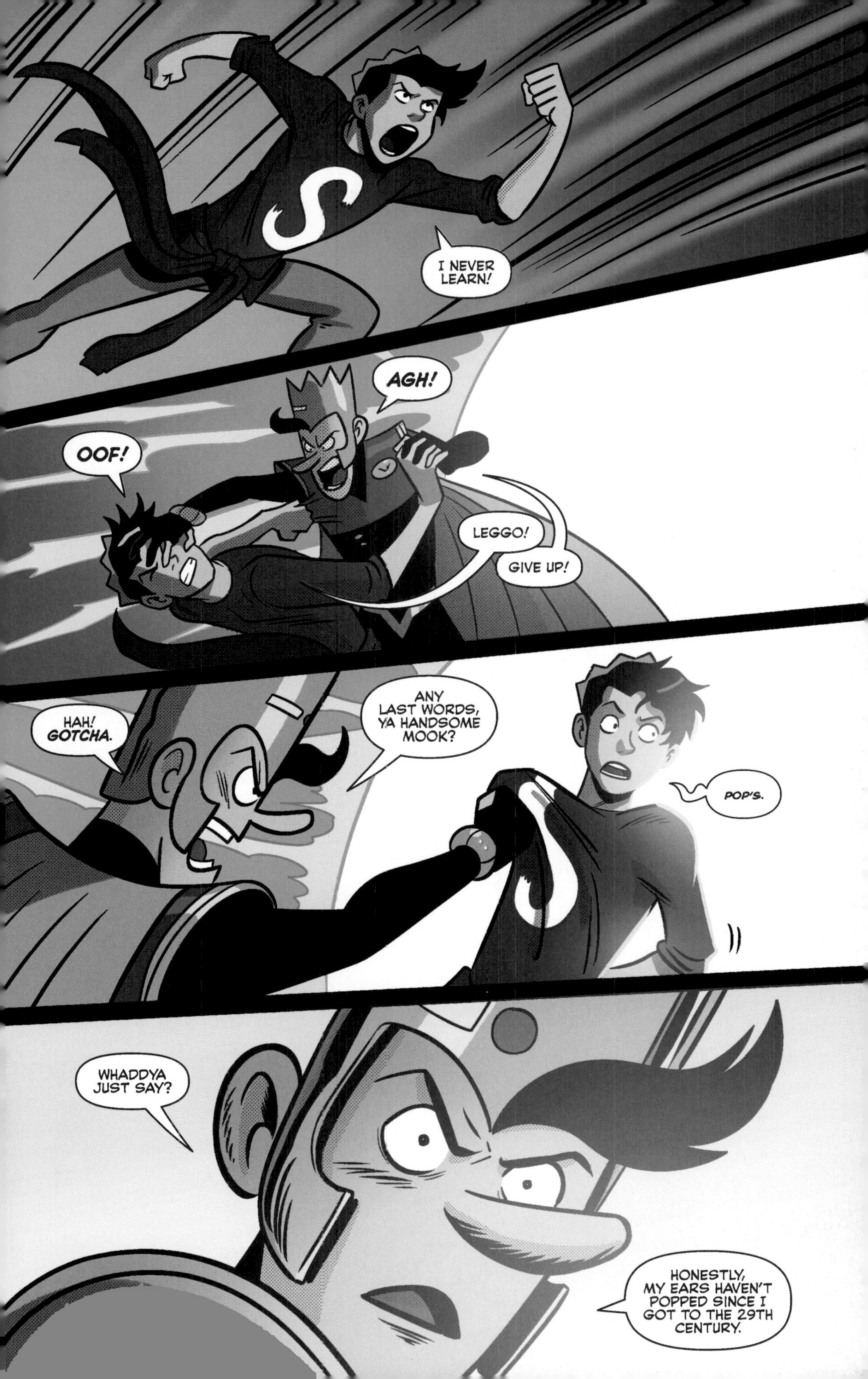
I NEVER LEARN!
AGH!
OOF!
LEGGO!
GIVE UP!
HAH! GOTCHA.
ANY LAST WORDS, YA HANDSOME MOOK?
POP'S.
WHADDYA JUST SAY?
HONESTLY, MY EARS HAVEN'T POPPED SINCE I GOT TO THE 29TH CENTURY.

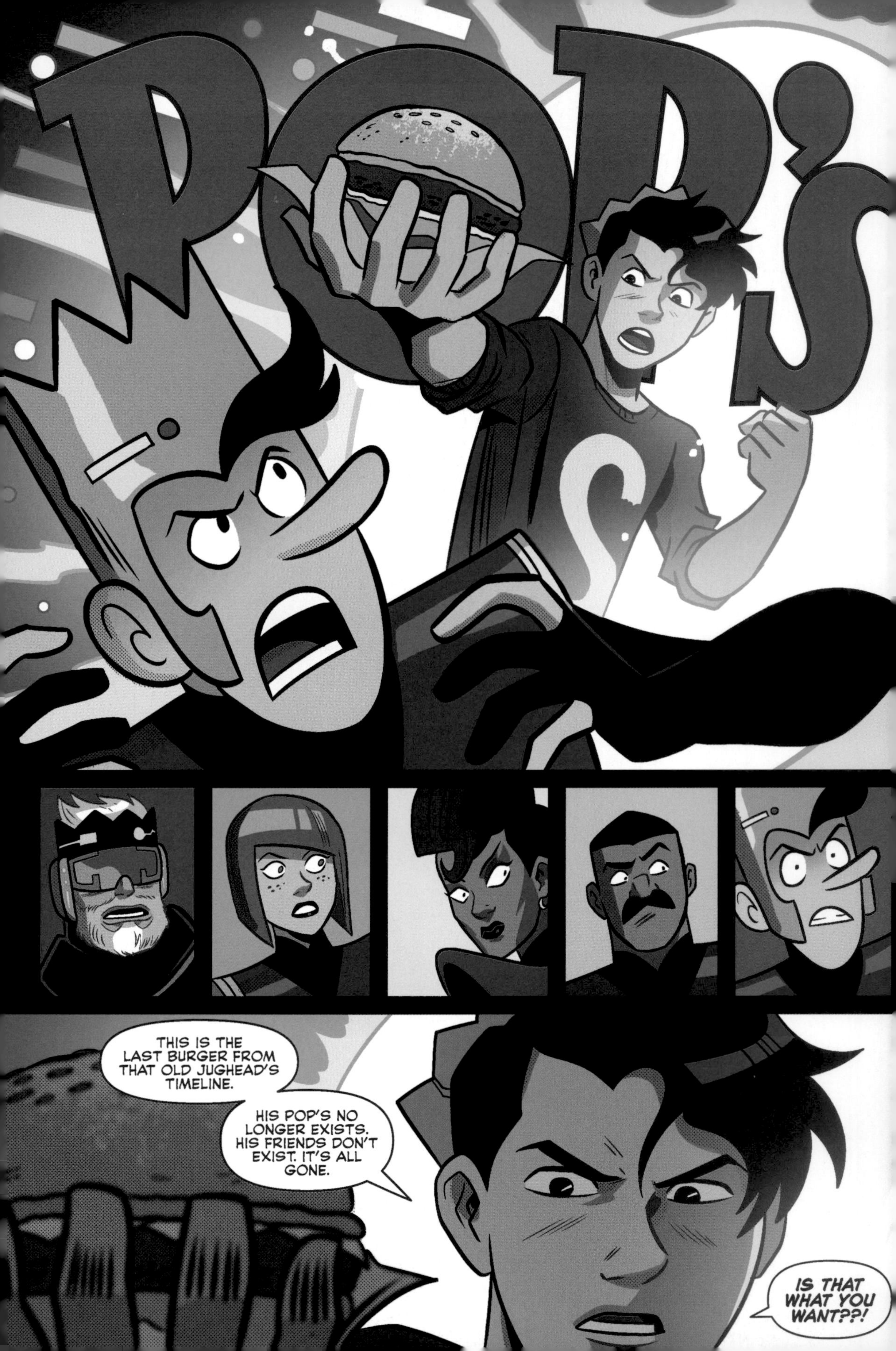
POP'S
THIS IS THE LAST BURGER FROM THAT OLD JUGHEAD'S TIMELINE.
HIS POP'S NO LONGER EXISTS. HIS FRIENDS DON'T EXIST. IT'S ALL GONE.
IS THAT WHAT YOU WANT??!

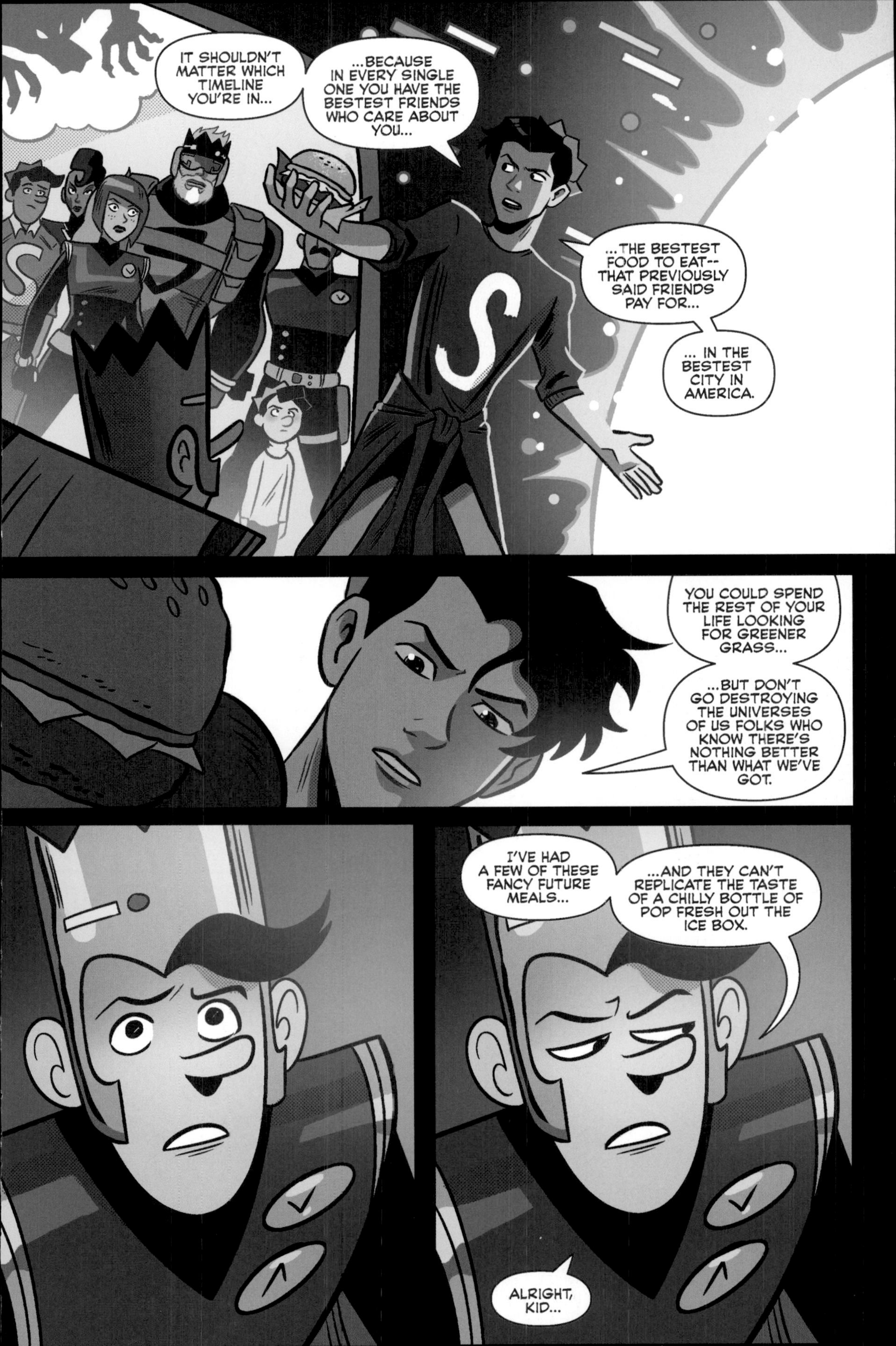
IT SHOULDN'T MATTER WHICH TIMELINE YOU'RE IN...
...BECAUSE IN EVERY SINGLE ONE YOU HAVE THE BESTEST FRIENDS WHO CARE ABOUT YOU...
...THE BESTEST FOOD TO EAT--THAT PREVIOUSLY SAID FRIENDS PAY FOR...
... IN THE BESTEST CITY IN AMERICA.
YOU COULD SPEND THE REST OF YOUR LIFE LOOKING FOR GREENER GRASS...
...BUT DON'T GO DESTROYING THE UNIVERSES OF US FOLKS WHO KNOW THERE'S NOTHING BETTER THAN WHAT WE'VE GOT.
I'VE HAD A FEW OF THESE FANCY FUTURE MEALS...
...AND THEY CAN'T REPLICATE THE TASTE OF A CHILLY BOTTLE OF POP FRESH OUT THE ICE BOX.
ALRIGHT, KID...

"...YOU WIN."

FZZTPOP FZZTPOP

JUST LIKE THAT, EVERYONE'S REALITIES GO BACK TO NORMAL--

--EVERY-BODY'S...BUT *YOURS*.

Oh, HEYA, JAN.

MY RIVERDALE'S PROBABLY DISINTEGRATED BY NOW...GUESS I'LL HAVE TO FIND A SUNSET TO RIDE OFF INTO.

OR, I COULD PERSUADE YOU TO STAY HERE?

WHILE THE DEPARTMENT HAS A DECENT HOLD ON TIME TRAVEL, MISHAPS LIKE THIS ARE STILL BOUND TO HAPPEN.

IT WOULD BEHOOVE US TO SPONSOR A TEAM OF INDIVIDUALS WITH EXPERTISE TO HANDLE SITUATIONS THAT MAY BE A TAD... TOUCHY, FROM AN OPTICS PERSPECTIVE.

LEMME GUESS...

...YOU ALSO OFFERED THOSE GLITZY TIME THIEVES REDUCED SENTENCES IF THEY JOINED YOUR WETWORKS GROUP?

I GOT NOWHERE BETTER TO BE.

Y'KNOW, ONE PIECE OF ADVICE: MAYBE WORK ON THE NOISES THESE LOOPER SCOOPERS MAKE?

AT THE END OF THE DAY, NO ONE WANTS THEIR LAST SOUND OF THE FUTURE TO BE THAT OF A--

FZZTPOP

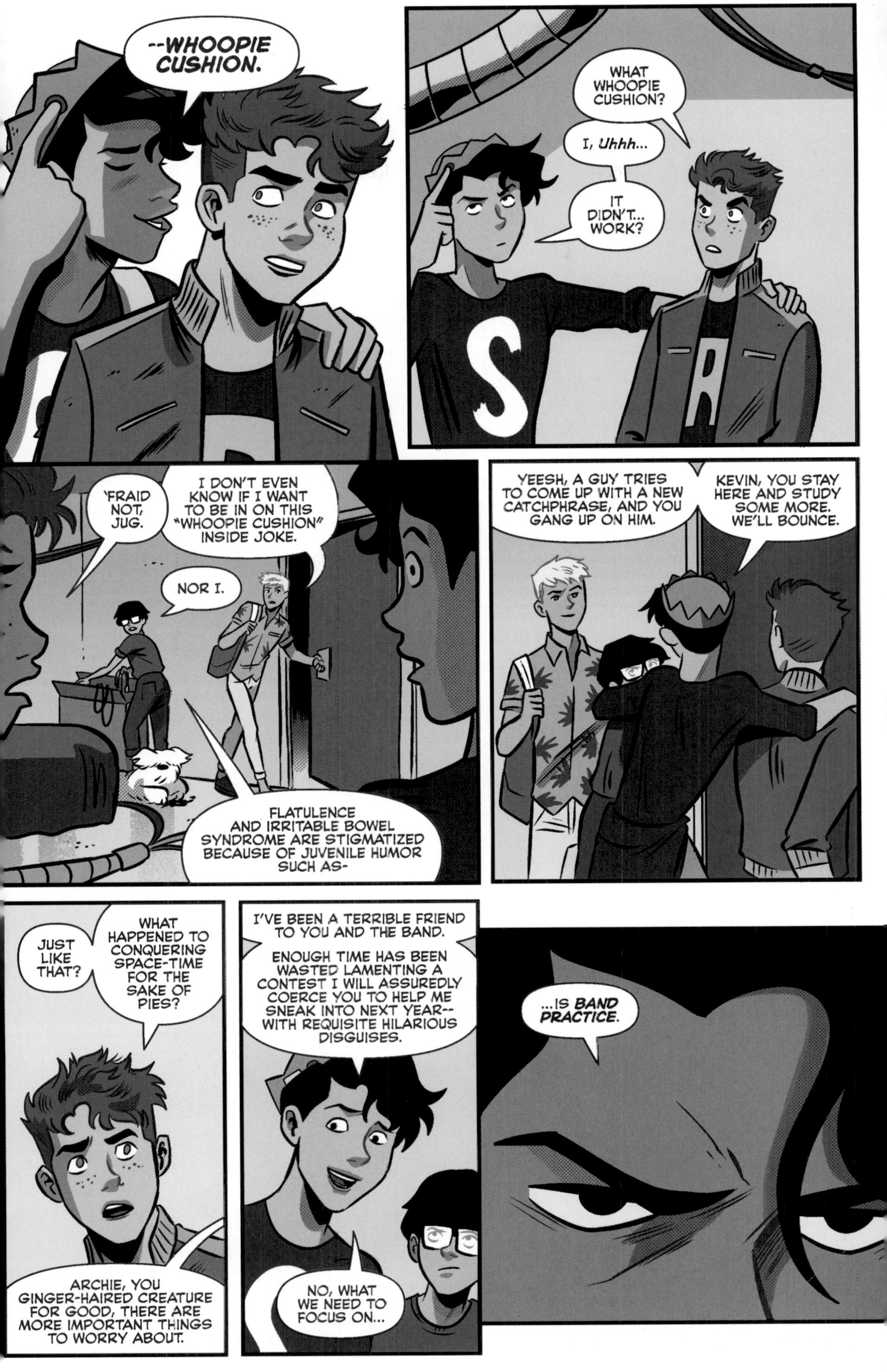
--WHOOPIE CUSHION.
WHAT WHOOPIE CUSHION?
I, Uhhh...
IT DIDN'T... WORK?
'FRAID NOT, JUG.
I DON'T EVEN KNOW IF I WANT TO BE IN ON THIS "WHOOPIE CUSHION" INSIDE JOKE.
NOR I.
FLATULENCE AND IRRITABLE BOWEL SYNDROME ARE STIGMATIZED BECAUSE OF JUVENILE HUMOR SUCH AS-
YEESH, A GUY TRIES TO COME UP WITH A NEW CATCHPHRASE, AND YOU GANG UP ON HIM.
KEVIN, YOU STAY HERE AND STUDY SOME MORE. WE'LL BOUNCE.
JUST LIKE THAT?
WHAT HAPPENED TO CONQUERING SPACE-TIME FOR THE SAKE OF PIES?
ARCHIE, YOU GINGER-HAIRED CREATURE FOR GOOD, THERE ARE MORE IMPORTANT THINGS TO WORRY ABOUT.
I'VE BEEN A TERRIBLE FRIEND TO YOU AND THE BAND.
ENOUGH TIME HAS BEEN WASTED LAMENTING A CONTEST I WILL ASSUREDLY COERCE YOU TO HELP ME SNEAK INTO NEXT YEAR--WITH REQUISITE HILARIOUS DISGUISES.
NO, WHAT WE NEED TO FOCUS ON...
...IS BAND PRACTICE.

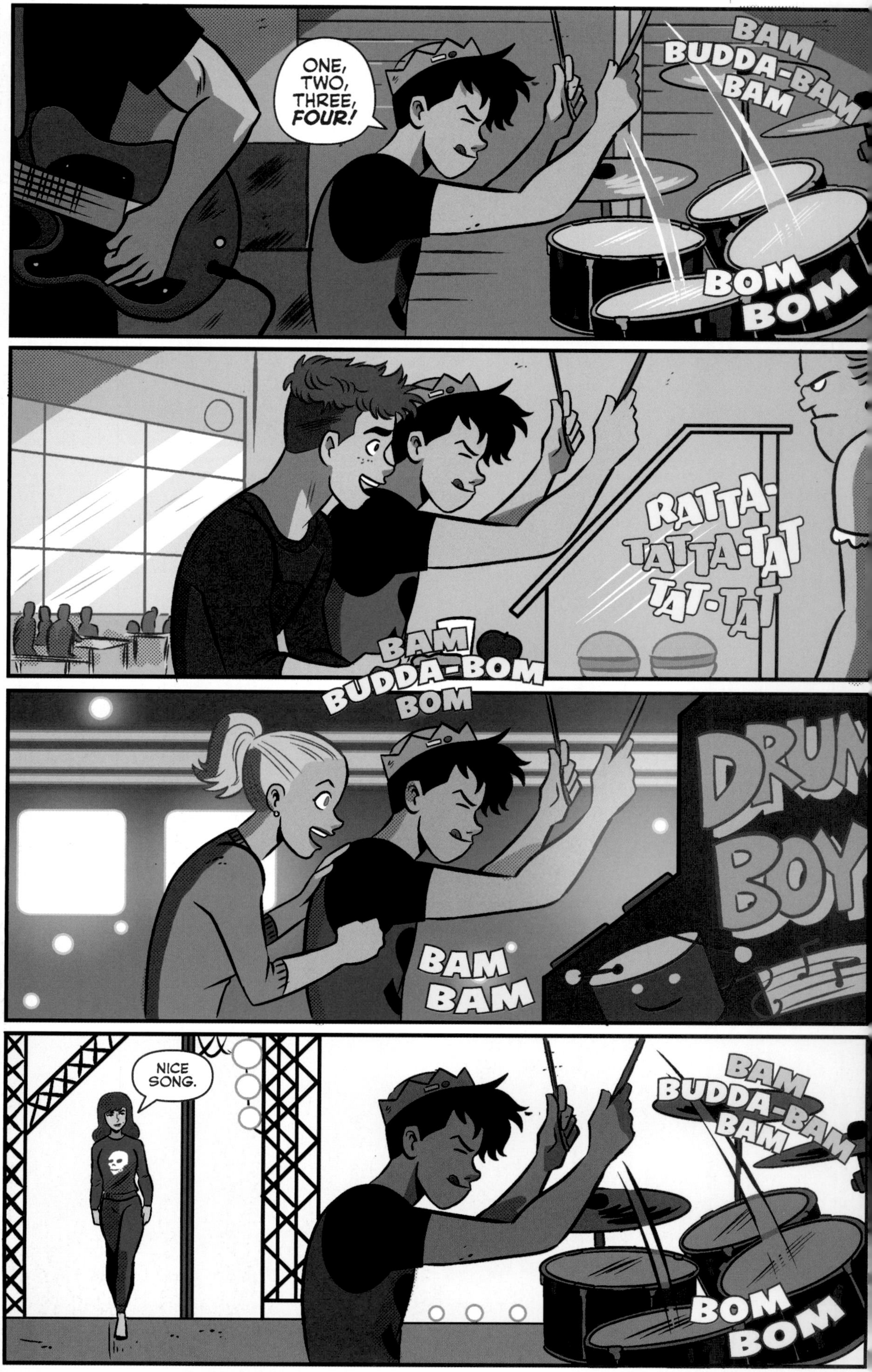
ONE, TWO, THREE, FOUR!
BAM BUDDA-BAM BAM
BOM BOM
RATTA-TATTA-TAT TAT-TAT
BAM BUDDA-BOM BOM
DRUM BOY
BAM BAM
NICE SONG.
BAM BUDDA-BAM BAM
BOM BOM

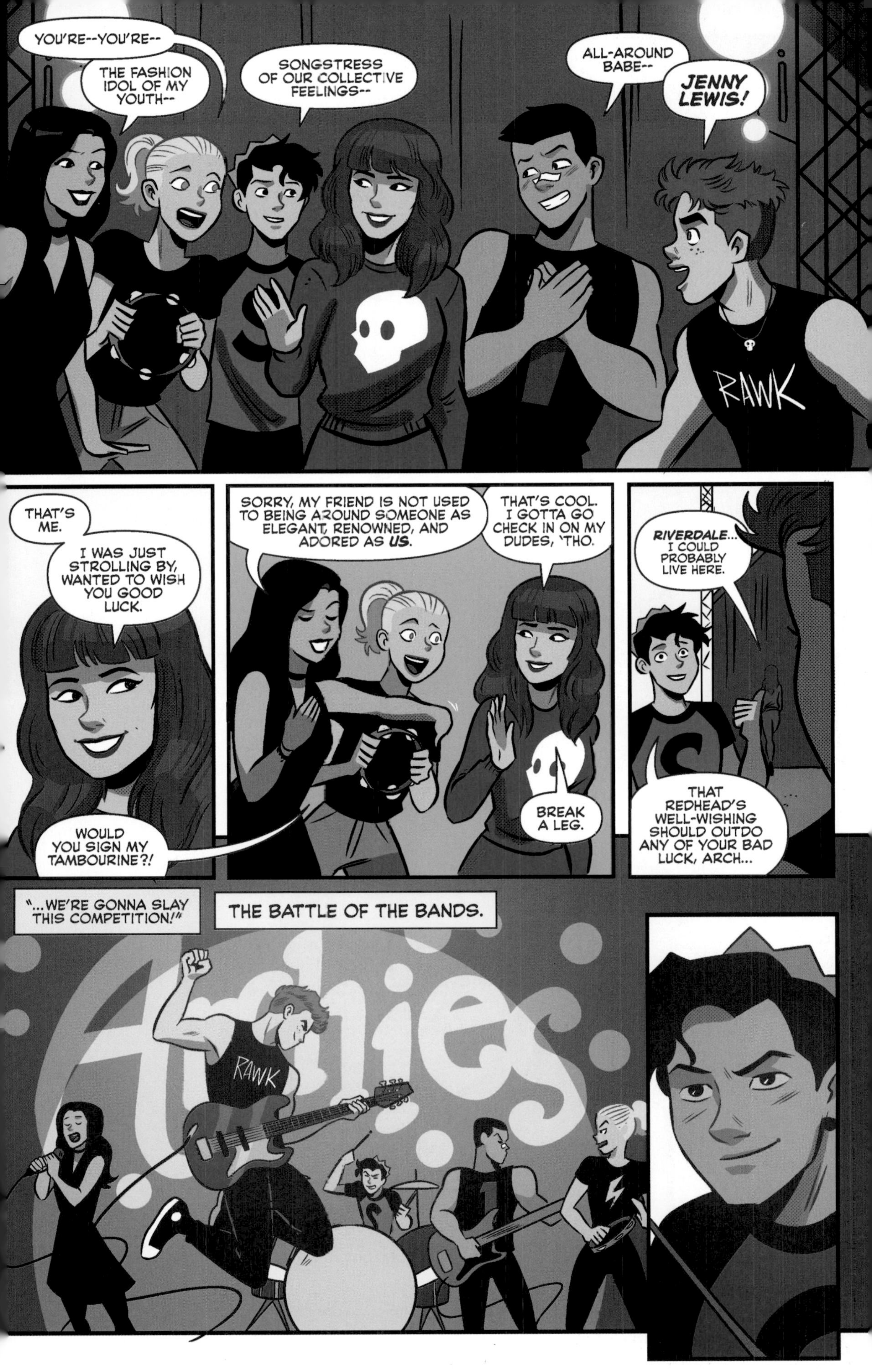

YOU'RE--YOU'RE--
THE FASHION IDOL OF MY YOUTH--
SONGSTRESS OF OUR COLLECTIVE FEELINGS--
ALL-AROUND BABE--
JENNY LEWIS!
RAWK
THAT'S ME.
I WAS JUST STROLLING BY, WANTED TO WISH YOU GOOD LUCK.
WOULD YOU SIGN MY TAMBOURINE?!
SORRY, MY FRIEND IS NOT USED TO BEING AROUND SOMEONE AS ELEGANT, RENOWNED, AND ADORED AS US.
THAT'S COOL. I GOTTA GO CHECK IN ON MY DUDES, 'THO.
BREAK A LEG.
RIVERDALE... I COULD PROBABLY LIVE HERE.
THAT REDHEAD'S WELL-WISHING SHOULD OUTDO ANY OF YOUR BAD LUCK, ARCH...
"...WE'RE GONNA SLAY THIS COMPETITION!"
THE BATTLE OF THE BANDS.
Archies
RAWK

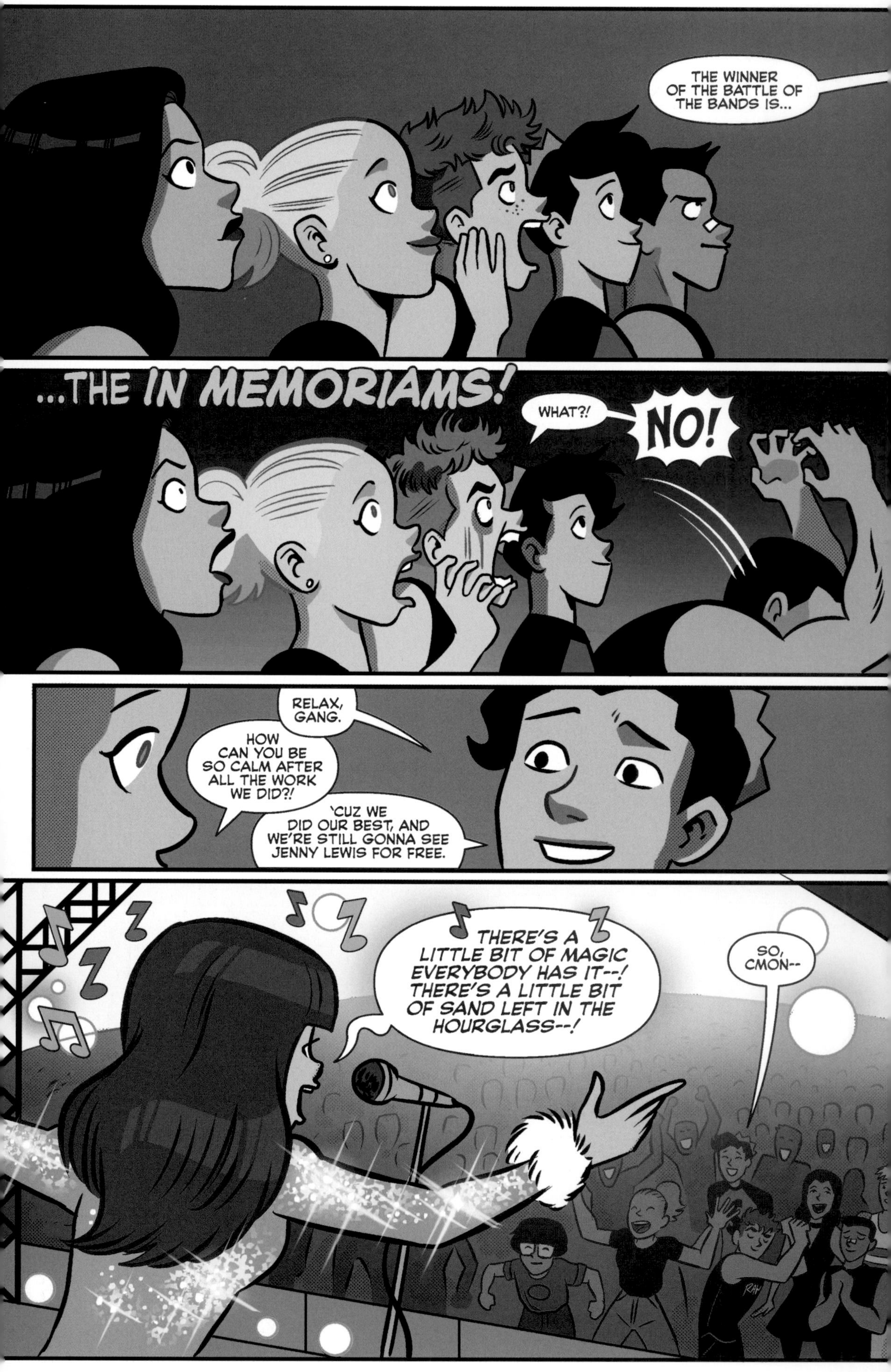
THE WINNER OF THE BATTLE OF THE BANDS IS...
...THE IN MEMORIAMS!
WHAT?!
NO!
RELAX, GANG.
HOW CAN YOU BE SO CALM AFTER ALL THE WORK WE DID?!
'CUZ WE DID OUR BEST, AND WE'RE STILL GONNA SEE JENNY LEWIS FOR FREE.
THERE'S A LITTLE BIT OF MAGIC EVERYBODY HAS IT--! THERE'S A LITTLE BIT OF SAND LEFT IN THE HOURGLASS--!
SO, CMON--

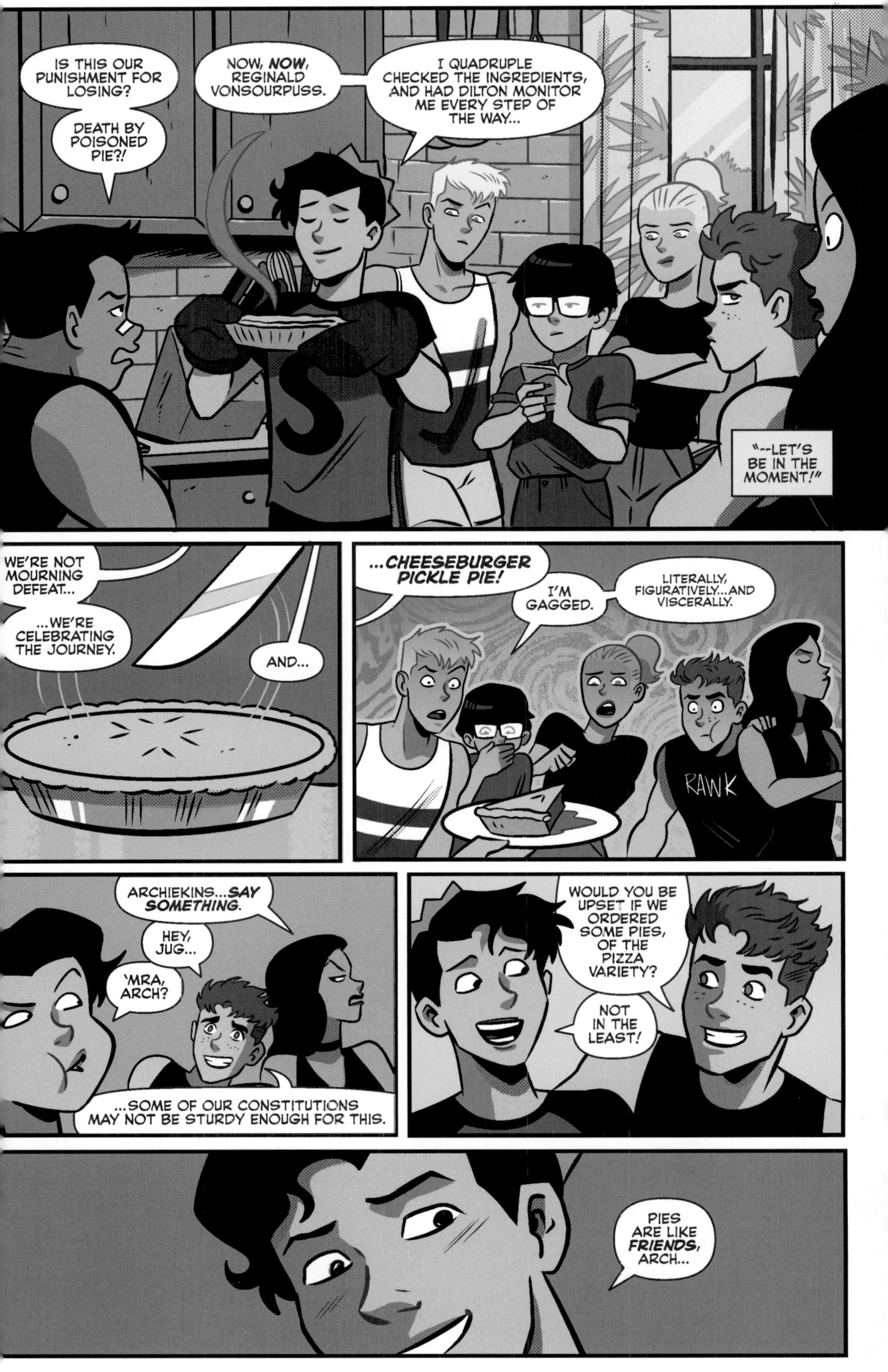
IS THIS OUR PUNISHMENT FOR LOSING?
DEATH BY POISONED PIE?!
NOW, *NOW*, REGINALD VONSOURPUSS.
I QUADRUPLE CHECKED THE INGREDIENTS, AND HAD DILTON MONITOR ME EVERY STEP OF THE WAY...
"--LET'S BE IN THE MOMENT!"
WE'RE NOT MOURNING DEFEAT...
...WE'RE CELEBRATING THE JOURNEY.
AND...
...*CHEESEBURGER PICKLE PIE!*
I'M GAGGED.
LITERALLY, FIGURATIVELY...AND VISCERALLY.
RAWK
ARCHIEKINS...*SAY SOMETHING*.
HEY, JUG...
'MRA, ARCH?
...SOME OF OUR CONSTITUTIONS MAY NOT BE STURDY ENOUGH FOR THIS.
WOULD YOU BE UPSET IF WE ORDERED SOME PIES, OF THE PIZZA VARIETY?
NOT IN THE LEAST!
PIES ARE LIKE *FRIENDS*, ARCH...

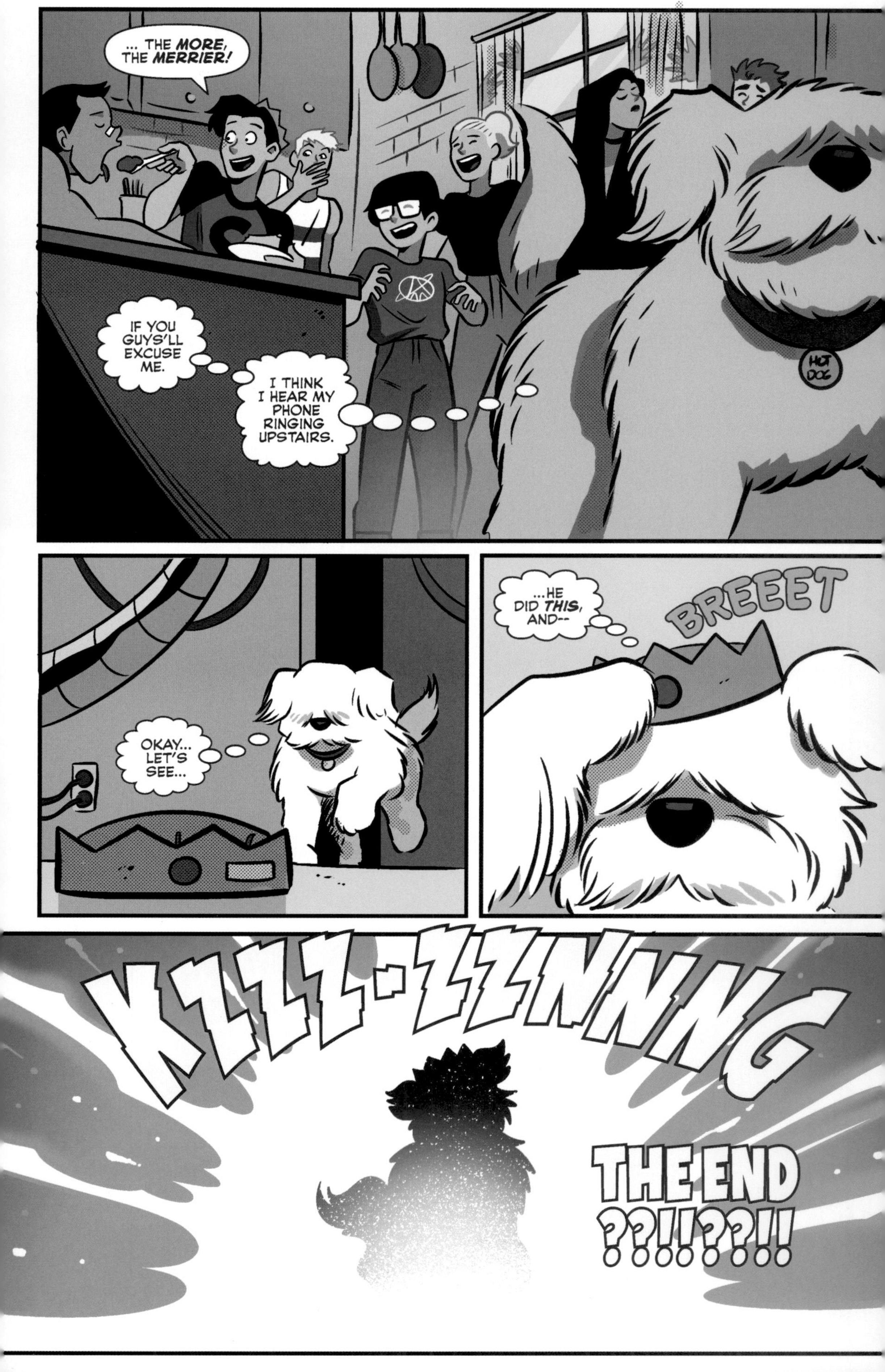
... THE MORE, THE MERRIER!
IF YOU GUYS'LL EXCUSE ME.
I THINK I HEAR MY PHONE RINGING UPSTAIRS.
HOT DOG
OKAY... LET'S SEE...
...HE DID THIS, AND--
BREEET
KZZZZ-ZZNNNG
THE END ??!!??!!

VARIANT COVERY GALLERY

ISSUE 1

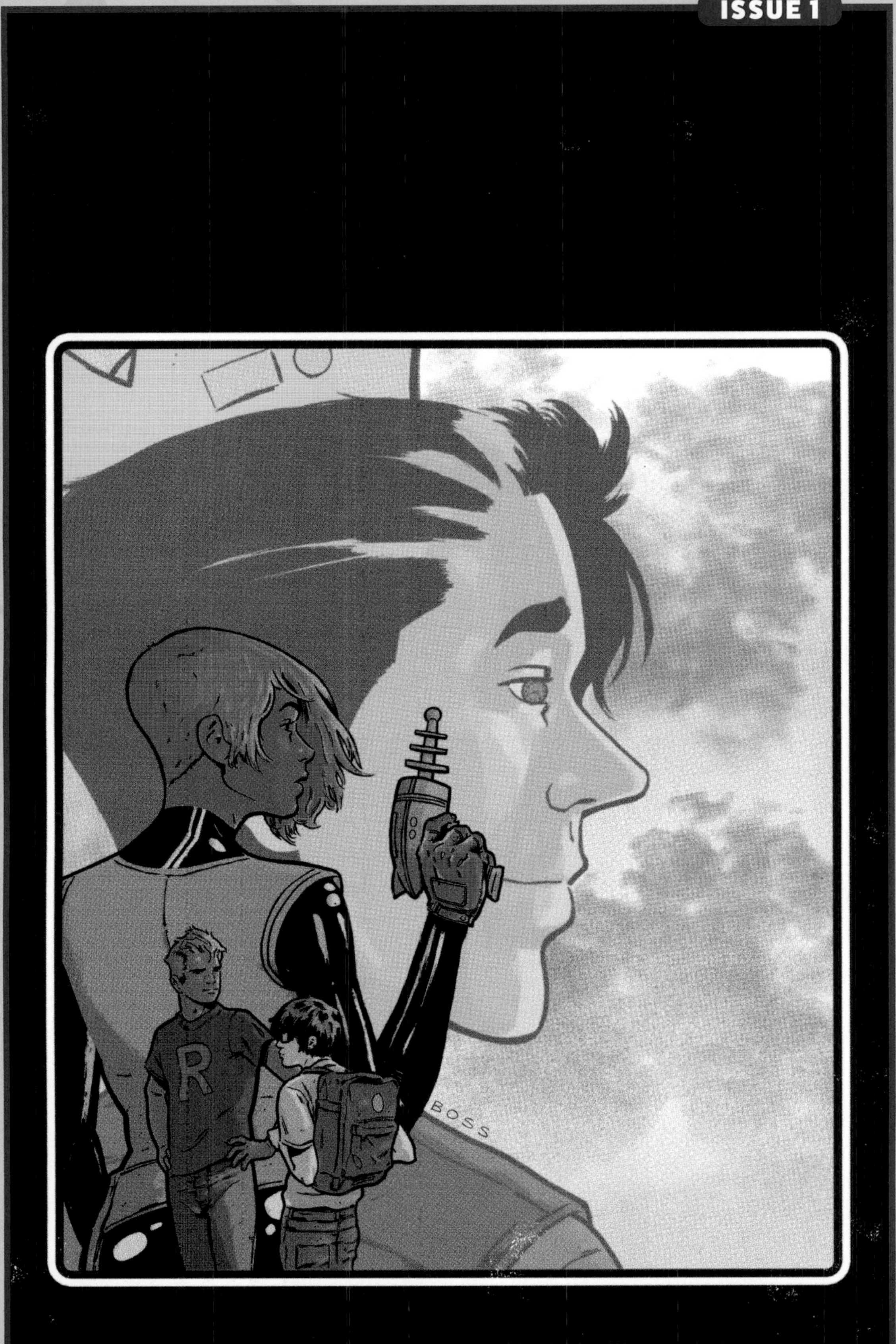

R
BOSS

ART BY TYLER BOSS

ISSUE 1

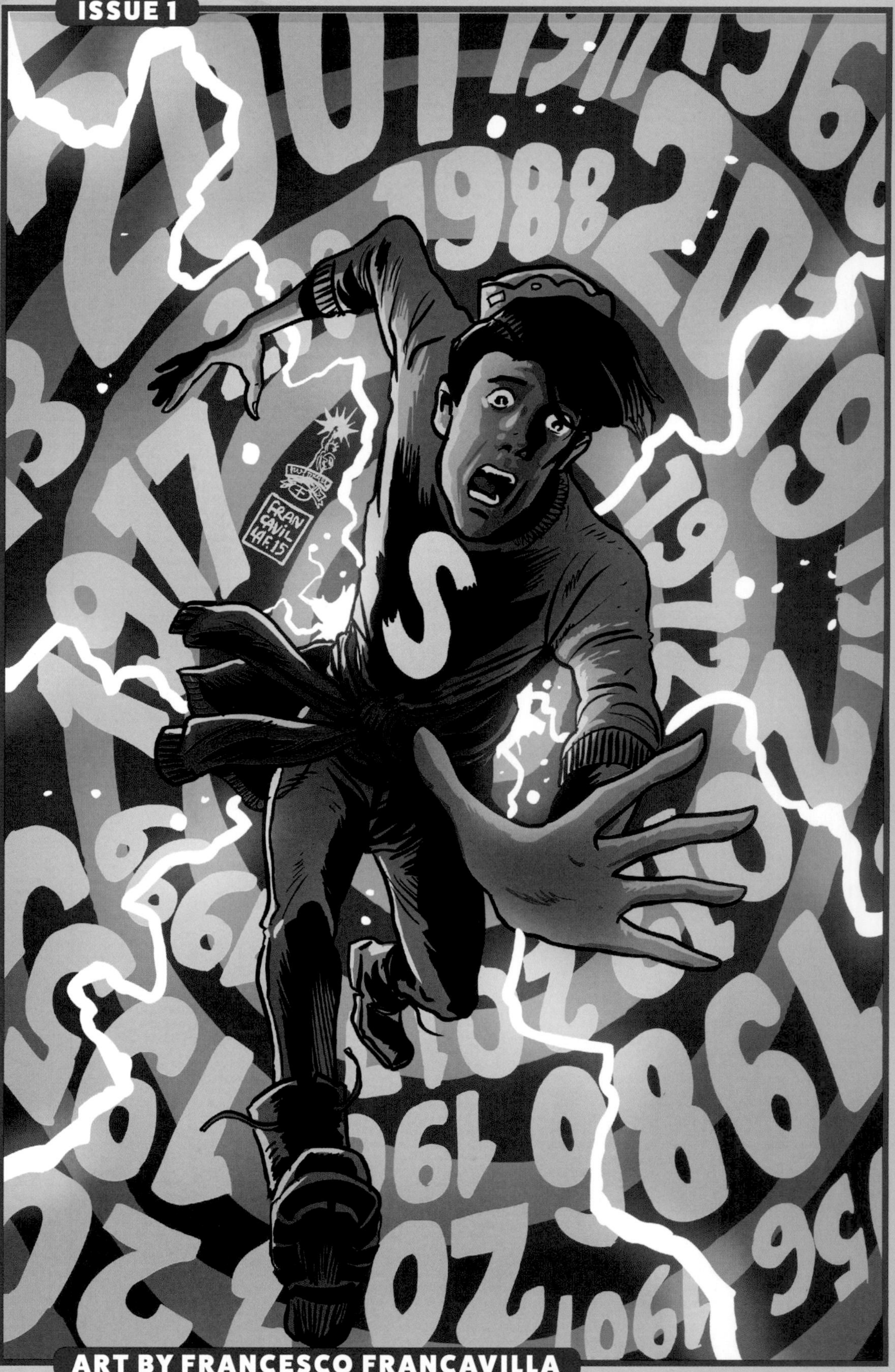
1988

ART BY FRANCESCO FRANCAVILLA

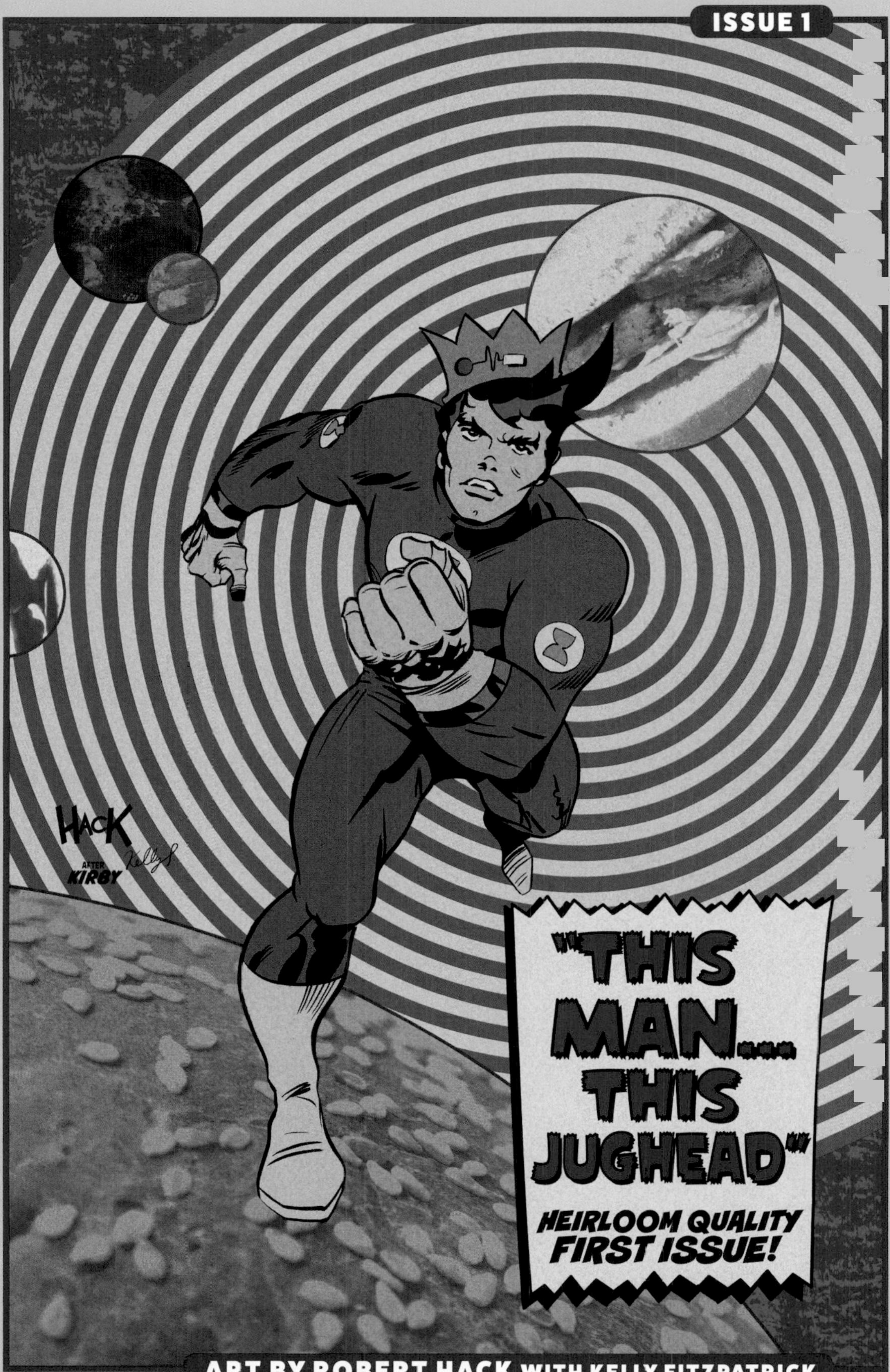
ISSUE 1
HACK
AFTER KIRBY
"THIS MAN... THIS JUGHEAD"
HEIRLOOM QUALITY FIRST ISSUE!
ART BY ROBERT HACK WITH KELLY FITZPATRICK

ISSUE 1

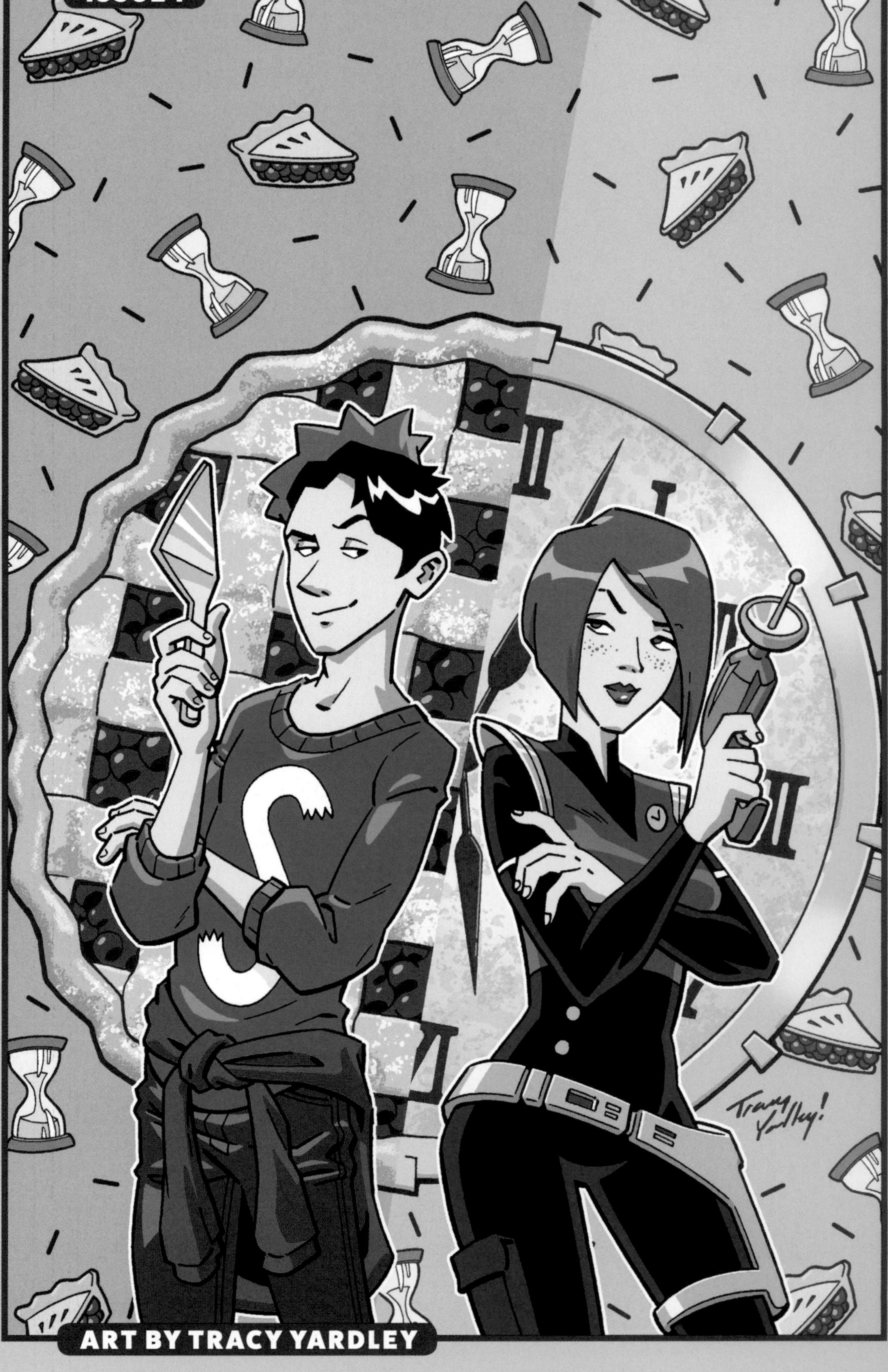

Tracy Yardley!

ART BY TRACY YARDLEY

ISSUE 1 (RETAILER VARIANT: PHAT COLLECTIBLES, ANAHEIM, CALIFORNIA)

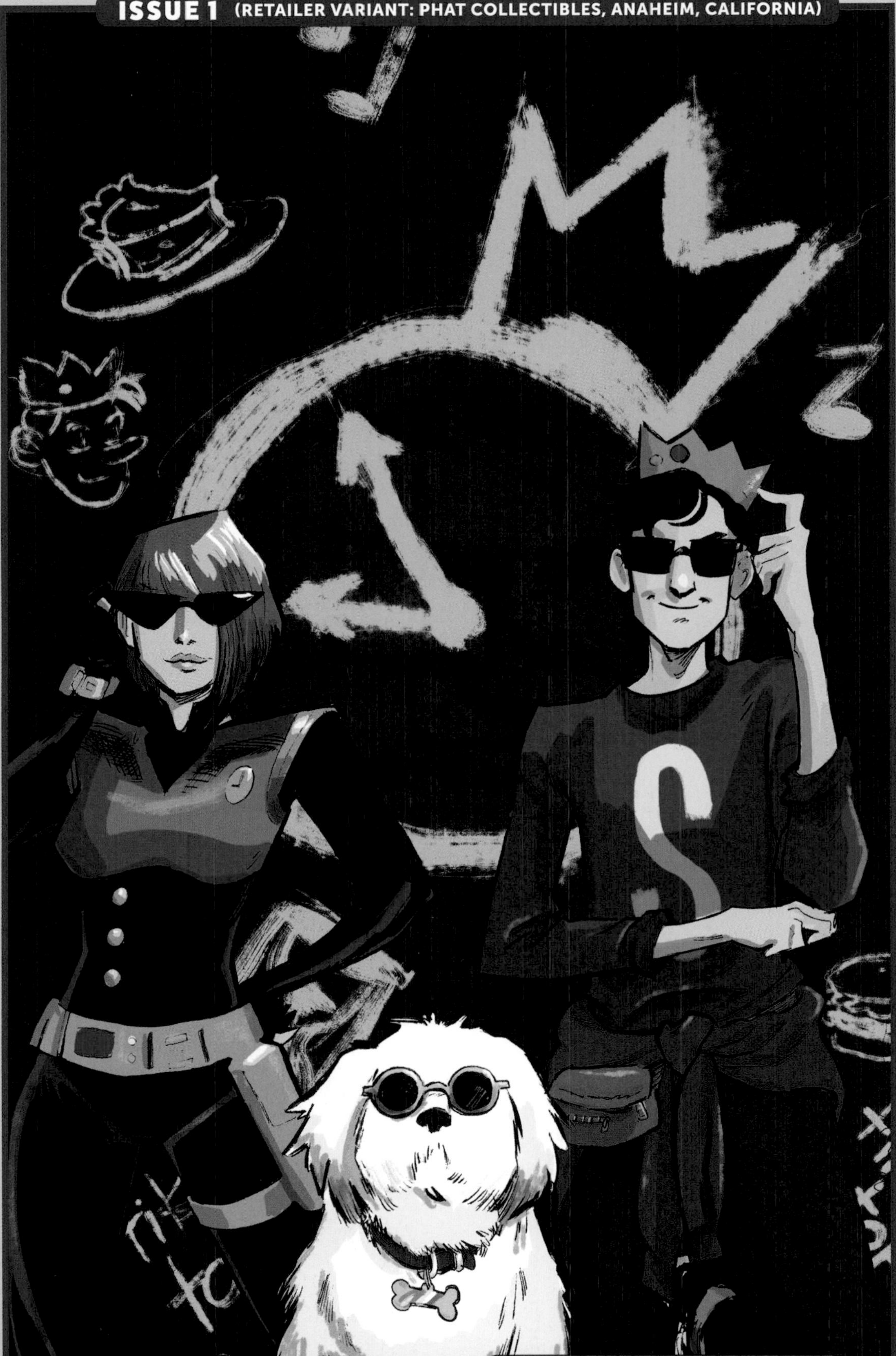

ART BY SINA GRACE

ISSUE 2

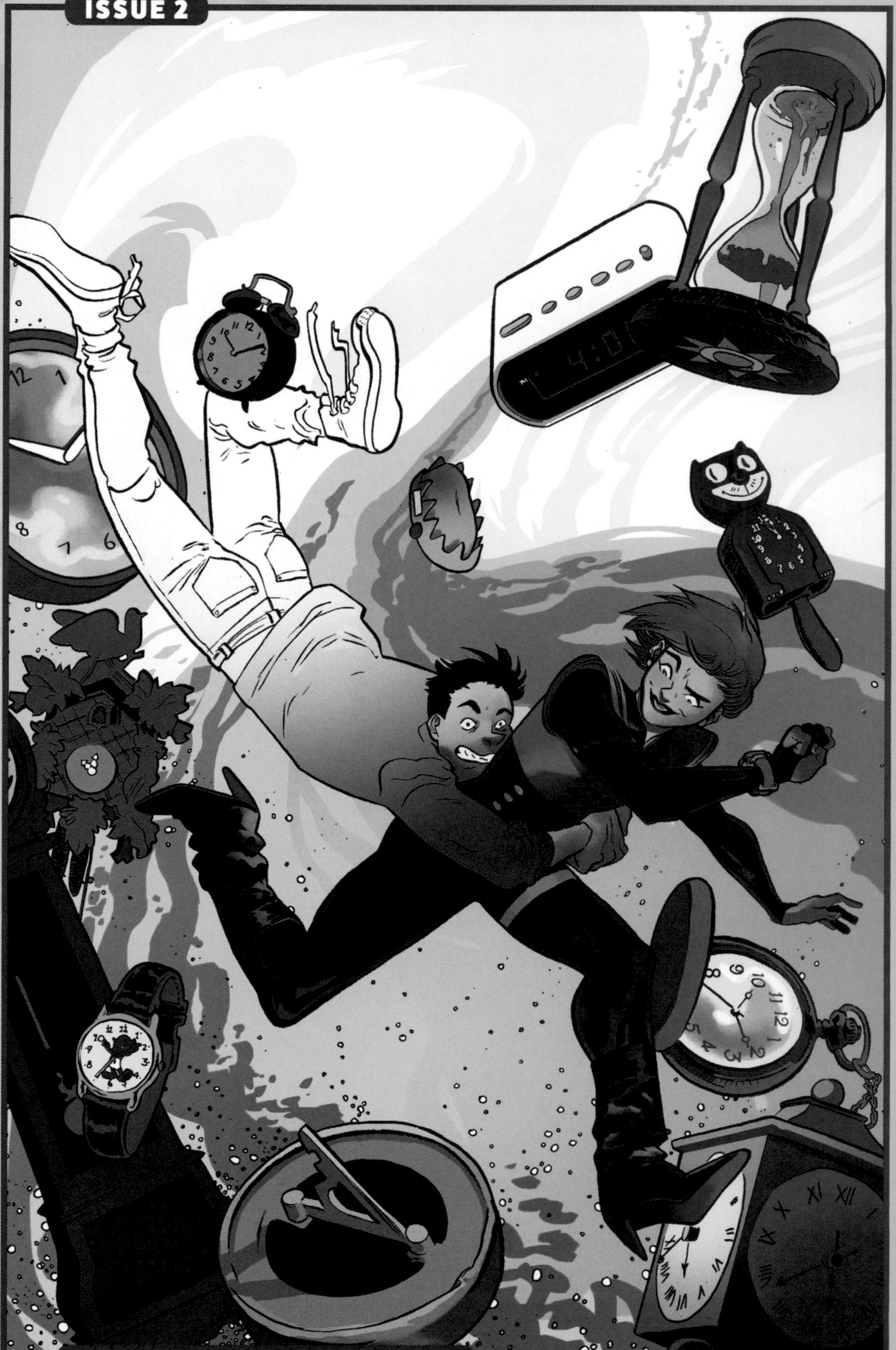

ART BY ERICA HENDERSON

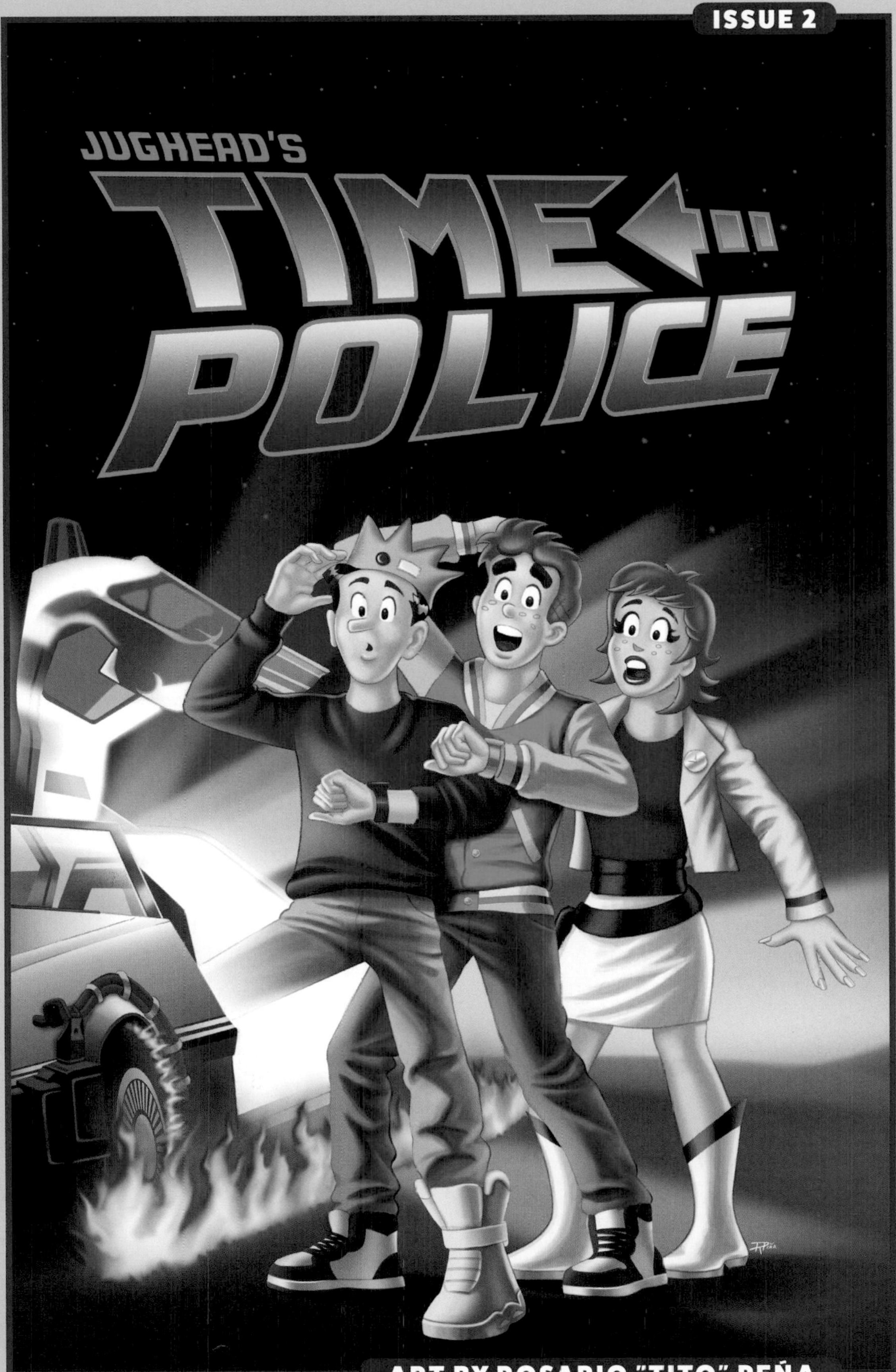
ISSUE 2
JUGHEAD'S
TIME POLICE
ART BY ROSARIO "TITO" PEÑA

ISSUE 3

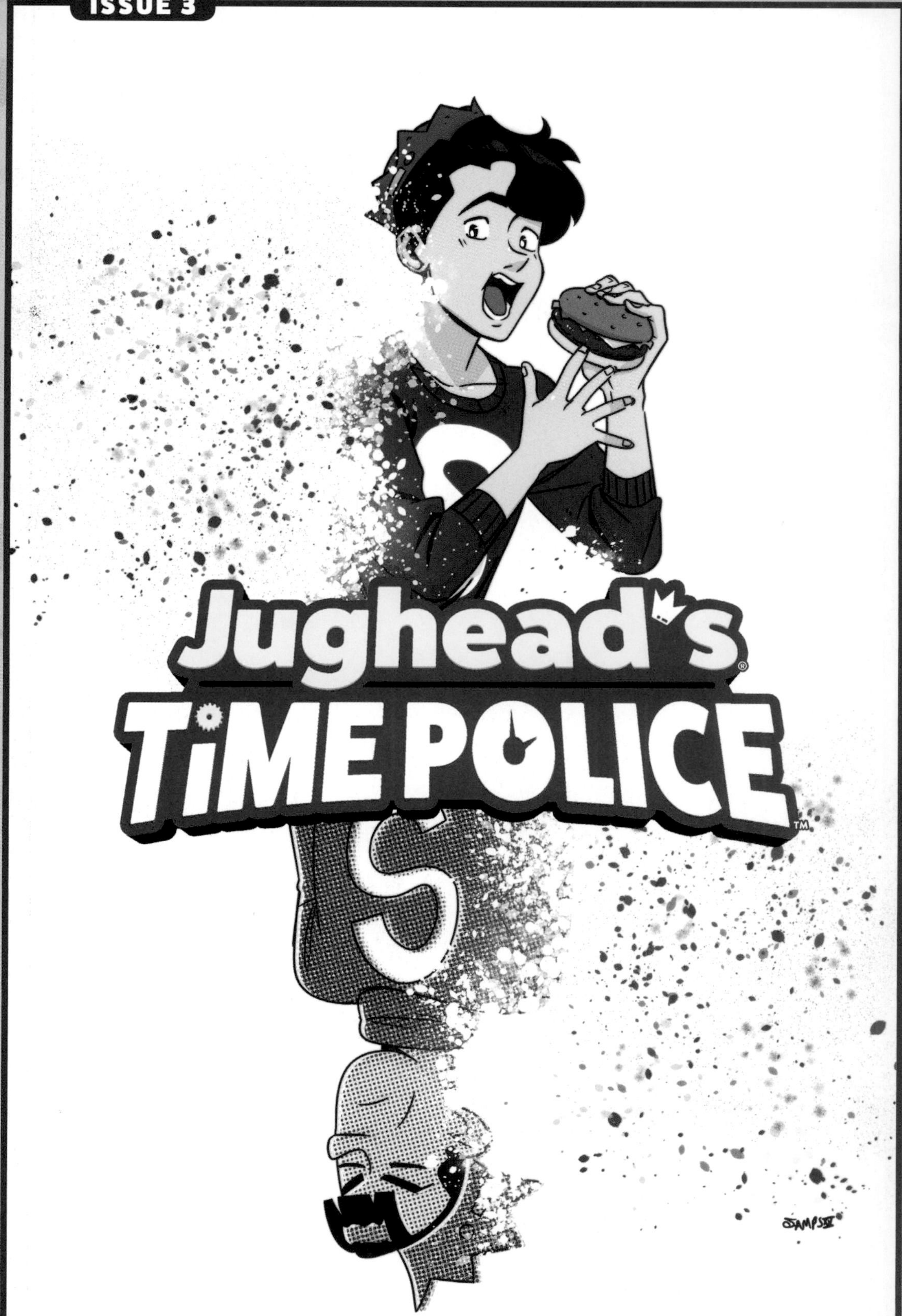
Jughead's
TIME POLICE
JAMPS

ART BY RYAN JAMPOLE

ISSUE 3

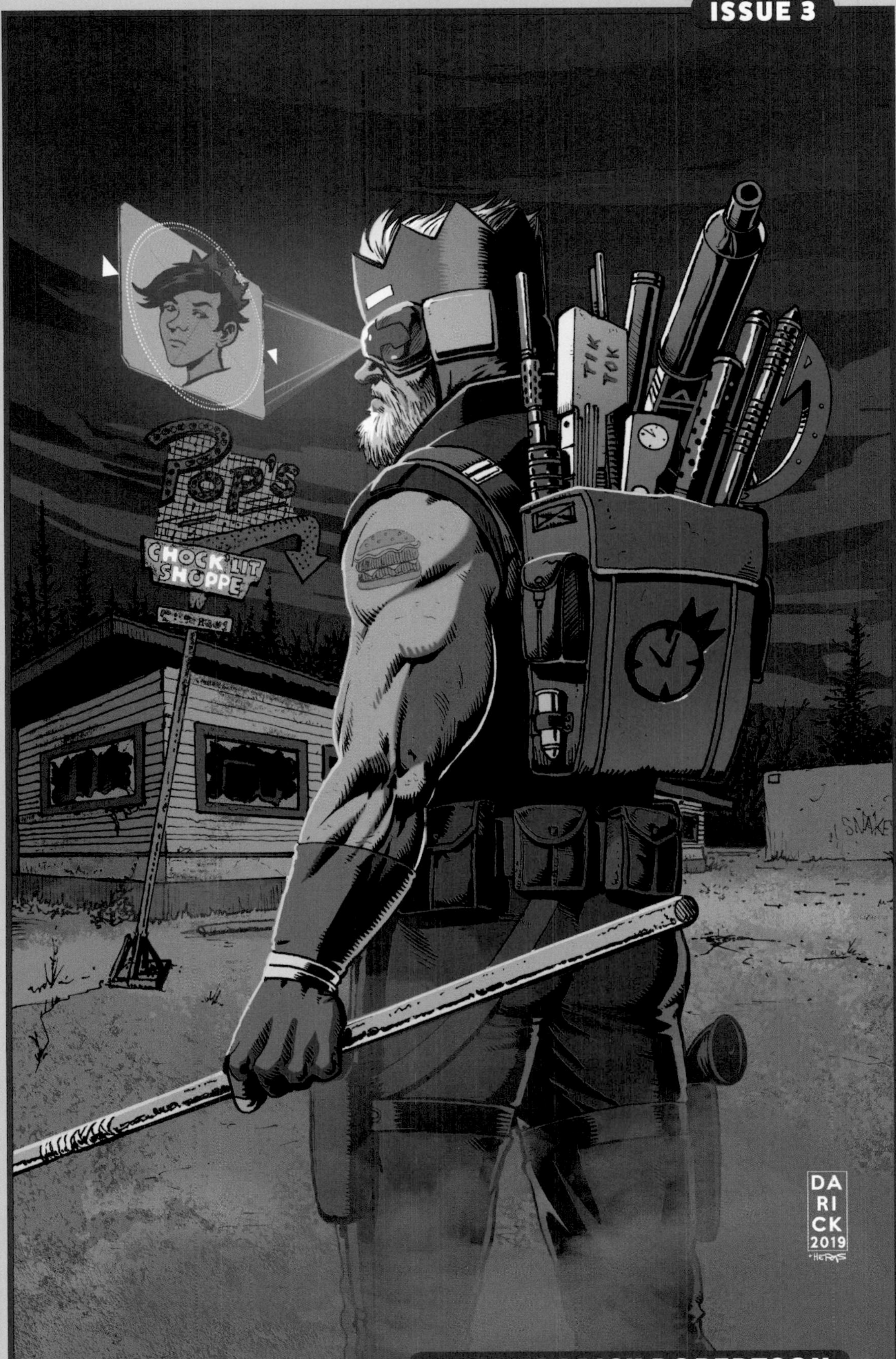
Pop's
CHOCK'LIT SHOPPE
TIK TOK
SNAKE
DA RI CK 2019

ART BY DARICK ROBERTSON

ISSUE 4

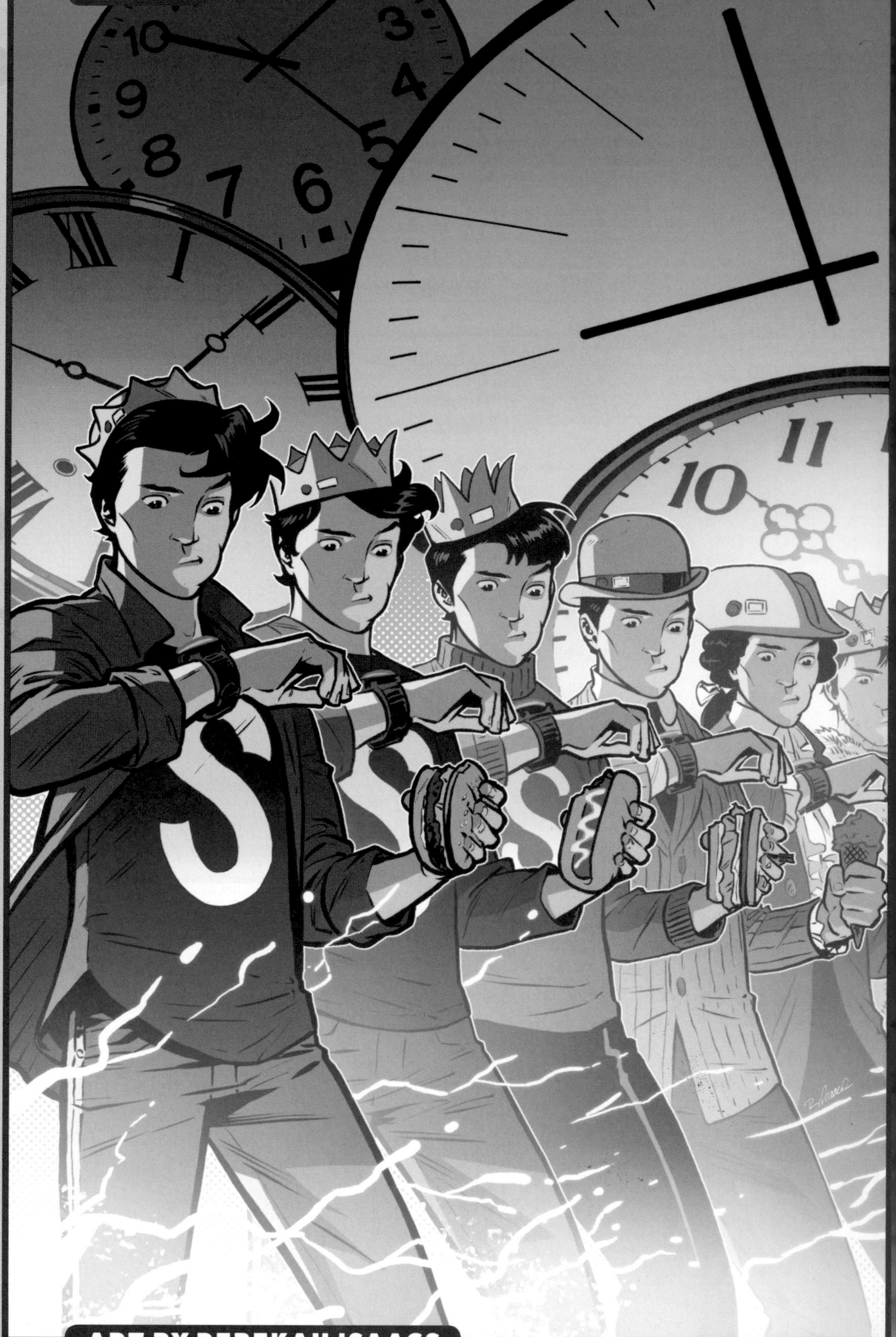

ART BY REBEKAH ISAACS

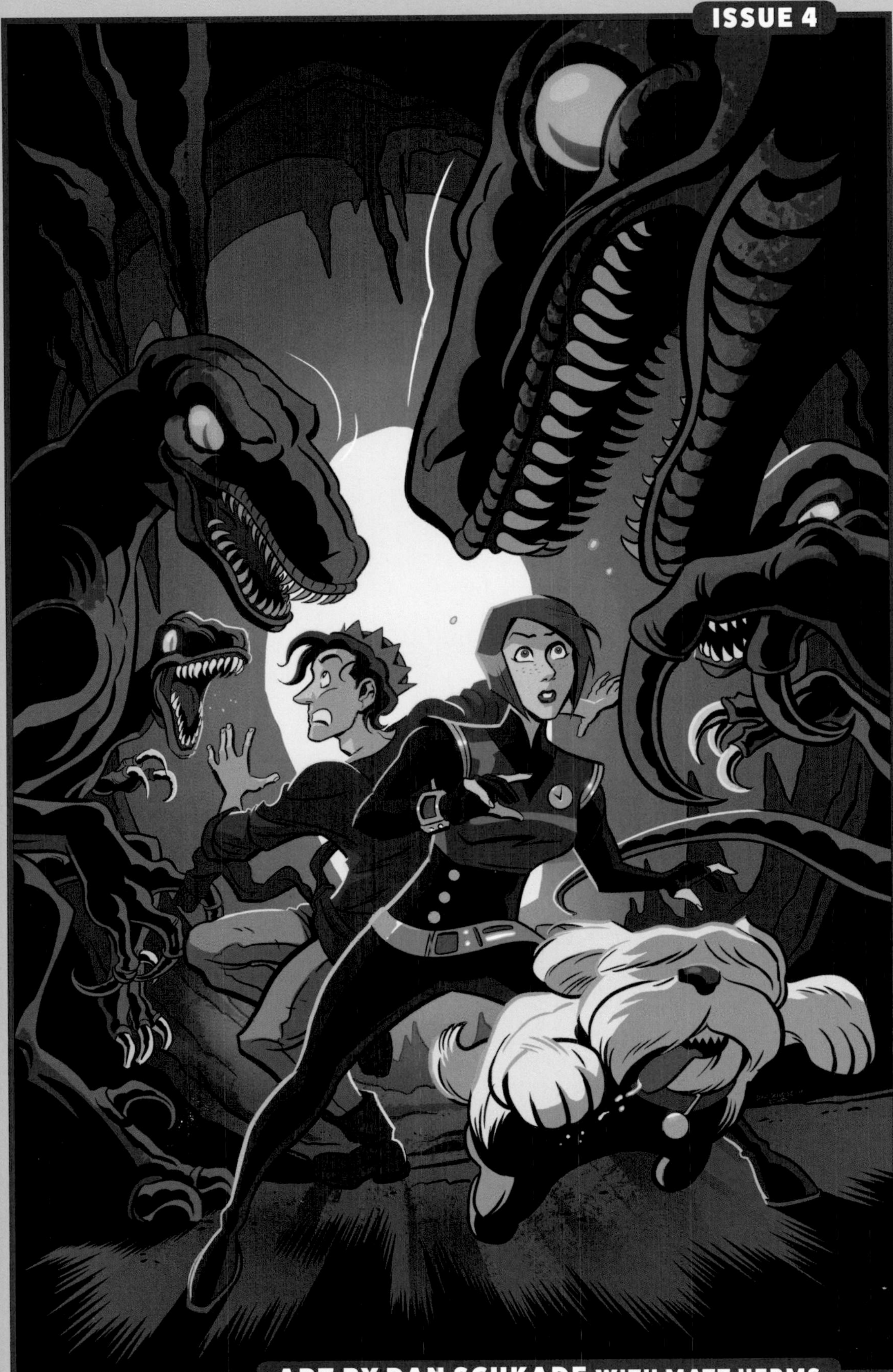
ISSUE 4
ART BY DAN SCHKADE WITH MATT HERMS

ISSUE 5

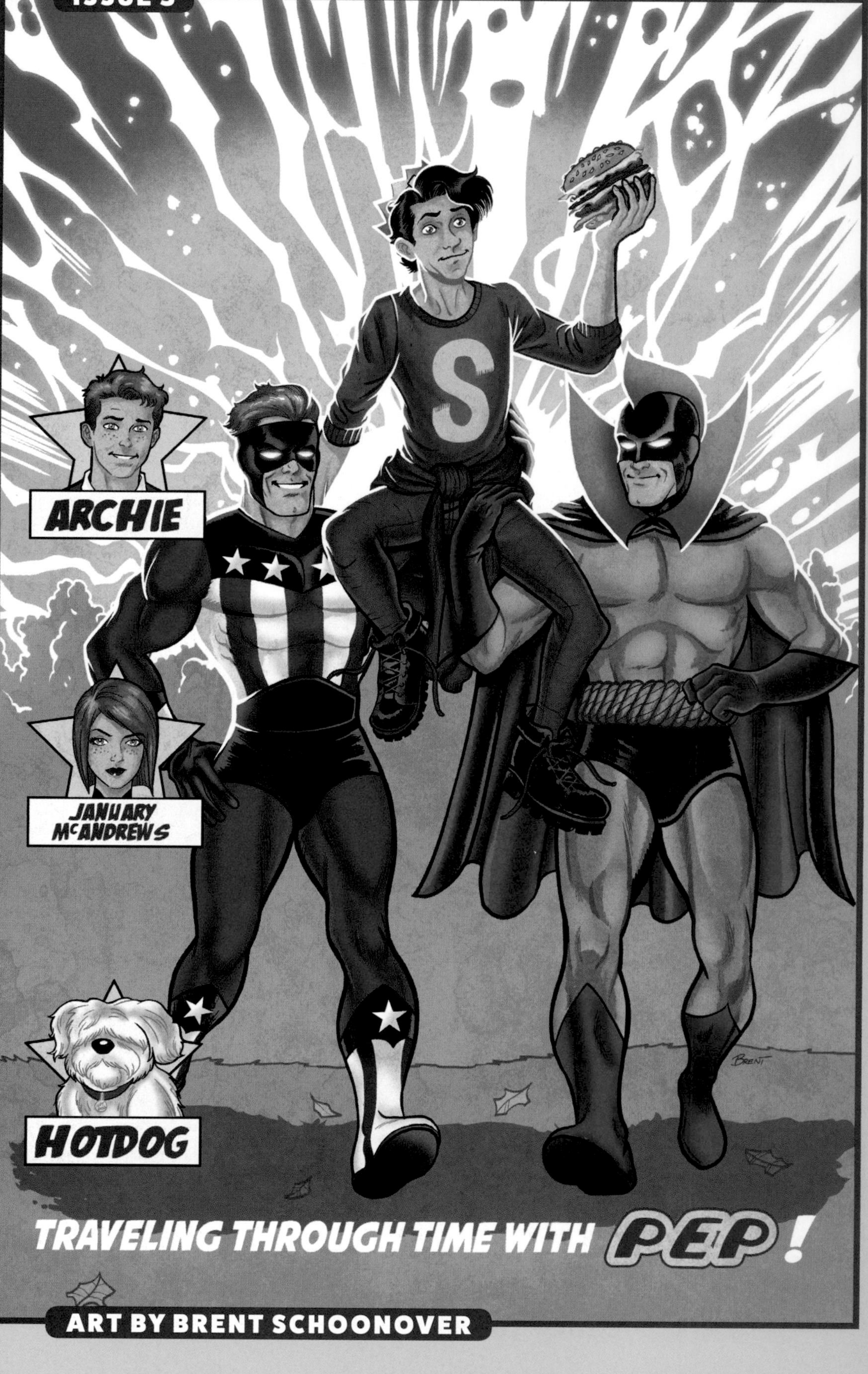
ARCHIE
JANUARY McANDREWS
HOTDOG
BRENT
TRAVELING THROUGH TIME WITH PEP!

ART BY BRENT SCHOONOVER

ISSUE 5

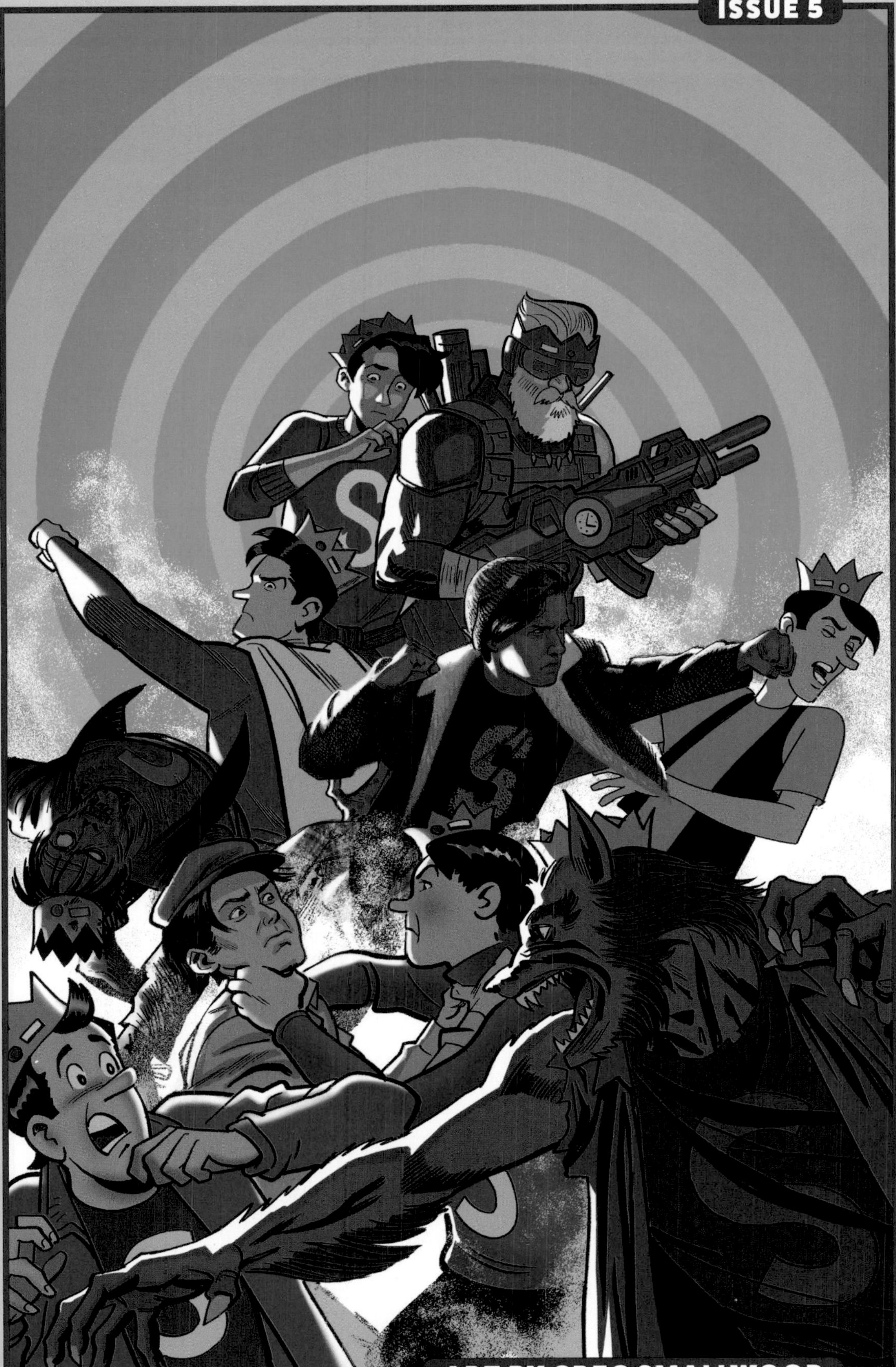

ART BY GREG SMALLWOOD

BONUS COMIC: BACK FROM THE FUTURE

Originally printed in ARCHIE GIANT SERIES #590, October 1988

SCRIPT: RICH MARGOPOULOS PENCILS: REX LINDSEY INKS: JON D'AGOSTINO
LETTERING: BILL YOSHIDA COLORS: BARRY GROSSMAN

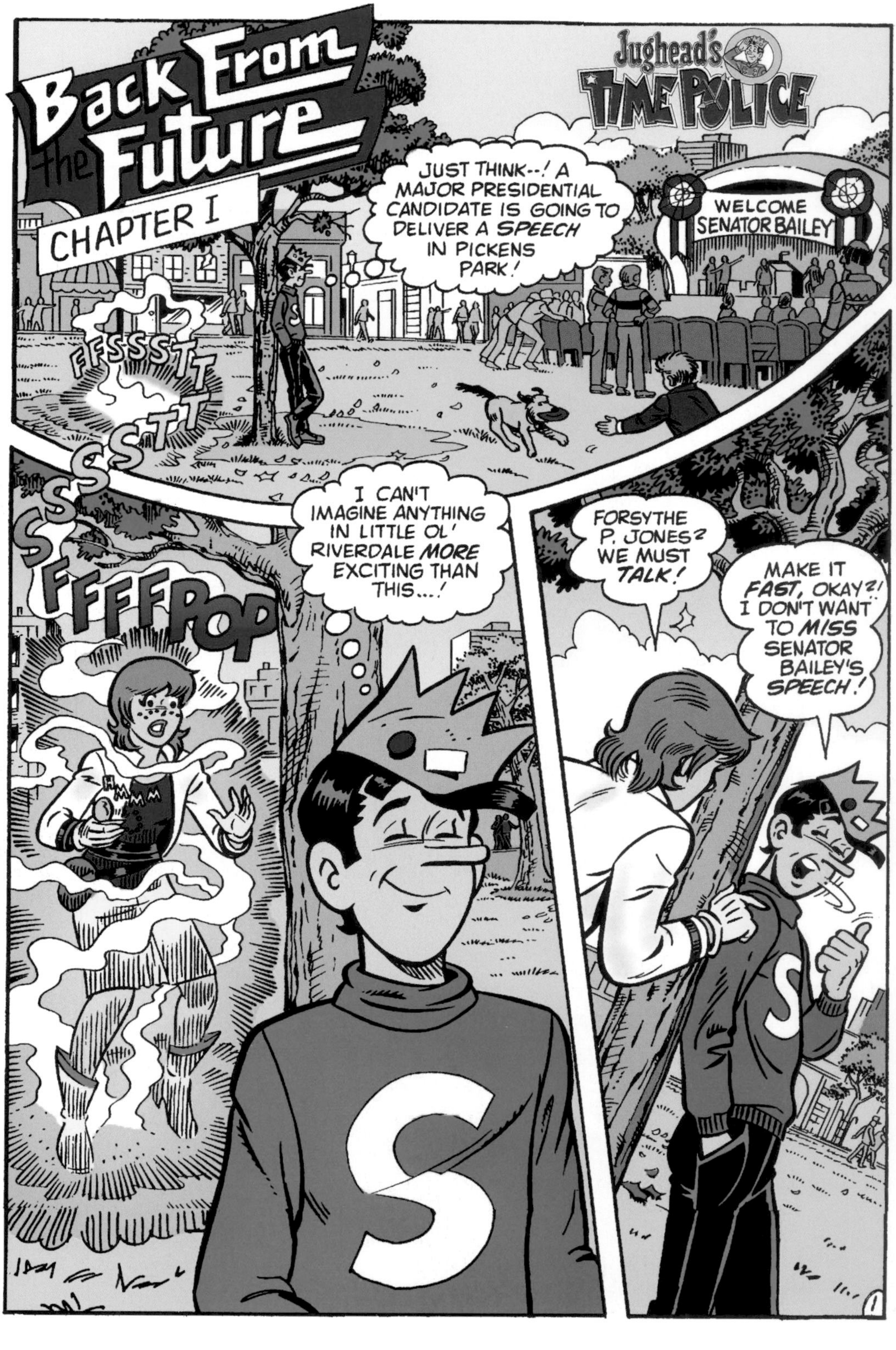

Back From the Future
Jughead's TIME POLICE
CHAPTER I
JUST THINK--! A MAJOR PRESIDENTIAL CANDIDATE IS GOING TO DELIVER A SPEECH IN PICKENS PARK!
WELCOME SENATOR BAILEY
FFSSSSTT
SSSTT
SSS
FFFFPOP
I CAN'T IMAGINE ANYTHING IN LITTLE OL' RIVERDALE MORE EXCITING THAN THIS...!
FORSYTHE P. JONES? WE MUST TALK!
MAKE IT FAST, OKAY?! I DON'T WANT TO MISS SENATOR BAILEY'S SPEECH!
1

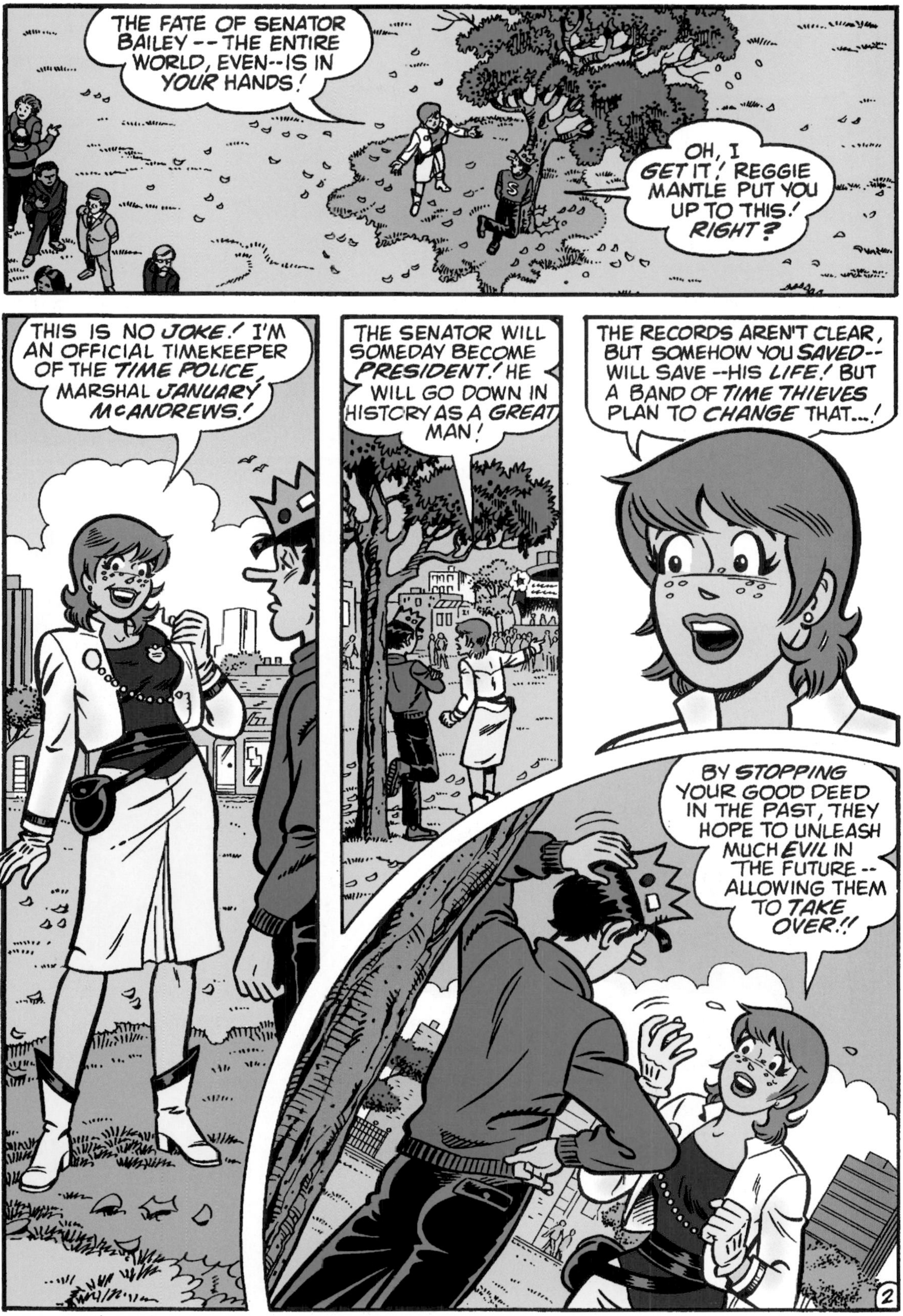
THE FATE OF SENATOR BAILEY -- THE ENTIRE WORLD, EVEN--IS IN YOUR HANDS!
OH, I GET IT! REGGIE MANTLE PUT YOU UP TO THIS! RIGHT?
THIS IS NO JOKE! I'M AN OFFICIAL TIMEKEEPER OF THE TIME POLICE, MARSHAL JANUARY McANDREWS!
THE SENATOR WILL SOMEDAY BECOME PRESIDENT! HE WILL GO DOWN IN HISTORY AS A GREAT MAN!
THE RECORDS AREN'T CLEAR, BUT SOMEHOW YOU SAVED-- WILL SAVE --HIS LIFE! BUT A BAND OF TIME THIEVES PLAN TO CHANGE THAT...!
BY STOPPING YOUR GOOD DEED IN THE PAST, THEY HOPE TO UNLEASH MUCH EVIL IN THE FUTURE -- ALLOWING THEM TO TAKE OVER!!

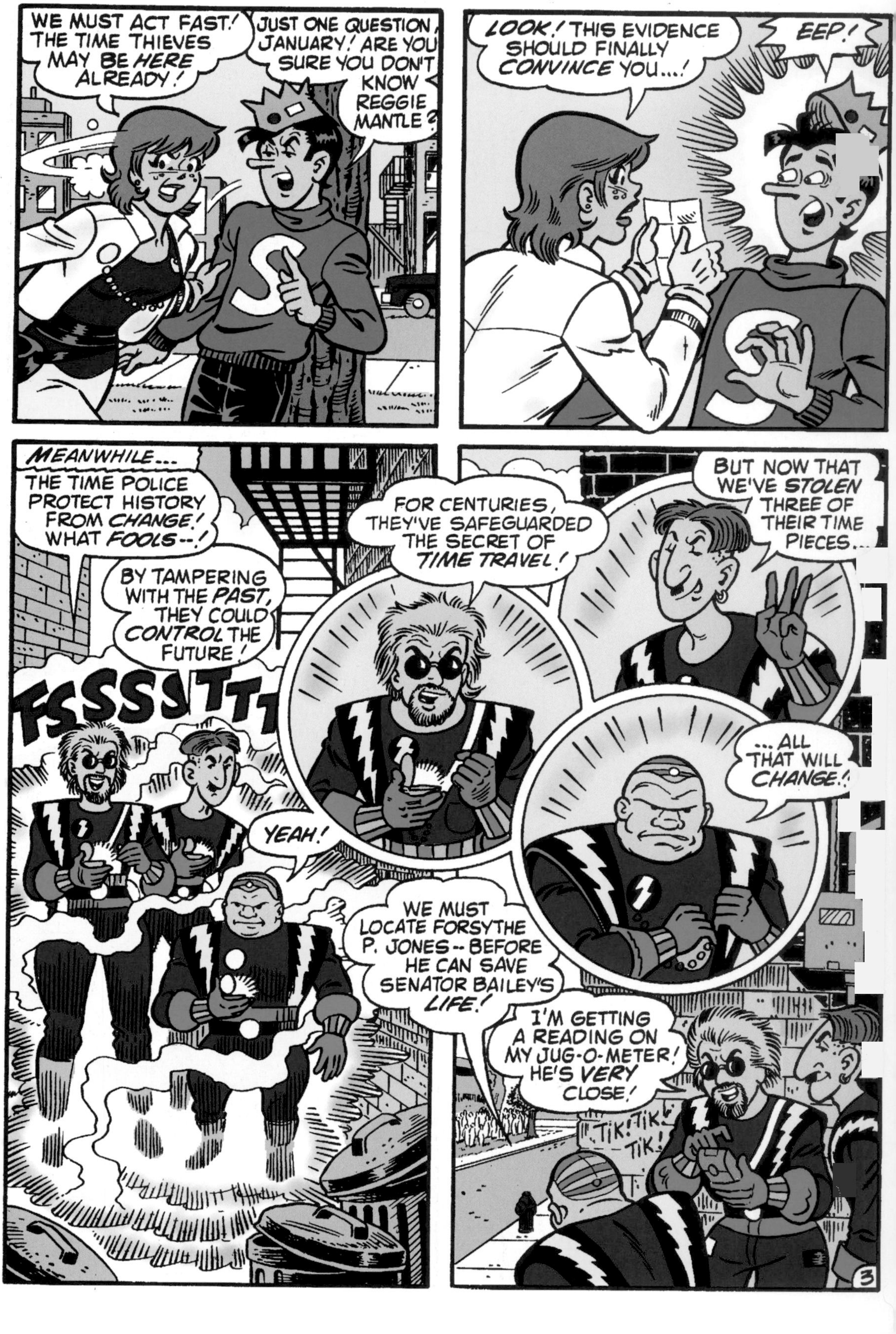

WE MUST ACT FAST! THE TIME THIEVES MAY BE HERE ALREADY!
JUST ONE QUESTION, JANUARY! ARE YOU SURE YOU DON'T KNOW REGGIE MANTLE?
LOOK! THIS EVIDENCE SHOULD FINALLY CONVINCE YOU...!
EEP!
MEANWHILE...
THE TIME POLICE PROTECT HISTORY FROM CHANGE! WHAT FOOLS--!
BY TAMPERING WITH THE PAST, THEY COULD CONTROL THE FUTURE!
FSSSTTT
YEAH!
FOR CENTURIES, THEY'VE SAFEGUARDED THE SECRET OF TIME TRAVEL!
BUT NOW THAT WE'VE STOLEN THREE OF THEIR TIME PIECES...
...ALL THAT WILL CHANGE!
WE MUST LOCATE FORSYTHE P. JONES--BEFORE HE CAN SAVE SENATOR BAILEY'S LIFE!
I'M GETTING A READING ON MY JUG-O-METER! HE'S VERY CLOSE!
TIK! TIK! TIK!

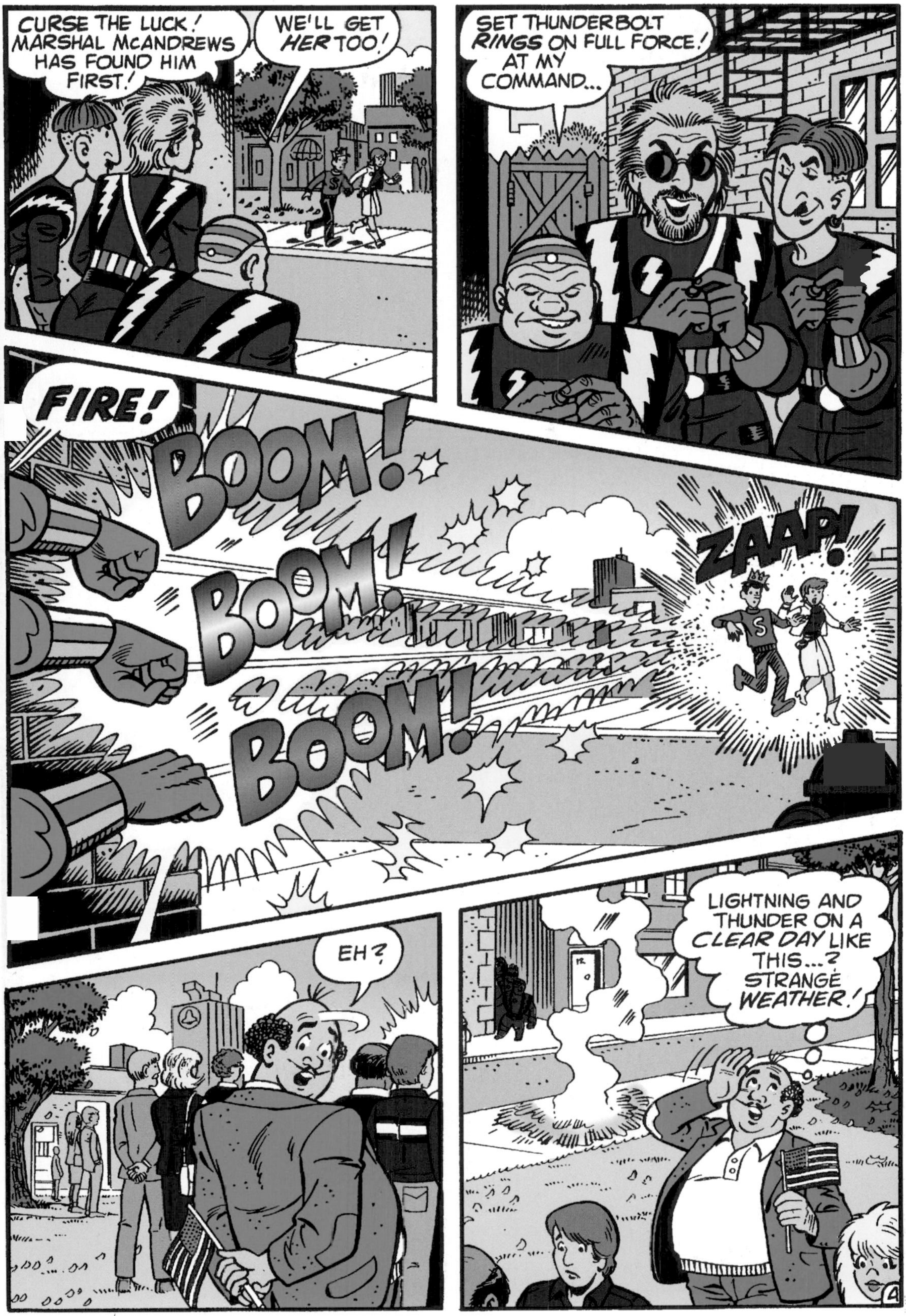

CURSE THE LUCK! MARSHAL McANDREWS HAS FOUND HIM FIRST!
WE'LL GET HER TOO!
SET THUNDERBOLT RINGS ON FULL FORCE! AT MY COMMAND...
FIRE!
BOOM!
BOOM!
BOOM!
ZAAP!
EH?
LIGHTNING AND THUNDER ON A CLEAR DAY LIKE THIS...? STRANGE WEATHER!
4

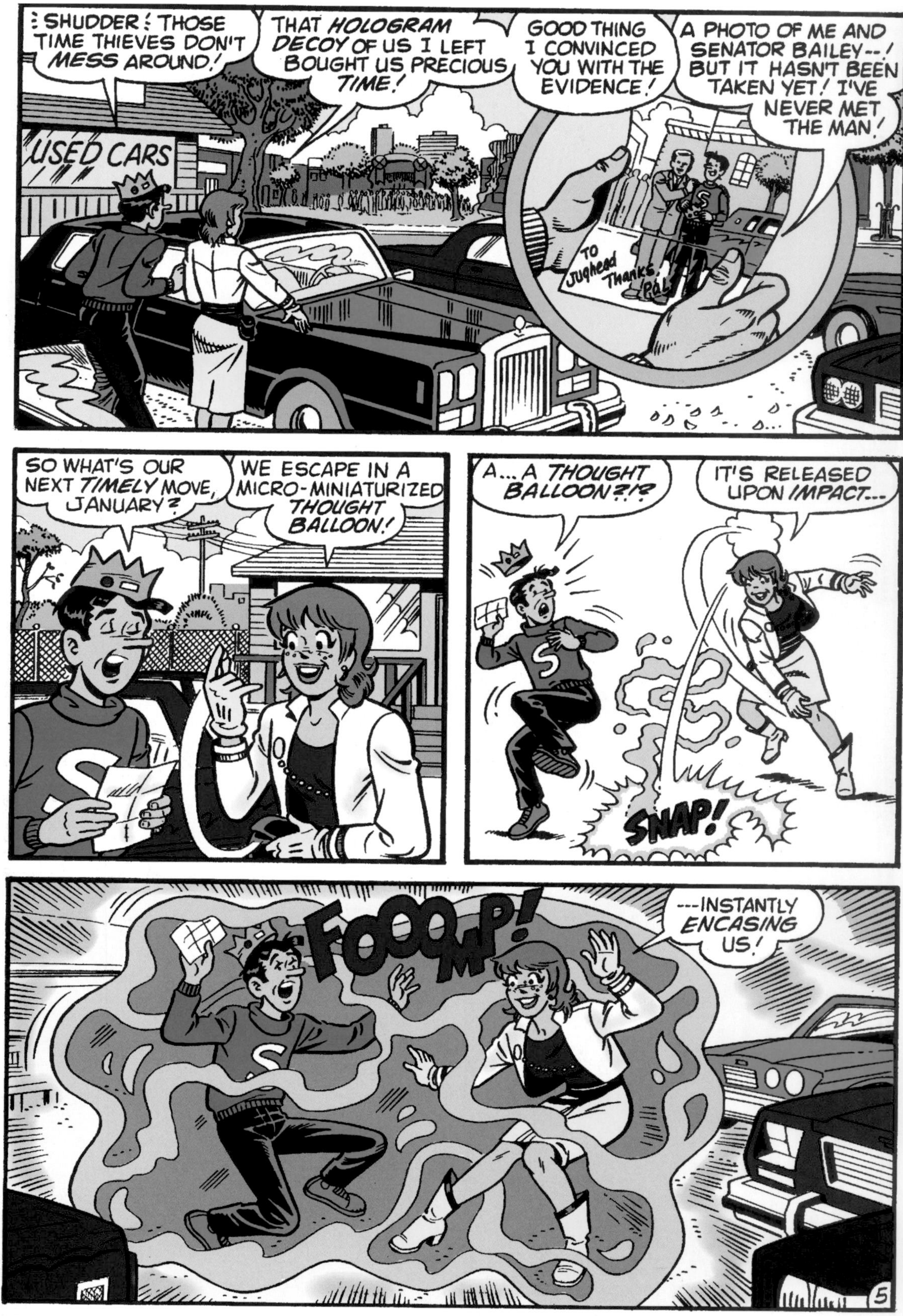
SHUDDER! THOSE TIME THIEVES DON'T MESS AROUND!
THAT HOLOGRAM DECOY OF US I LEFT BOUGHT US PRECIOUS TIME!
GOOD THING I CONVINCED YOU WITH THE EVIDENCE!
A PHOTO OF ME AND SENATOR BAILEY--! BUT IT HASN'T BEEN TAKEN YET! I'VE NEVER MET THE MAN!
USED CARS
TO Jughead Thanks PAL
SO WHAT'S OUR NEXT TIMELY MOVE, JANUARY?
WE ESCAPE IN A MICRO-MINIATURIZED THOUGHT BALLOON!
A... A THOUGHT BALLOON?!?
IT'S RELEASED UPON IMPACT...
SNAP!
FOOOMP!
---INSTANTLY ENCASING US!

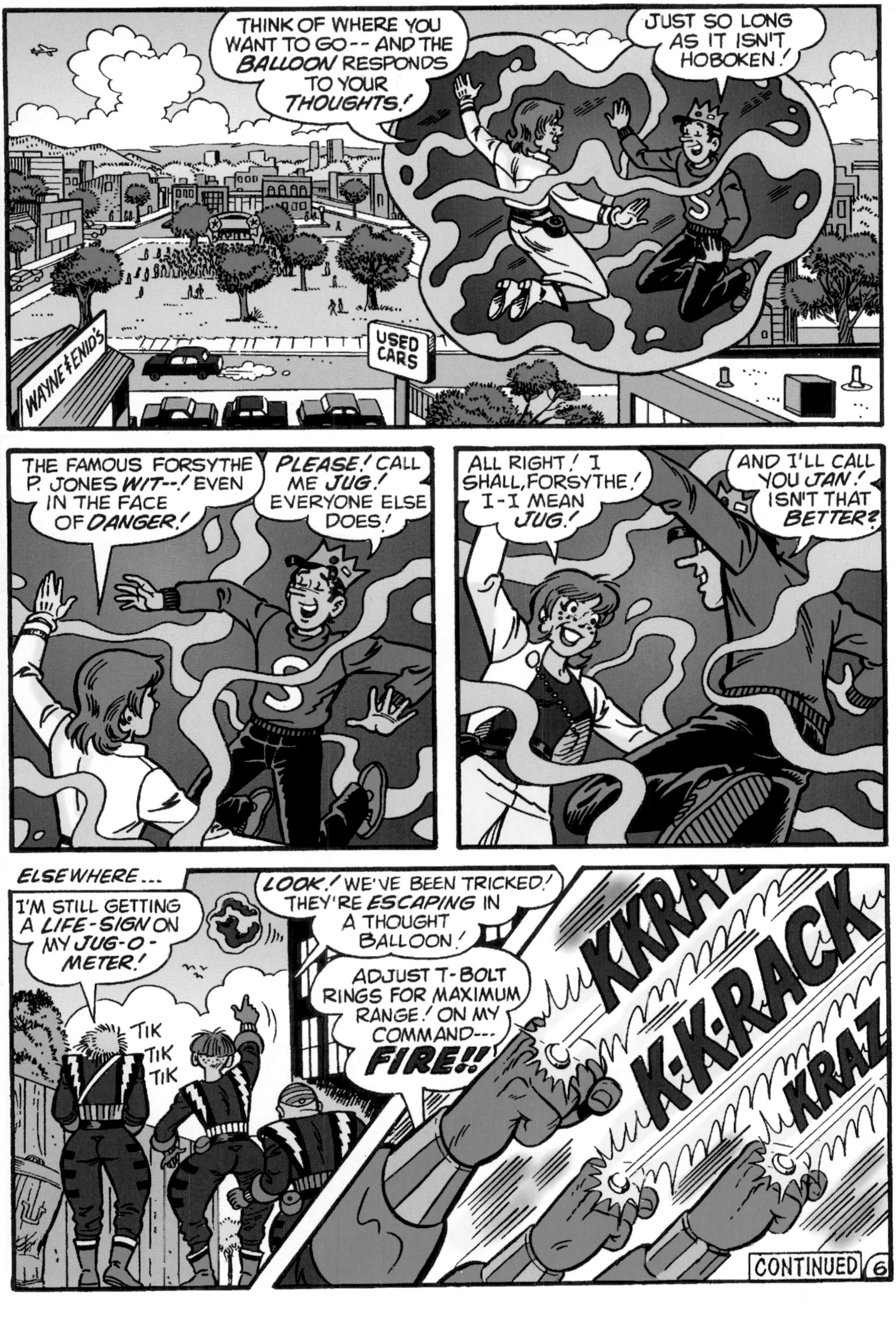
THINK OF WHERE YOU WANT TO GO-- AND THE BALLOON RESPONDS TO YOUR THOUGHTS!
JUST SO LONG AS IT ISN'T HOBOKEN!
WAYNE & ENID'S
USED CARS
THE FAMOUS FORSYTHE P. JONES WIT--! EVEN IN THE FACE OF DANGER!
PLEASE! CALL ME JUG! EVERYONE ELSE DOES!
ALL RIGHT! I SHALL, FORSYTHE! I-I MEAN JUG!
AND I'LL CALL YOU JAN! ISN'T THAT BETTER?
ELSEWHERE...
I'M STILL GETTING A LIFE-SIGN ON MY JUG-O-METER!
TIK TIK TIK
LOOK! WE'VE BEEN TRICKED! THEY'RE ESCAPING IN A THOUGHT BALLOON!
ADJUST T-BOLT RINGS FOR MAXIMUM RANGE! ON MY COMMAND--- FIRE!!
K-K-RACK
KRAZ
CONTINUED

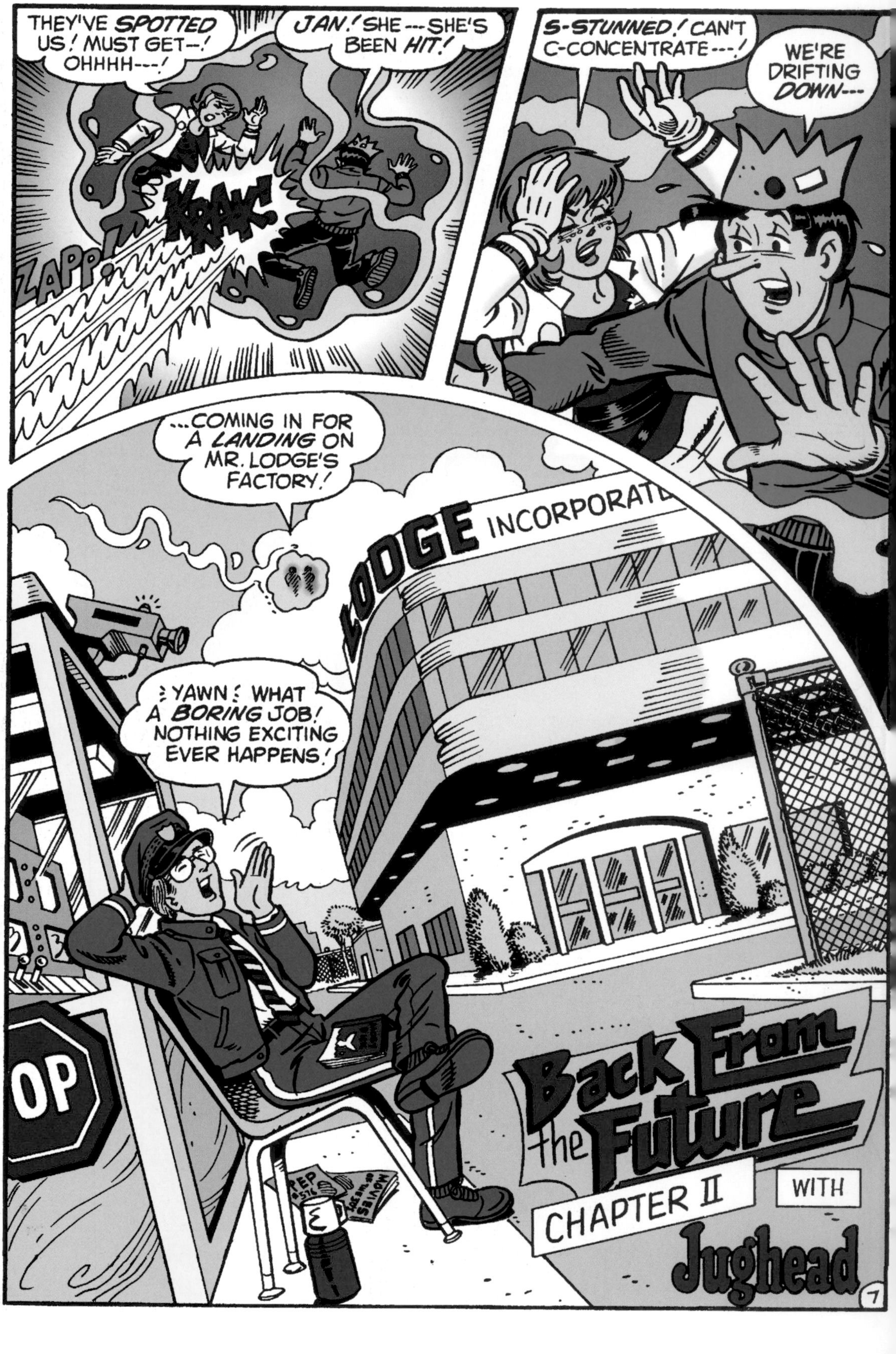
THEY'VE SPOTTED US! MUST GET--! OHHHH---!
JAN! SHE---SHE'S BEEN HIT!
ZAPP!
KRAK!
S-STUNNED! CAN'T C-CONCENTRATE---!
WE'RE DRIFTING DOWN---
...COMING IN FOR A LANDING ON MR. LODGE'S FACTORY!
LODGE INCORPORATE
YAWN WHAT A BORING JOB! NOTHING EXCITING EVER HAPPENS!
OP
Back From the Future
CHAPTER II
WITH
Jughead

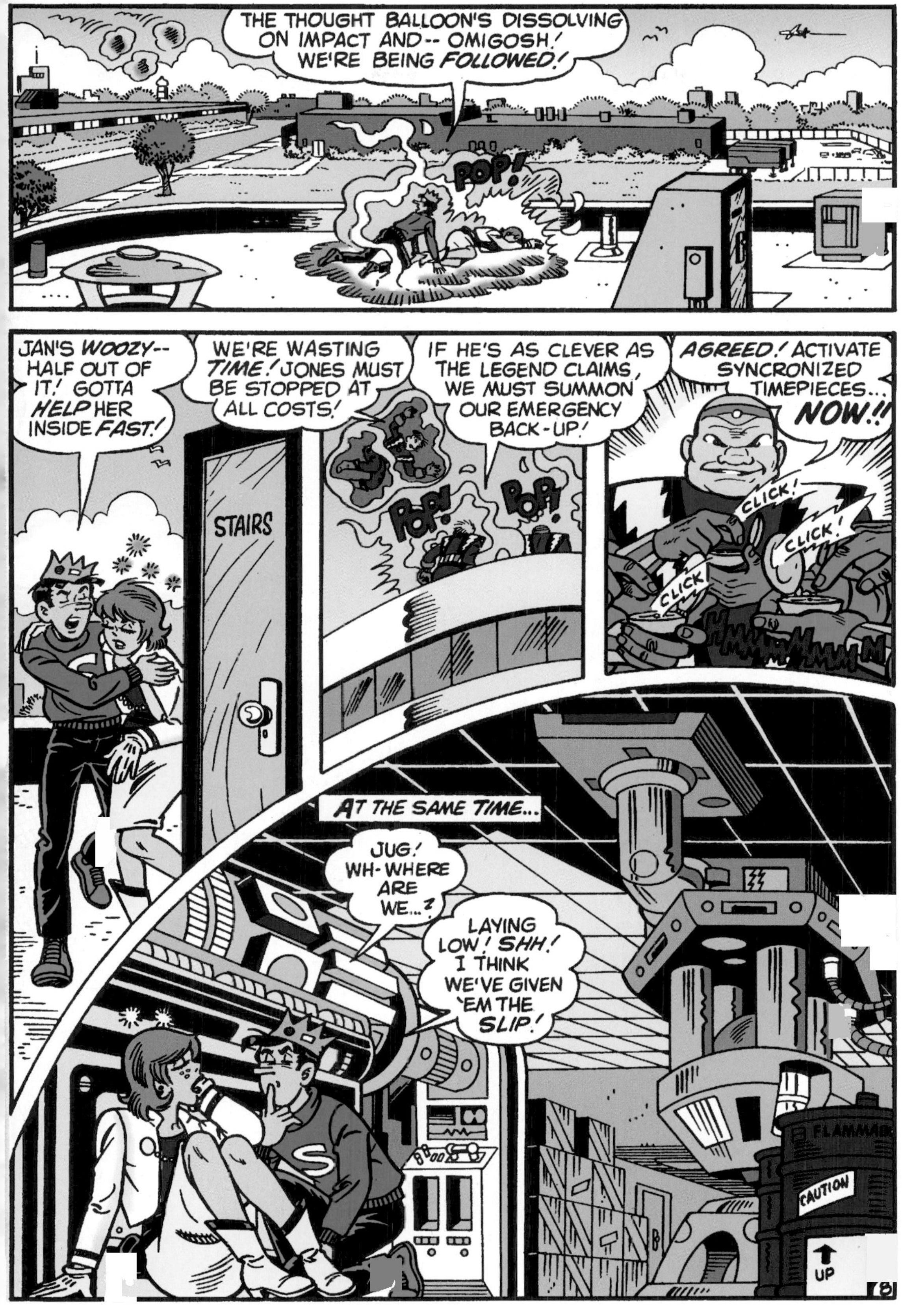
THE THOUGHT BALLOON'S DISSOLVING ON IMPACT AND -- OMIGOSH! WE'RE BEING FOLLOWED!
POP!
JAN'S WOOZY-- HALF OUT OF IT! GOTTA HELP HER INSIDE FAST!
STAIRS
WE'RE WASTING TIME! JONES MUST BE STOPPED AT ALL COSTS!
IF HE'S AS CLEVER AS THE LEGEND CLAIMS, WE MUST SUMMON OUR EMERGENCY BACK-UP!
POP!
POP!
AGREED! ACTIVATE SYNCRONIZED TIMEPIECES... NOW!!
CLICK!
CLICK!
CLICK
HMMMMMMMMM
AT THE SAME TIME...
JUG! WH-WHERE ARE WE...?
LAYING LOW! SHH! I THINK WE'VE GIVEN 'EM THE SLIP!
CAUTION
UP
8

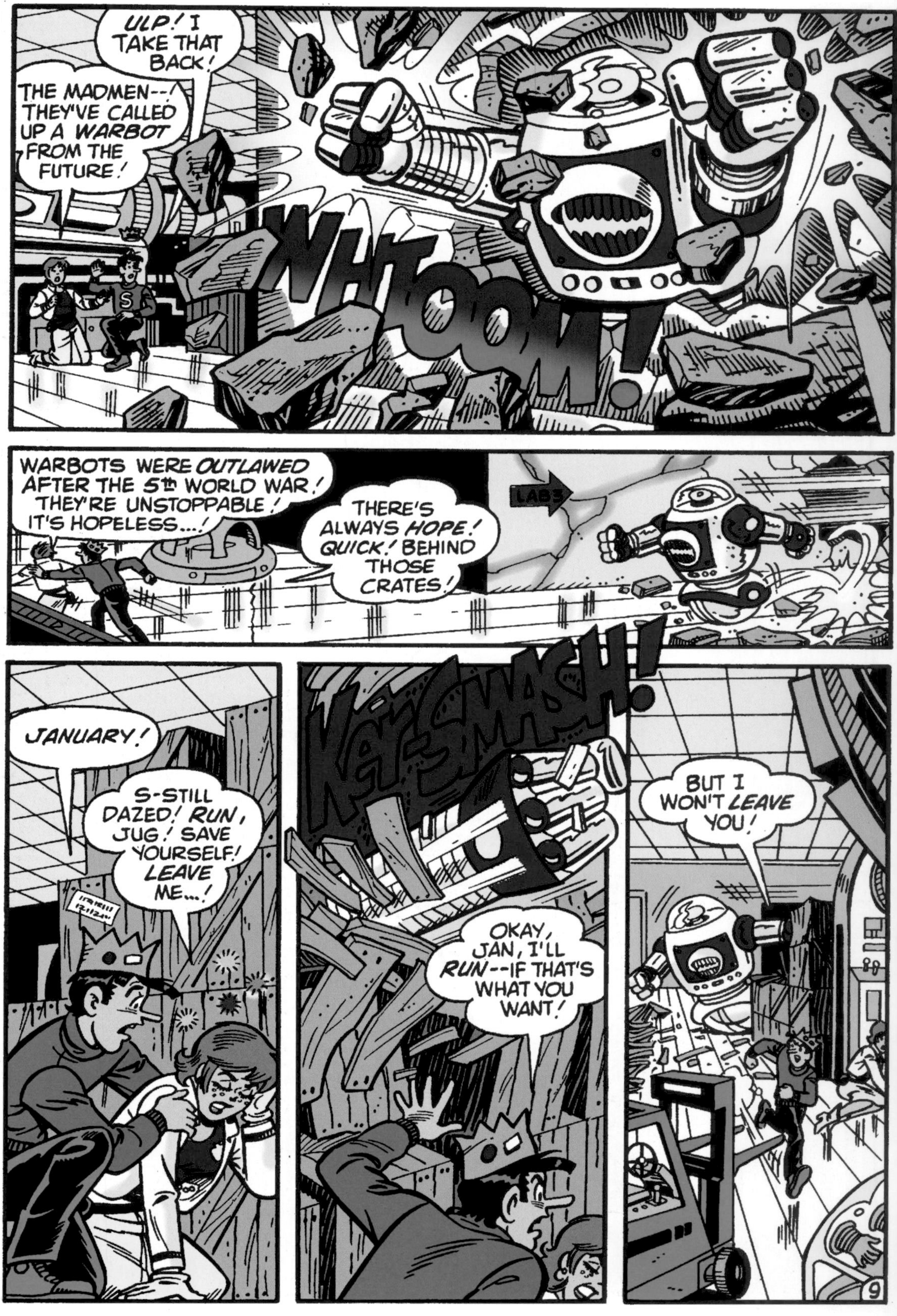
ULP! I TAKE THAT BACK!
THE MADMEN--! THEY'VE CALLED UP A WARBOT FROM THE FUTURE!
WHOOOM!
WARBOTS WERE OUTLAWED AFTER THE 5th WORLD WAR! THEY'RE UNSTOPPABLE! IT'S HOPELESS...!
THERE'S ALWAYS HOPE! QUICK! BEHIND THOSE CRATES!
LAB3
JANUARY!
S-STILL DAZED! RUN, JUG! SAVE YOURSELF! LEAVE ME...!
KER-SMASH!
OKAY, JAN, I'LL RUN--IF THAT'S WHAT YOU WANT!
BUT I WON'T LEAVE YOU!
9

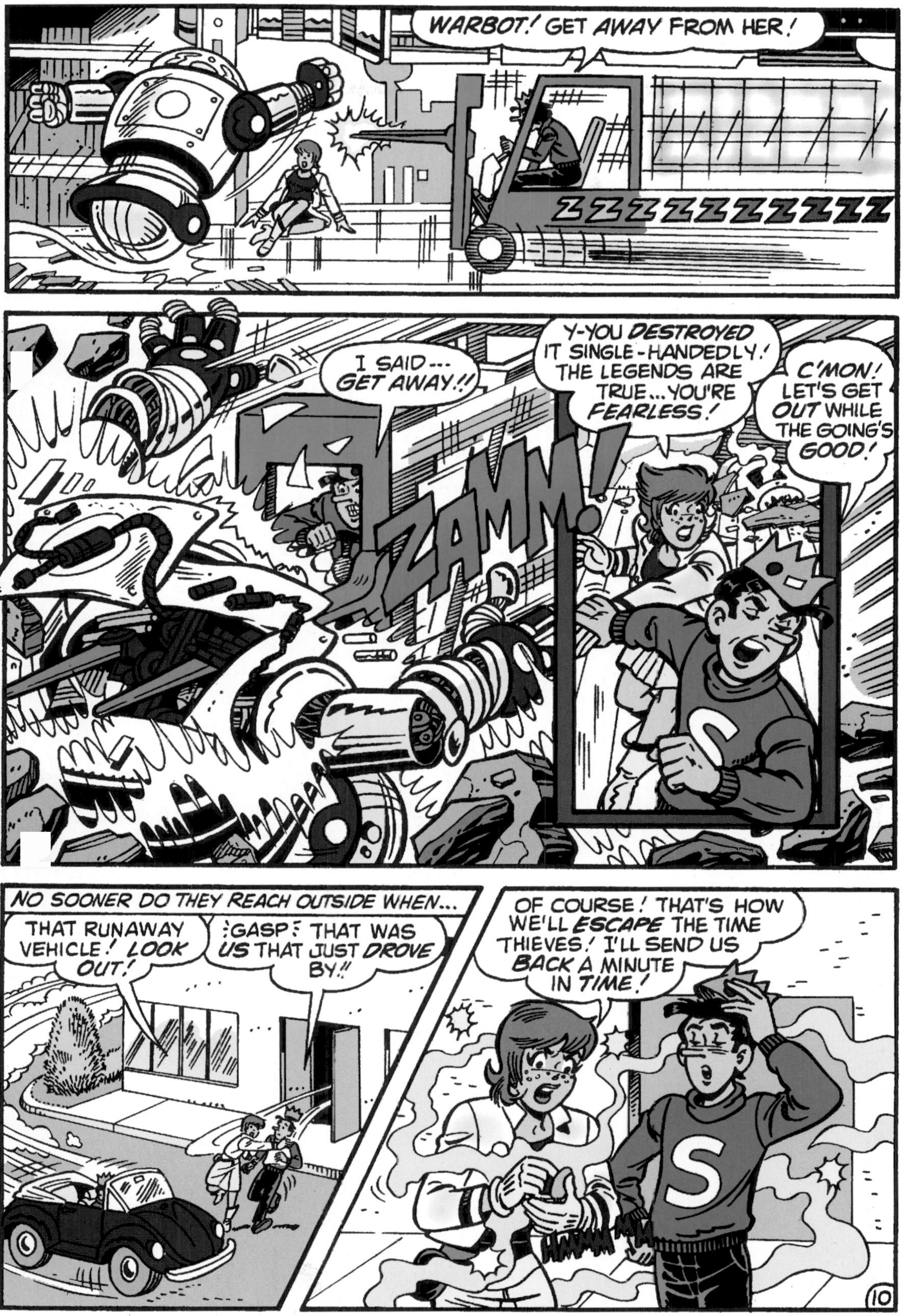
WARBOT! GET AWAY FROM HER!
ZZZZZZZZZZZZ
I SAID--- GET AWAY!!
ZAMM!
Y-YOU DESTROYED IT SINGLE-HANDEDLY! THE LEGENDS ARE TRUE...YOU'RE FEARLESS!
C'MON! LET'S GET OUT WHILE THE GOING'S GOOD!
NO SOONER DO THEY REACH OUTSIDE WHEN...
THAT RUNAWAY VEHICLE! LOOK OUT!
GASP THAT WAS US THAT JUST DROVE BY!!
OF COURSE! THAT'S HOW WE'LL ESCAPE THE TIME THIEVES! I'LL SEND US BACK A MINUTE IN TIME!
HMMMMM

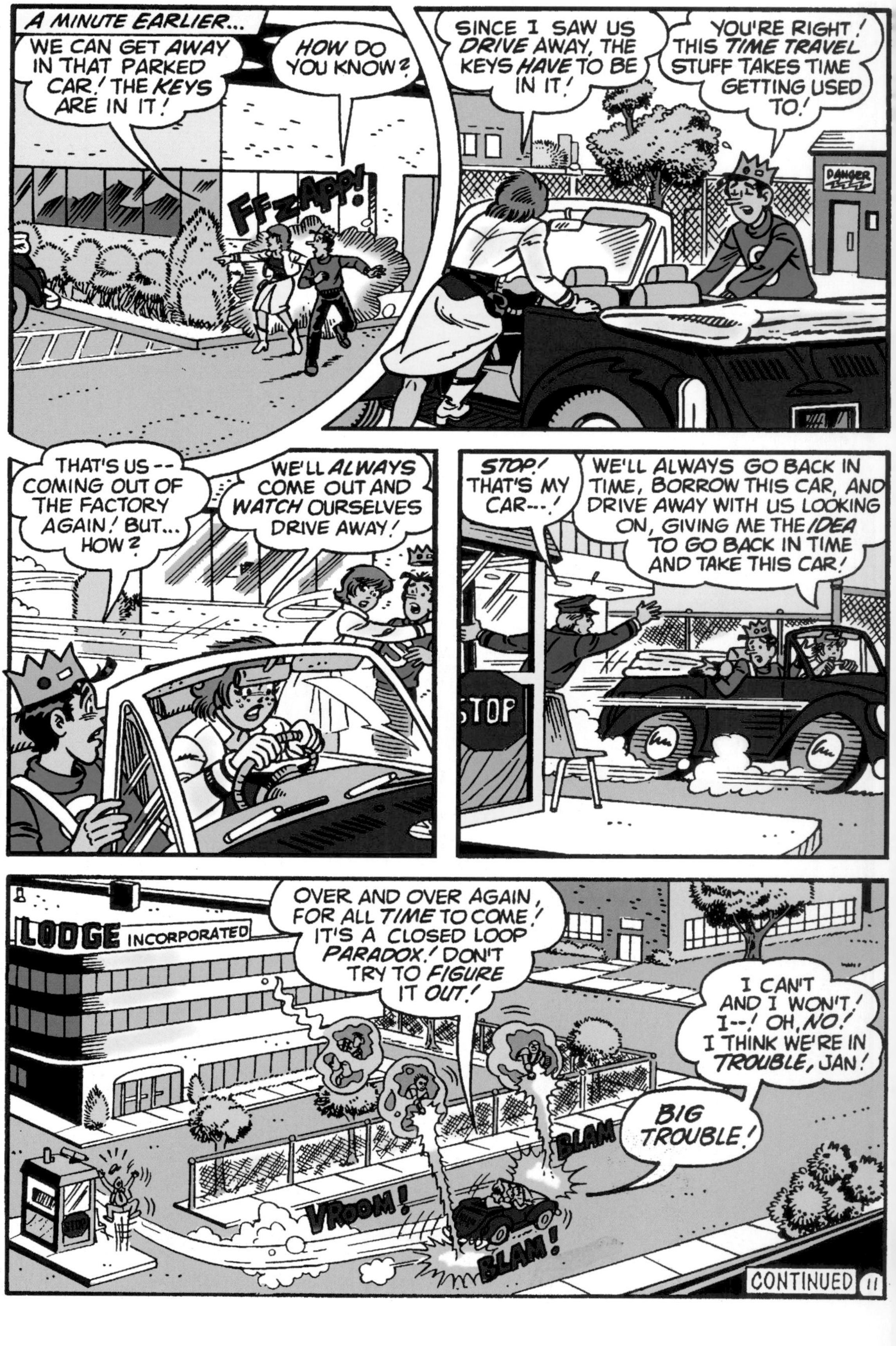
A MINUTE EARLIER...
WE CAN GET AWAY IN THAT PARKED CAR! THE KEYS ARE IN IT!
HOW DO YOU KNOW?
FFZAPP!
SINCE I SAW US DRIVE AWAY, THE KEYS HAVE TO BE IN IT!
YOU'RE RIGHT! THIS TIME TRAVEL STUFF TAKES TIME GETTING USED TO!
DANGER
THAT'S US -- COMING OUT OF THE FACTORY AGAIN! BUT... HOW?
WE'LL ALWAYS COME OUT AND WATCH OURSELVES DRIVE AWAY!
STOP! THAT'S MY CAR---!
WE'LL ALWAYS GO BACK IN TIME, BORROW THIS CAR, AND DRIVE AWAY WITH US LOOKING ON, GIVING ME THE IDEA TO GO BACK IN TIME AND TAKE THIS CAR!
STOP
LODGE INCORPORATED
OVER AND OVER AGAIN, FOR ALL TIME TO COME! IT'S A CLOSED LOOP PARADOX! DON'T TRY TO FIGURE IT OUT!
I CAN'T AND I WON'T! I--! OH, NO! I THINK WE'RE IN TROUBLE, JAN!
BIG TROUBLE!
BLAM
VROOM!
BLAM!
CONTINUED

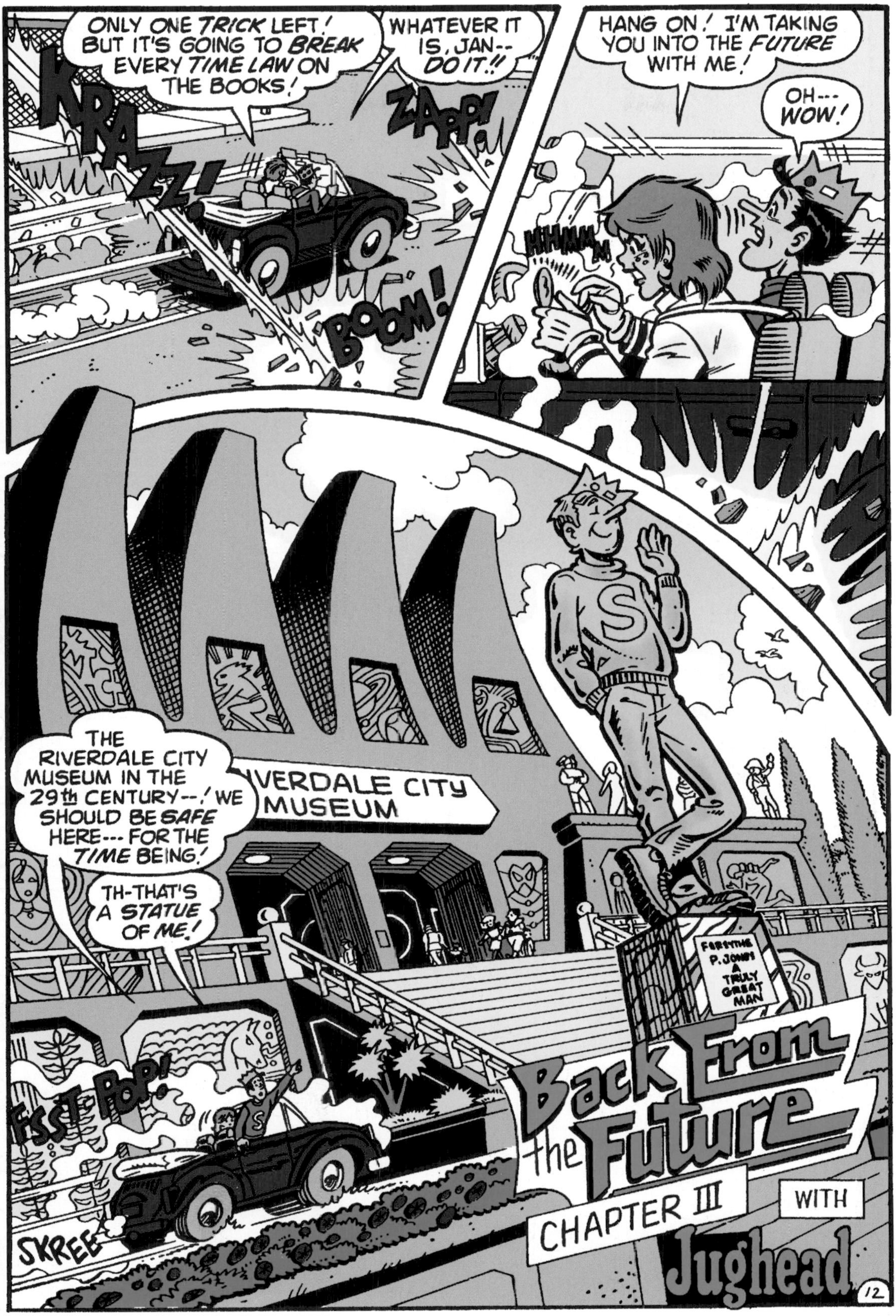
ONLY ONE TRICK LEFT! BUT IT'S GOING TO BREAK EVERY TIME LAW ON THE BOOKS!
WHATEVER IT IS, JAN-- DO IT!!
KRAZZZ!
ZAPP!
BOOM!
HANG ON! I'M TAKING YOU INTO THE FUTURE WITH ME!
OH--- WOW!
HHHMMMM
THE RIVERDALE CITY MUSEUM IN THE 29th CENTURY--! WE SHOULD BE SAFE HERE--- FOR THE TIME BEING!
TH-THAT'S A STATUE OF ME!
VERDALE CITY MUSEUM
FORSYTHE P. JONES A TRULY GREAT MAN
FSST POP!
SKREE
Back From the Future
CHAPTER III
WITH
Jughead
12

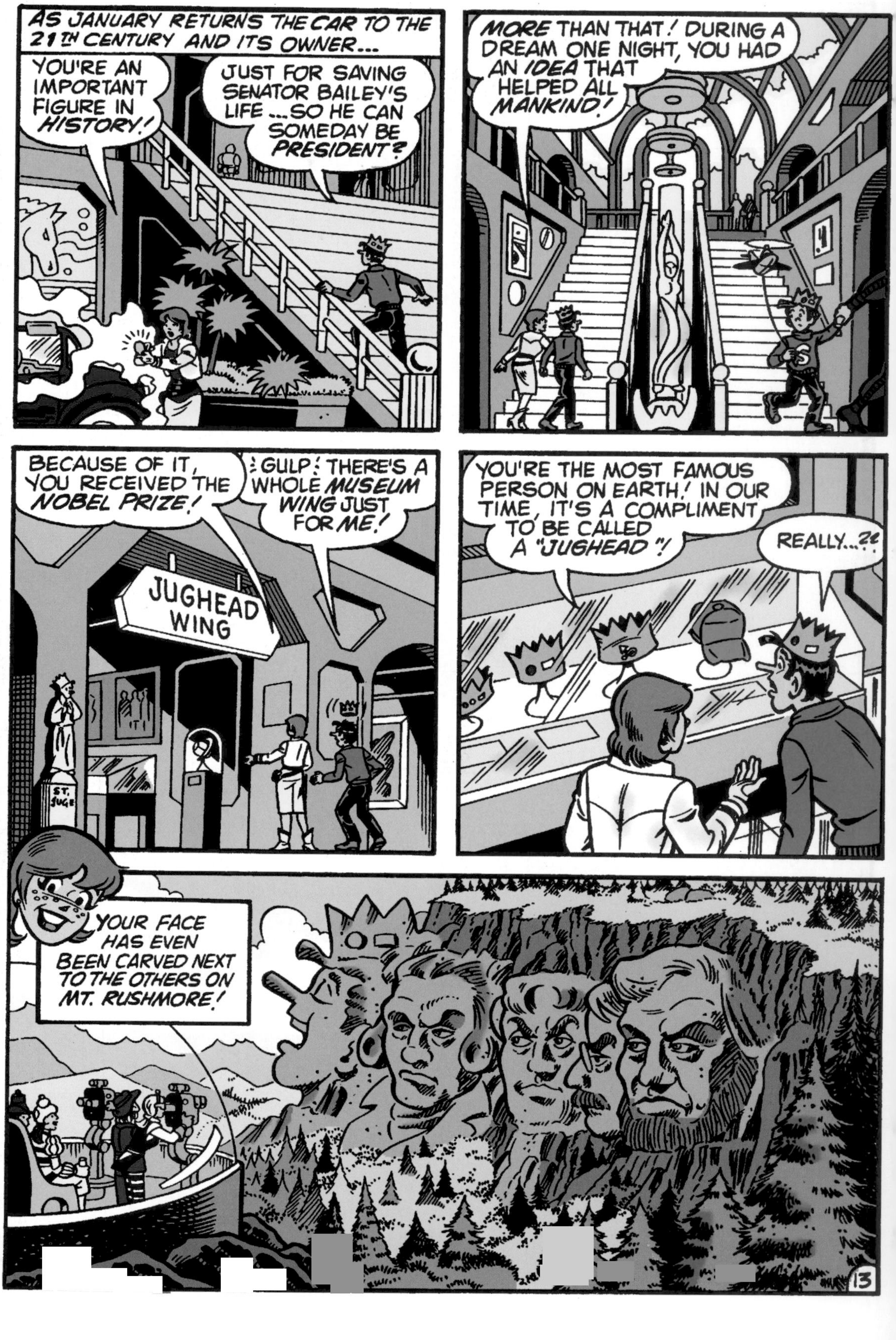
AS JANUARY RETURNS THE CAR TO THE 21TH CENTURY AND ITS OWNER...
YOU'RE AN IMPORTANT FIGURE IN HISTORY!
JUST FOR SAVING SENATOR BAILEY'S LIFE ...SO HE CAN SOMEDAY BE PRESIDENT?
MORE THAN THAT! DURING A DREAM ONE NIGHT, YOU HAD AN IDEA THAT HELPED ALL MANKIND!
BECAUSE OF IT, YOU RECEIVED THE NOBEL PRIZE!
GULP! THERE'S A WHOLE MUSEUM WING JUST FOR ME!
JUGHEAD WING
ST. JUGE
YOU'RE THE MOST FAMOUS PERSON ON EARTH! IN OUR TIME, IT'S A COMPLIMENT TO BE CALLED A "JUGHEAD"!
REALLY...??
YOUR FACE HAS EVEN BEEN CARVED NEXT TO THE OTHERS ON MT. RUSHMORE!

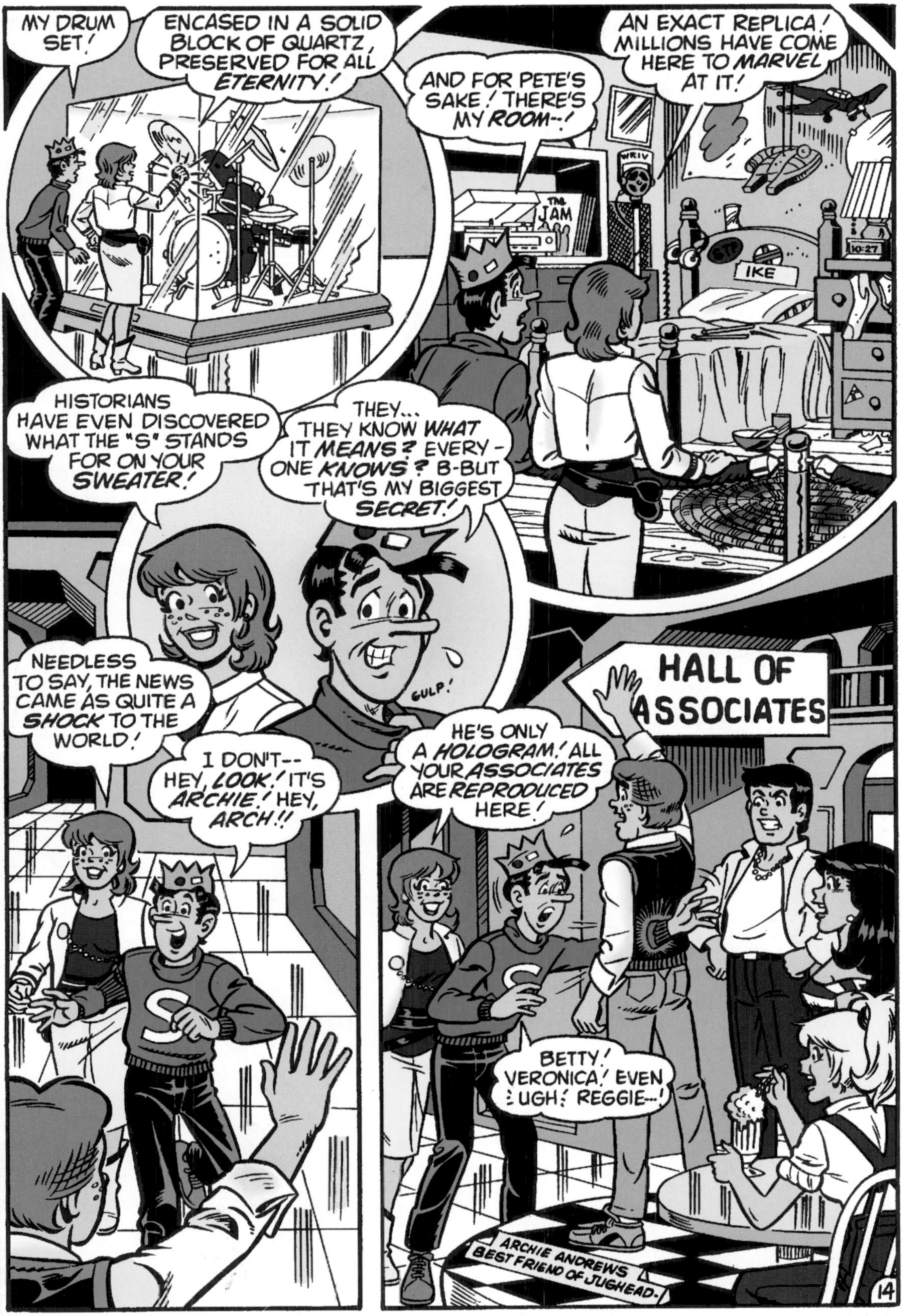
MY DRUM SET!
ENCASED IN A SOLID BLOCK OF QUARTZ, PRESERVED FOR ALL ETERNITY!
AND FOR PETE'S SAKE! THERE'S MY ROOM--!
AN EXACT REPLICA! MILLIONS HAVE COME HERE TO MARVEL AT IT!
WRIV
THE JAM
IKE
10:27
HISTORIANS HAVE EVEN DISCOVERED WHAT THE "S" STANDS FOR ON YOUR SWEATER!
THEY... THEY KNOW WHAT IT MEANS? EVERY-ONE KNOWS? B-BUT THAT'S MY BIGGEST SECRET!
GULP!
NEEDLESS TO SAY, THE NEWS CAME AS QUITE A SHOCK TO THE WORLD!
I DON'T-- HEY, LOOK! IT'S ARCHIE! HEY, ARCH!!
HALL OF ASSOCIATES
HE'S ONLY A HOLOGRAM! ALL YOUR ASSOCIATES ARE REPRODUCED HERE!
BETTY! VERONICA! EVEN UGH! REGGIE--!
ARCHIE ANDREWS BEST FRIEND OF JUGHEAD.

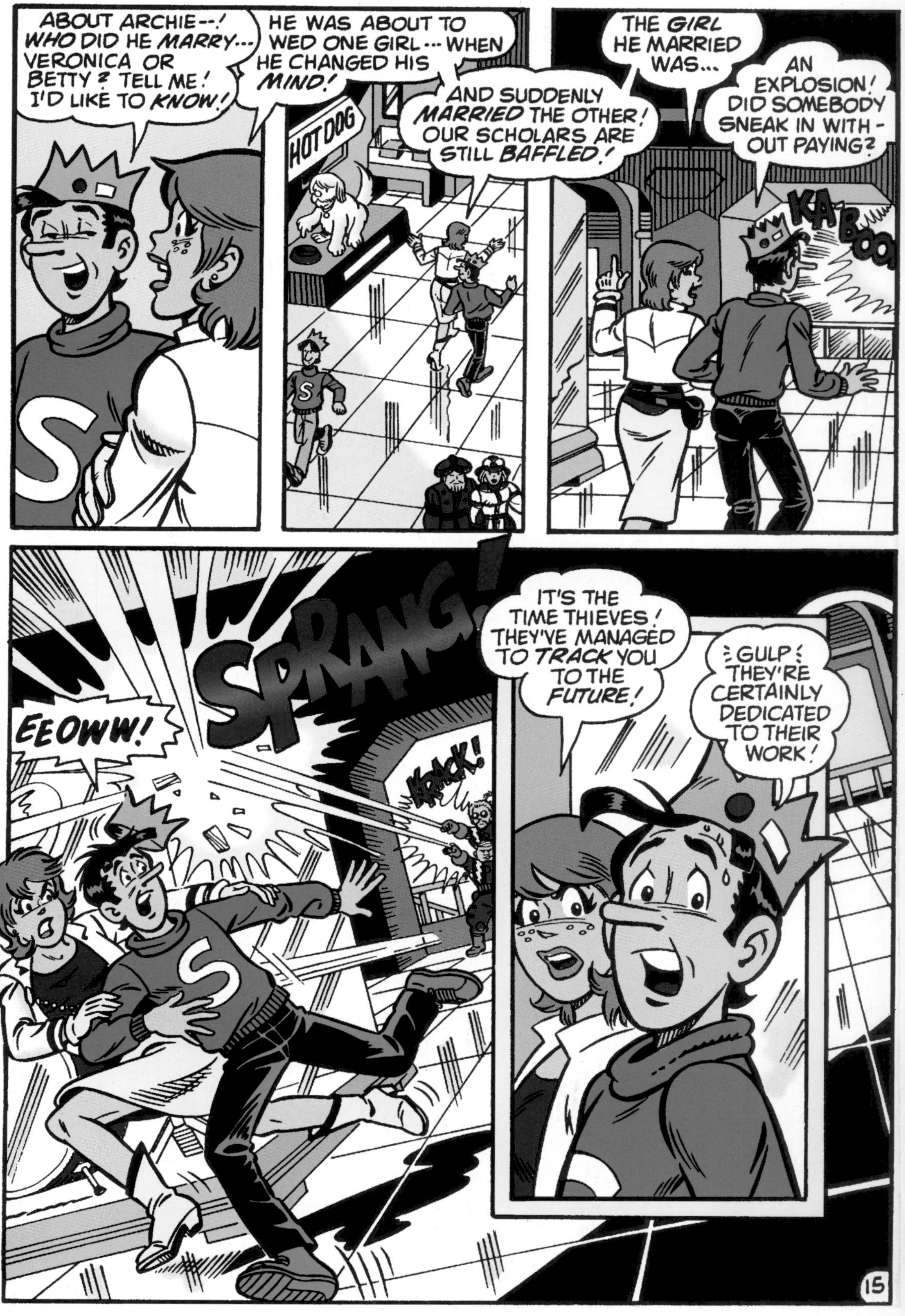
ABOUT ARCHIE--! WHO DID HE MARRY... VERONICA OR BETTY? TELL ME! I'D LIKE TO KNOW!
HE WAS ABOUT TO WED ONE GIRL... WHEN HE CHANGED HIS MIND!
HOT DOG
AND SUDDENLY MARRIED THE OTHER! OUR SCHOLARS ARE STILL BAFFLED!
THE GIRL HE MARRIED WAS...
AN EXPLOSION! DID SOMEBODY SNEAK IN WITH-OUT PAYING?
KA BOOM
SPRANG!
EEOWW!
KRACK!
IT'S THE TIME THIEVES! THEY'VE MANAGED TO TRACK YOU TO THE FUTURE!
GULP! THEY'RE CERTAINLY DEDICATED TO THEIR WORK!

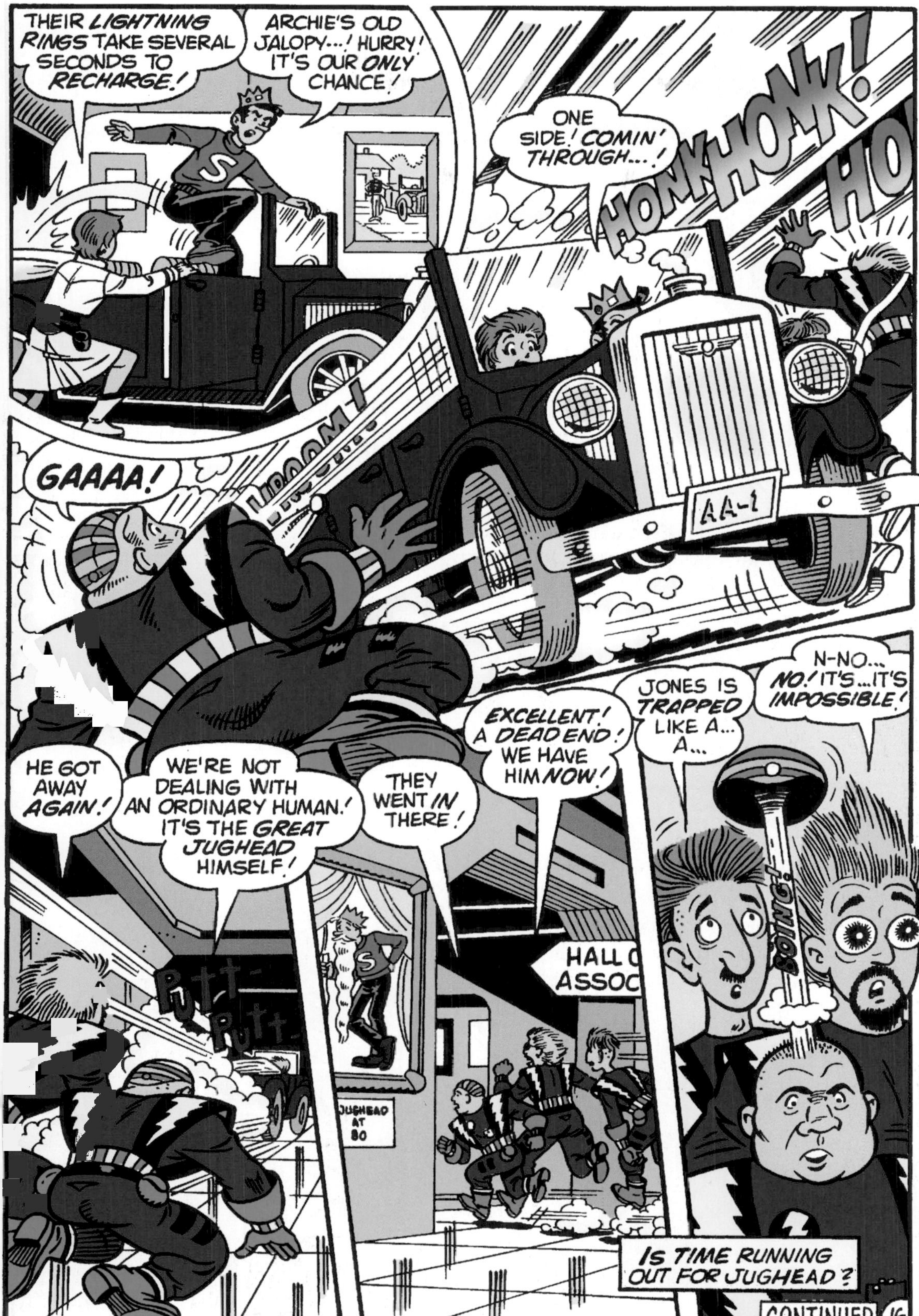
THEIR LIGHTNING RINGS TAKE SEVERAL SECONDS TO RECHARGE!
ARCHIE'S OLD JALOPY...! HURRY! IT'S OUR ONLY CHANCE!
ONE SIDE! COMIN' THROUGH...!
HONK HONK!
HO
VROOM!
GAAAA!
HE GOT AWAY AGAIN!
WE'RE NOT DEALING WITH AN ORDINARY HUMAN! IT'S THE GREAT JUGHEAD HIMSELF!
PUTT-PUTT-PUTT
THEY WENT IN THERE!
EXCELLENT! A DEAD END! WE HAVE HIM NOW!
HALL O
ASSOC
JUGHEAD AT 80
JONES IS TRAPPED LIKE A... A...
N-NO... NO! IT'S...IT'S IMPOSSIBLE!
BOING!
IS TIME RUNNING OUT FOR JUGHEAD?
CONTINUED

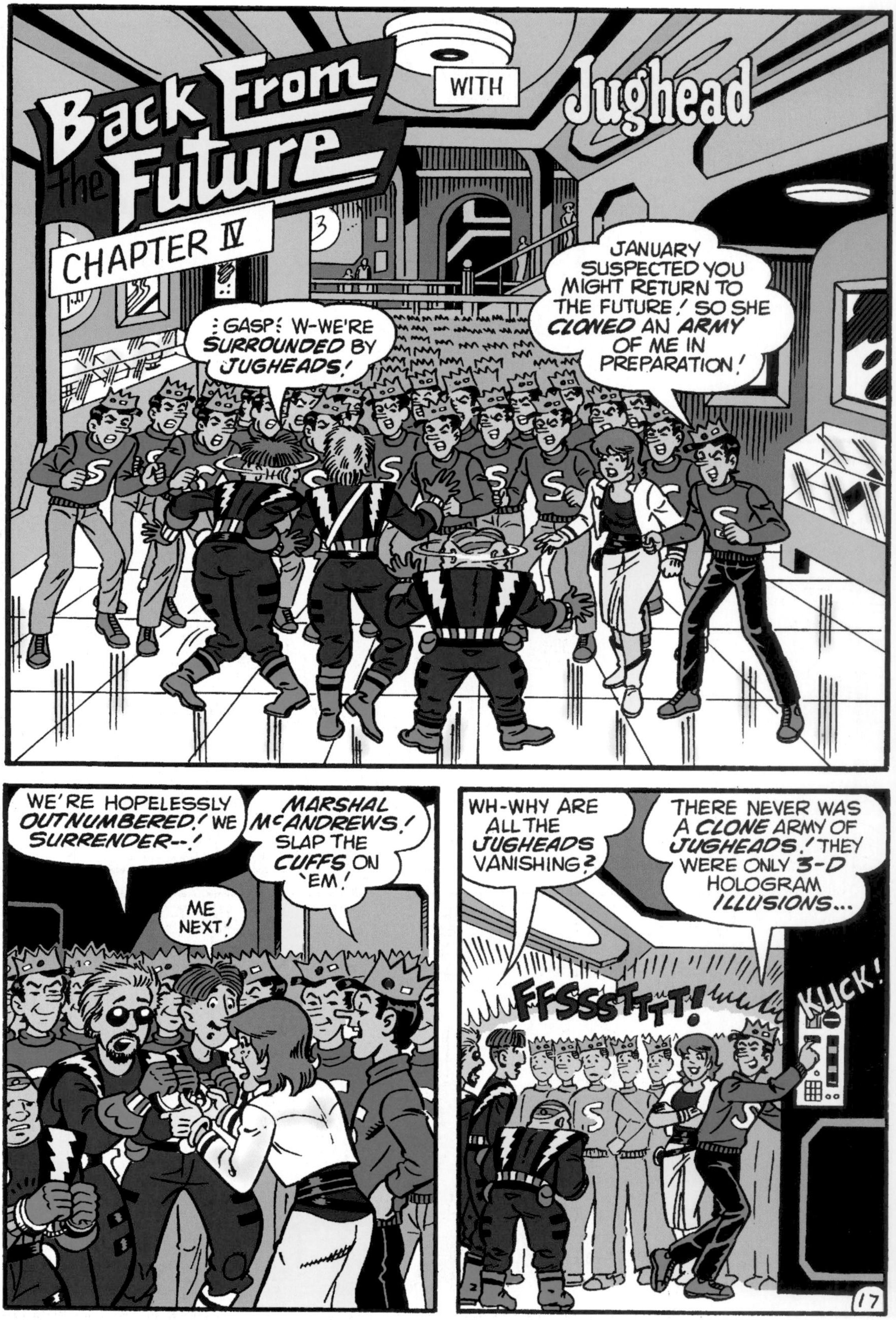
Back From the Future
WITH
Jughead
CHAPTER IV
:GASP: W-WE'RE SURROUNDED BY JUGHEADS!
JANUARY SUSPECTED YOU MIGHT RETURN TO THE FUTURE! SO SHE CLONED AN ARMY OF ME IN PREPARATION!
WE'RE HOPELESSLY OUTNUMBERED! WE SURRENDER--!
MARSHAL McANDREWS! SLAP THE CUFFS ON 'EM!
ME NEXT!
WH-WHY ARE ALL THE JUGHEADS VANISHING?
THERE NEVER WAS A CLONE ARMY OF JUGHEADS! THEY WERE ONLY 3-D HOLOGRAM ILLUSIONS...
FFSSSTTTT!
KLICK!
17

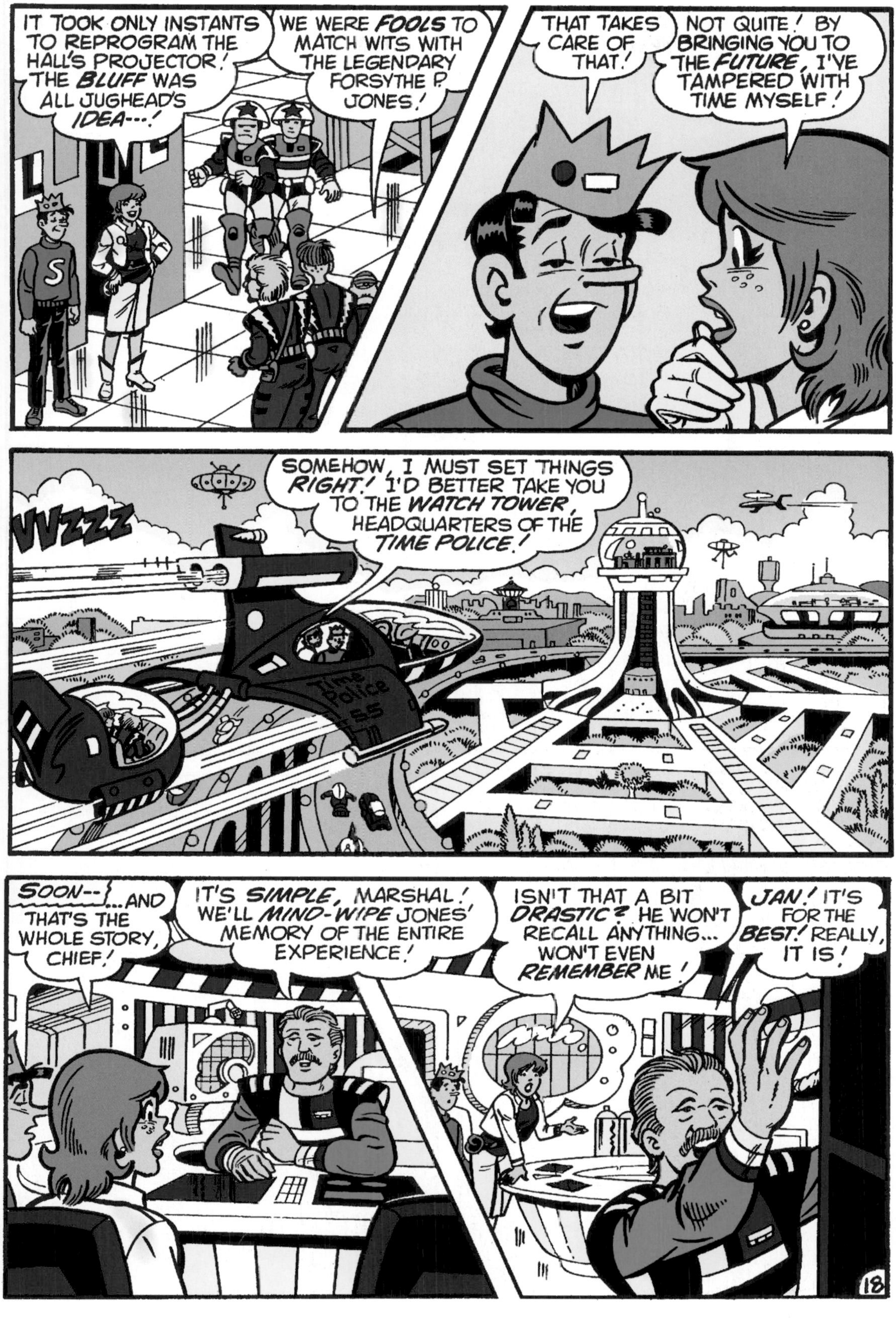
IT TOOK ONLY INSTANTS TO REPROGRAM THE HALL'S PROJECTOR! THE BLUFF WAS ALL JUGHEAD'S IDEA---!
WE WERE FOOLS TO MATCH WITS WITH THE LEGENDARY FORSYTHE P. JONES!
THAT TAKES CARE OF THAT!
NOT QUITE! BY BRINGING YOU TO THE FUTURE, I'VE TAMPERED WITH TIME MYSELF!
VVZZZ
SOMEHOW, I MUST SET THINGS RIGHT! I'D BETTER TAKE YOU TO THE WATCH TOWER, HEADQUARTERS OF THE TIME POLICE!
Time Police 55
SOON--
...AND THAT'S THE WHOLE STORY, CHIEF!
IT'S SIMPLE, MARSHAL! WE'LL MIND-WIPE JONES' MEMORY OF THE ENTIRE EXPERIENCE!
ISN'T THAT A BIT DRASTIC? HE WON'T RECALL ANYTHING... WON'T EVEN REMEMBER ME!
JAN! IT'S FOR THE BEST! REALLY, IT IS!
18

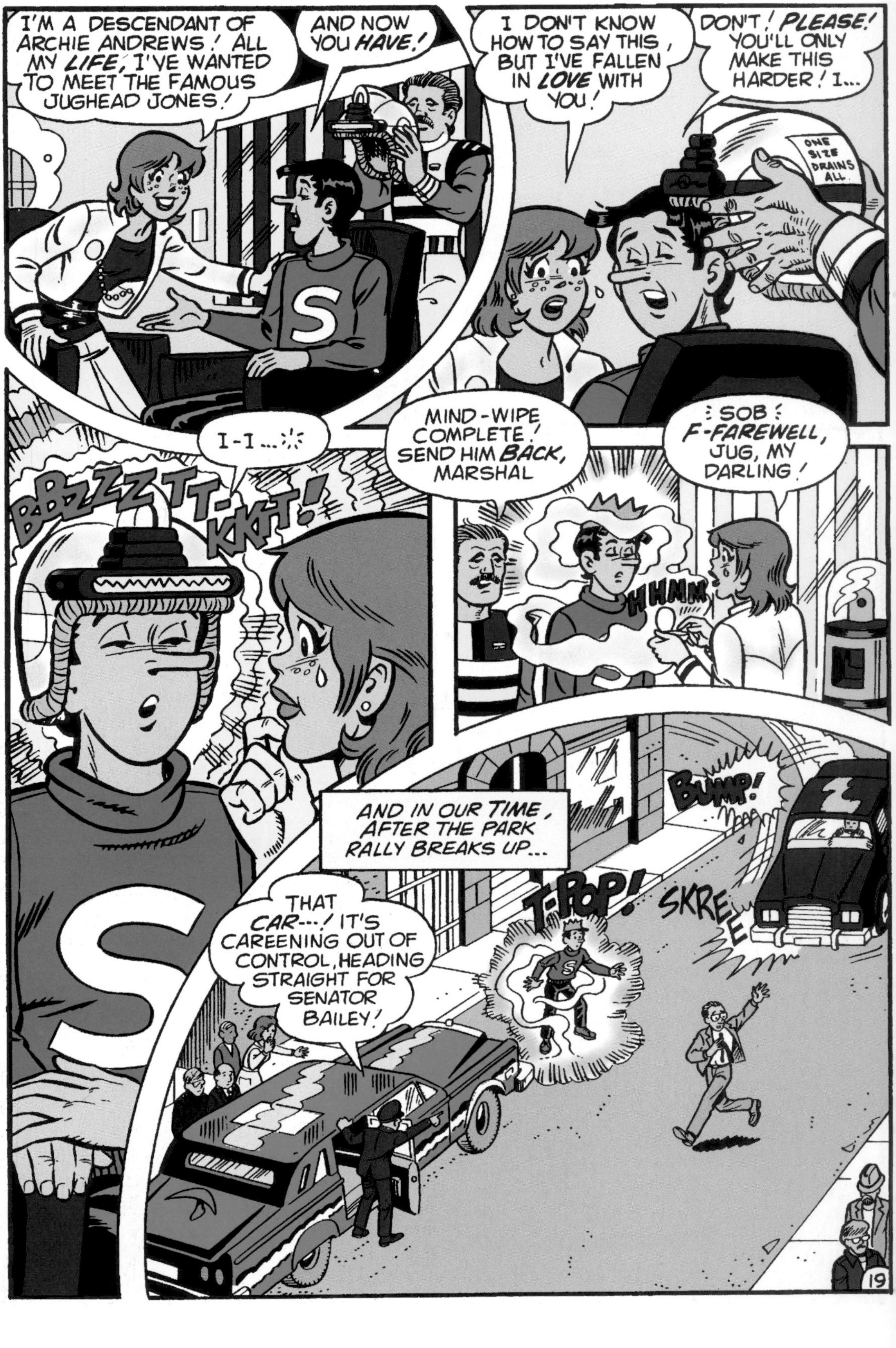
I'M A DESCENDANT OF ARCHIE ANDREWS! ALL MY LIFE, I'VE WANTED TO MEET THE FAMOUS JUGHEAD JONES!
AND NOW YOU HAVE!
I DON'T KNOW HOW TO SAY THIS, BUT I'VE FALLEN IN LOVE WITH YOU!
DON'T! PLEASE! YOU'LL ONLY MAKE THIS HARDER! I...
ONE SIZE DRAINS ALL
BBZZZZ TT-KKKT!
I-I...
MIND-WIPE COMPLETE! SEND HIM BACK, MARSHAL
SOB F-FAREWELL, JUG, MY DARLING!
HHMM
AND IN OUR TIME, AFTER THE PARK RALLY BREAKS UP...
BUMP!
T-POP!
SKREEE
THAT CAR---! IT'S CAREENING OUT OF CONTROL, HEADING STRAIGHT FOR SENATOR BAILEY!
19

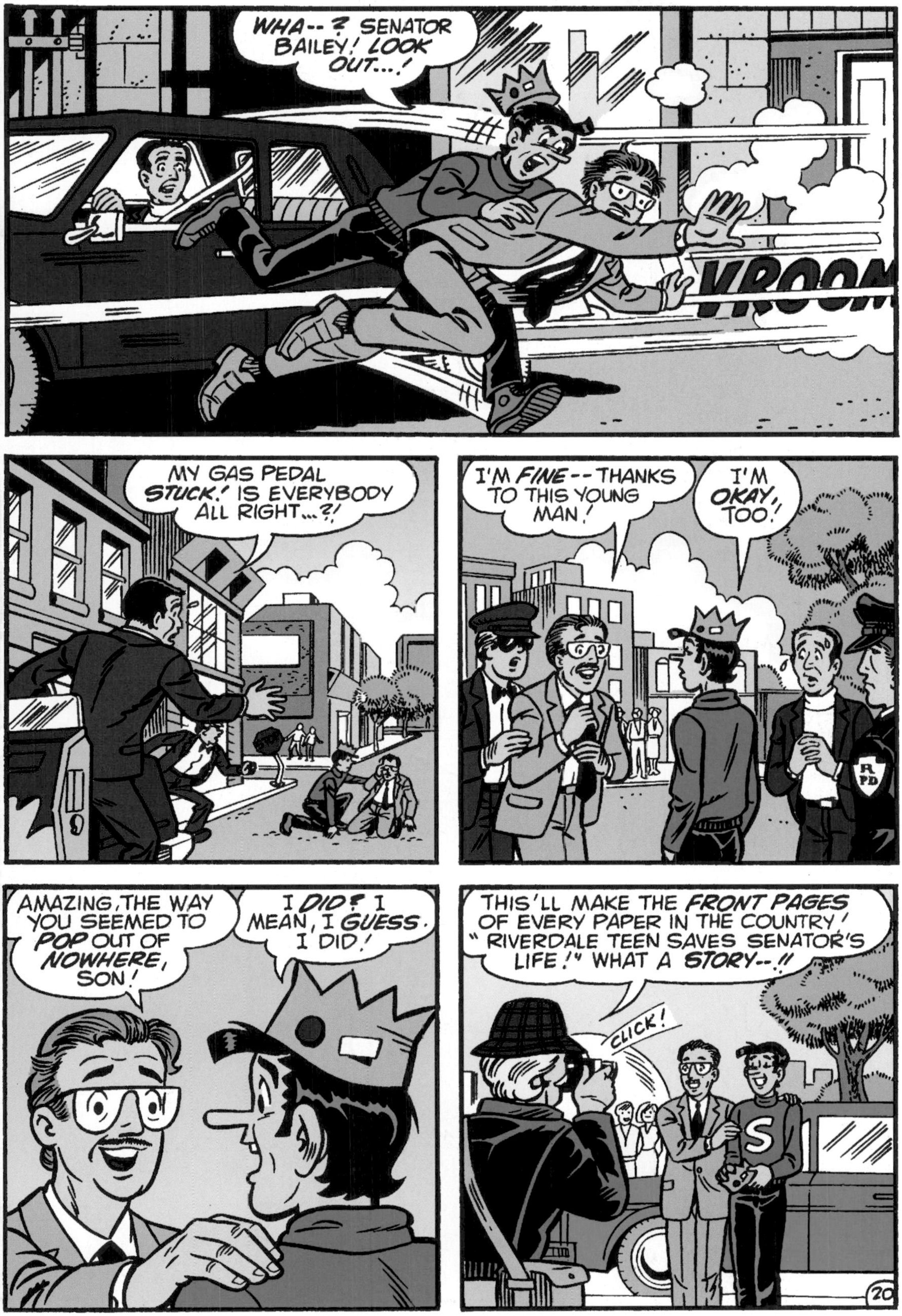
WHA--? SENATOR BAILEY! LOOK OUT...!
VROOM
MY GAS PEDAL STUCK! IS EVERYBODY ALL RIGHT...?!
I'M FINE--THANKS TO THIS YOUNG MAN!
I'M OKAY, TOO!
AMAZING, THE WAY YOU SEEMED TO POP OUT OF NOWHERE, SON!
I DID? I MEAN, I GUESS I DID!
THIS'LL MAKE THE FRONT PAGES OF EVERY PAPER IN THE COUNTRY! "RIVERDALE TEEN SAVES SENATOR'S LIFE!" WHAT A STORY--!!
CLICK!
20

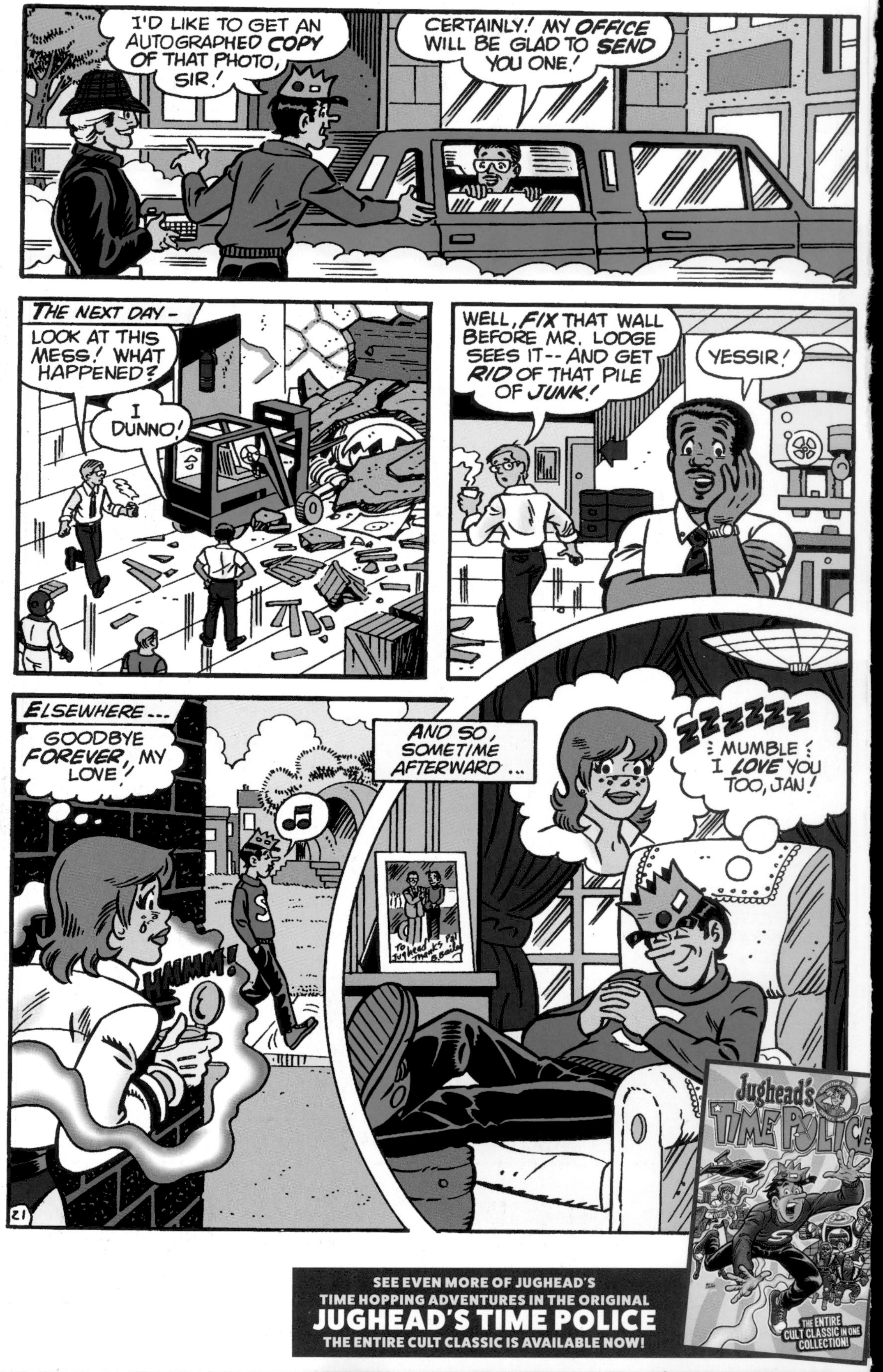
I'D LIKE TO GET AN AUTOGRAPHED COPY OF THAT PHOTO, SIR!
CERTAINLY! MY OFFICE WILL BE GLAD TO SEND YOU ONE!
THE NEXT DAY -
LOOK AT THIS MESS! WHAT HAPPENED?
I DUNNO!
WELL, FIX THAT WALL BEFORE MR. LODGE SEES IT-- AND GET RID OF THAT PILE OF JUNK!
YESSIR!
ELSEWHERE ...
GOODBYE FOREVER, MY LOVE!
AND SO, SOMETIME AFTERWARD ...
To Jughead Thanks Pal S. Bailey
ZZZZZZ
MUMBLE! I LOVE YOU TOO, JAN!
21